INTERNATIONAL PARTNERSHIPS
in Large Science Projects

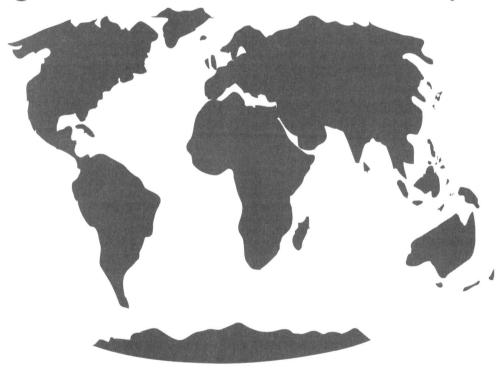

Congress of the United States ▲ Office of Technology Assessment

Recommended Citation: U.S. Congress, Office of Technology Assessment, *International Partnerships in Large Science Projects*, OTA-BP-ETI-150 (Washington, DC: U.S. Government Printing Office, July 1995).

For sale by the U.S. Government Printing Office
Superintendent of Documents, Mail Stop: SSOP, Washington, DC 20402-9328
ISBN 0-16-048166-X

Foreword

Federal investment in research and development (R&D) has been crucial to many of the nation's achievements in basic sciences. In recent years, however, budgetary pressures have made it difficult to sustain ongoing government R&D efforts and to initiate new ventures. These pressures and the growing international character of scientific research have focused greater attention on the potential contributions of international cooperation, particularly for large-scale, long-term science projects.

The United States has several decades of experience with international scientific collaborations. Numerous successful small-scale scientific cooperative efforts, largely through bilateral agreements, have been conducted. High-energy physics, fusion energy, and space are rich with examples of this type of cooperation. However, U.S. experience in the joint construction and operation of large-scale experiments and facilities is far more limited.

This background paper, requested by the Chairman and Ranking Minority Member of the House Committee on Science, reviews U.S. experience with collaborative projects in many different fields and their implications for future activities. It assesses the factors that facilitate international partnerships in big science projects and those that, conversely, favor the pursuit of purely national projects. The background paper also reviews and identifies several important issues to consider in structuring future collaborations. These include maintaining U.S. scientific expertise, setting research priorities, developing mechanisms to ensure long-term project stability, and safeguarding economic and national security interests.

In the course of this study, OTA drew on the experience of many organizations and individuals. In particular, we appreciate the invaluable assistance of the workshop participants, as well as the efforts of the project's contractors. We would also like to acknowledge the help of the many reviewers who gave their time to ensure the accuracy and comprehensiveness of this study. To all of them goes the gratitude of OTA and the personal thanks of the staff.

ROGER C. HERDMAN
Director

Workshop

International Collaboration in Large Science Projects
September 13, 1994

Nancy Carson
Chair
Nancy Carson Associates
Alexandria, VA

Phillip Anderson
Princeton University
Princeton, NJ

Charles Baker
ITER Project
University of California,
 San Diego
La Jolla, CA

David Burke
Stanford Linear Accelerator
 Center
Menlo Park, CA

James Decker
Department of Energy
Washington, DC

Lyndon Evans
European Organization for
 Nuclear Research
Geneva, Switzerland

Noel W. Hinners
Martin Marietta Astronautics
Denver, CO

John Logsdon
Space Policy Institute
George Washington University
Washington, DC

Akihiro Maki
Japan Society for the Promotion
 of Science
Washington, DC

Edward M. Malloy
Department of State
Washington, DC

Rodney W. Nichols
New York Academy of Sciences
New York, NY

David Overskei
General Atomics
San Diego, CA

Ian Pryke
European Space Agency
Washington, DC

J. Thomas Ratchford
George Mason University
Arlington, VA

John D. Schumacher
National Aeronautics and Space
 Administration
Washington, DC

Mr. Anatoliy A. Shurygin
Embassy of the Russian
 Federation
Washington, DC

Ken Stanfield
Fermi National Accelerator
 Laboratory
Batavia, IL

Note: OTA appreciates and is grateful for the valuable assistance and thoughtful critiques provided by the workshop participants. The participants do not, however, necessarily approve, disapprove, or endorse this report. OTA assumes full responsibility for the report and the accuracy of its contents.

Project Staff

Peter D. Blair
Assistant Director
Industry, Commerce, and
    International Security Division

Emilia L. Govan
Program Director
Industry, Commerce, and
    International Security Division

CONTRACTORS
Center for Science, Trade and
    Technology Policy
George Mason University

John Krige
European University Institute

Kenneth Pechter
Research Center for Advanced
    Science and Technology
University of Tokyo

Florence Poillon
Editor

PRINCIPAL STAFF
Joanne Sedor
Project Director

Matthew Weinberg
Project Director

Richard Brody
Analyst

Karen Larsen
Senior Analyst

Robin Roy
Senior Analyst[1]

ADMINISTRATIVE STAFF
Marsha Fenn
Office Administrator

Tina Aikens
Administrative Secretary

Gay Jackson
PC Specialist

Lillian Chapman
Division Administrator

PUBLISHING STAFF
Mary Lou Higgs
Manager, Publishing Services

Cheryl Davis
Electronic Publishing Specialist

Susan Hoffmeyer
Graphic Designer

Chip Moore
Production Editor

---

[1] Served as project director until January 1995.

v

Reviewers

Charles Baker
U.S. ITER Home Team Office
University of California,
  San Diego

Julie Baker
National Aeronautics and Space
  Administration

William A. Blanpied
National Science Foundation

David L. Burke
Stanford Linear Accelerator
  Center

Daryl Chubin
National Science Foundation

Alan T. Crane
Office of Technology Assessment

Stephen O. Dean
Fusion Power Associates

Sidney Drell
Stanford Linear Acclerator Center

Gerald Epstein
Office of Technology Assessment

Herman Feshbach
Center for Theoretical Physics
Massachusetts Institute of
  Technology

Wendell Fletcher
Office of Technology Assessment

Harold Jaffe
Department of Energy

Don Kash
George Mason University

Genevieve J. Knezo
Congressional Research Service

Akihiro Maki
Japan Society for the Promotion
  of Science

Beth A. Masters
National Aeronautics and Space
  Administration

John E. Metzler
Department of Energy

David Overskei
SAIC

Francoise Praderie
Megascience Forum
Organization for Economic
  Cooperation and Development

Ian Pryke
European Space Agency

J. Thomas Ratchford
George Mason University

Burton Richter
Stanford Linear Accelerator
  Center

Michael Roberts
Department of Energy

Don A. Rolt
British Embassy

Rustum Roy
The Pennsylvania State University

Alan Schriesheim
Argonne National Laboratory

Eugene B. Skolnikoff
Massachusetts Institute of
  Technology

Marcia Smith
Congressional Research Service

Peter Smith[1]
Office of Technology Assessment

Rodney Sobin
Office of Techology Assessment

Linda Staheli
Office of Science and Technology
  Policy

Albert Teich
American Association for the
  Advancement of Science

Alvin Trivelpiece
Oak Ridge National Laboratory

Paul F. Uhlir
National Research Council

Ray Williamson
Office of Technology Assessment

---

[1]On detail from the National Aeronautics and Space Administration.

Note: OTA appreciates and is grateful for the valuable assistance and thoughtful critiques provided by the reviewers. The reviewers do not, however, necessarily approve, disapprove, or endorse this report. OTA assumes full responsibility for the report and the accuracy of its contents.

Contents

Overview
and
Findings | 1

O ver the past several decades, the federal government has
supported a wide range of research projects in science
and technology. Federal support has been crucial to many
of the most important research and development (R&D)
achievements in defense, space, energy, environmental, and other
science and technology programs. Recently, however, federal
budget deficits and concerns about the effectiveness of research
efforts have intensified pressures on government R&D spending,
making it difficult to sustain many ongoing efforts and limiting
opportunities for new ventures. These pressures, coupled with the
increasingly international character of science and technology
R&D activities, have focused greater attention on bilateral and
multilateral collaborative arrangements, particularly for large-
scale, long-term projects in areas such as particle physics, energy
and environmental science, and space.

The United States has pursued international collaborative
projects in R&D to raise the likelihood of scientific success for
particularly complex endeavors, to take greater advantage of international scientific expertise and facilities, to address science
and technology issues that have global implications, to extend national scientific capabilities, and especially for very large science
projects, to share costs and risks with other nations. International
collaboration, however, poses special challenges, such as establishing R&D priorities within and across different scientific disciplines, developing funding and planning mechanisms that ensure
the long-term stability of projects, and maintaining U.S. economic and national security interests.

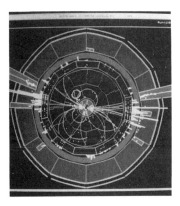

This background paper, requested by the Chairman and Ranking Minority Member of the House Committee on Science,[1] examines the factors that may warrant or facilitate international collaboration in large science projects or, conversely, that may favor the United States pursuing projects independently. It identifies the challenges raised by international collaboration, such as reconciling collaboration with U.S. science goals, achieving equitable distribution of costs and benefits among nations, understanding the advantages and disadvantages of technology transfer, and dealing with increased project management complexity. In addition, the paper explores approaches that can promote the successful planning and execution of international projects.

Chapter 1 presents the principal findings of this background paper. Chapter 2 provides an overview of the broad trends in science and the rise of large projects. Chapter 3 examines U.S. science goals, the U.S. experience with collaborative projects in science, and their implications for future activities. The areas discussed include high-energy physics, fusion, space, neutron sources, and synchrotron radiation facilities. Chapter 4 explores the benefits and disadvantages of participating in international partnerships.

The issues addressed here are relevant to congressional authorization, appropriation, and oversight of ongoing and upcoming large science projects. These include the International Space Station and the International Thermonuclear Experimental Reactor (ITER), as well as U.S. participation in the Large Hadron Collider (LHC) project at the European Laboratory for Particle Physics (CERN).

Other important issues, however, are beyond the scope of this background paper. The overall process of priority setting and planning in federal research is not examined, nor are the relative benefits of big versus small science.[2] Also, the role of international collaboration as it relates to the area of defense R&D is not addressed.[3] In addition, the paper does not examine the broad commercial aspects of government-sponsored basic science research. Basic research can provide the underpinning for commercial innovation and technology development. The possible commercial implications of large science research projects (which are not limited to the consequences of basic research) will continue to be an important issue in structuring international partnerships, selecting projects for collaboration, and sharing their benefits and burdens (see chapter 2).

BACKGROUND

■ The Internationalization of Science and the Role of Big Science Projects

International collaboration in scientific research and the rise of large science projects are two significant outgrowths of the scientific revolution of the past century. This revolution has brought unprecedented increases in the speed of scientific and technical innovation. The sheer pace of this change has transformed the fabric of daily life, affecting the course of economic and social development as well as the relationship between society and the natural world. Along with an increased rate of scientific innovation and knowledge generation, there has also been (especially in the past 50 years) a marked expansion of the breadth, cre-

---

[1]Previously, the House Committee on Science, Space, and Technology.

[2]For a discussion of these issues see U.S. Congress, Office of Technology Assessment, *Federally Funded Research: Decisions for a Decade*, OTA-SET-490 (Washington, DC: U.S. Government Printing Office, May 1991).

[3]Cooperation with its allies in the supply and joint production of defense technology has been an important element of U.S. national security policy over the past four decades. See U.S. Congress, Office of Technology Assessment, *Arming Our Allies: Cooperation and Competition in Defense Technology*, OTA-ISC-449 (Washington, DC: U.S. Government Printing Office, May 1990).

ativity, and sophistication of basic and applied research.[4] These qualitative changes have been accompanied by the growth of interdisciplinary research, which in turn has opened up new fields of inquiry. With the development and diffusion of powerful information and communications technologies,[5] the extraordinary pace of scientific discovery continues to accelerate. These new technologies have facilitated collaboration within and across scientific disciplines.

The expanding range of scientific and technological undertakings, and the development of new tools to expedite the exchange of information, have reinforced and augmented the international dimension of scientific research. This internationalization affects the nature of scientific inquiry, the transmission of information among scientists and programs, the development of interdisciplinary research, and the structure of transnational research initiatives. For example:

- The increased ability to coordinate research across international borders has stimulated ambitious research on global scientific questions such as climate change.
- The rapid global exchange of information has internationalized the results of almost all scientific research, even projects and investigations that are essentially national in character.
- The growth of cross-disciplinary research has been closely linked to greater interaction among researchers across international borders, stimulating the expansion of international scientific collaborations supported by a variety of national and international agencies and institutions.

The scale and scope of scientific research have expanded simultaneously with the growth of international activities. Although much research is still conducted on a small scale by individual investigators working in small laboratories, the past few decades have witnessed the development of very large science projects—called big science or megascience projects.

■ Defining "Big Science"

Although it is relatively easy to identify certain extremely large projects as megascience, it is more difficult to devise a generic definition of the term. Big science projects exist in a range of fields and share a number of common traits. Typically, and most simply, big science has meant "big money plus big machines." Megascience projects involve large, interdisciplinary teams of researchers, including both engineers and scientists. Such projects usually employ more complex and hierarchical management structures than smaller science projects. Big science ventures are almost always supported by governments. However, industry plays a more central role (as a contractor and recipient of federal funds) than it does in "small" science because of the need to build large, capital-intensive, high-technology facilities. Big science projects vary in scale and complexity, and reflect the different R&D goals and scientific capabilities of nations. They also vary in their commercialization potential and in the degree to which they address broad national or global needs. Some big science projects are based around a single facility, whereas others are distributed among several locations and institutions.[6]

---

[4]Although there is some overlap between basic and applied research, the following distinction can be offered: "Basic research pursues fundamental concepts and knowledge (theories, methods, and findings), while applied research focuses on the problems in utilizing these concepts and knowledge." Office of Technology Assessment, *Federally Funded Research*, see footnote 2.

[5]For example, the Internet—a set of interconnected computer networks that share a common set of communications protocols—links tens of millions of users worldwide via electronic mail and other communications services. Internet access is currently available in more than 160 countries, with connections being added almost daily.

[6]This aspect of project structure—single-site versus distributed projects—can profoundly alter the character of international collaboration and the benefits and challenges that underlie it. For example, the siting of international scientific facilities has been a contentious issue in some collaborations. See finding below.

Project	Year of completion (estimated)	Capital cost[a]	Participants
High-energy and nuclear physics			
Stanford Linear Collider	1987	$115 million	U.S.
Continuous Electron Beam Accelerator Facility	1995	$513 million	U.S.
Advanced Photon Source	1996	$812 million	U.S.
B-Factory	1998	$293 million	U.S.
Japanese Spring-8 Synchrotron	1998	$1 billion	Japan
Relativistic Heavy Ion Collider	1999	$595 million	U.S.
Superconducting Super Collider	Canceled	$8 billion-$11 billion	U.S.
Proposed neutron spallation source[b]	2005—preliminary planning stage	~$1 billion (no definite estimate available)	U.S.
Large Hadron Collider (LHC)	2005	$2.3 billion[c]	Europe (CERN), U.S., Japan
Fusion			
Tokamak Physics Experiment	2001	$694 million	U.S.
International Thermonuclear Experimental Reactor (ITER)	2005	$8 billion-$10 billion[d]	U.S., Europe (Euratom) Japan, Russia

TABLE 1-1: Total Estimated Costs of Selected Big Science Projects

(continued on next page)

Although it downplays other factors, cost is probably the most important characteristic of big science projects. If project funding is used as the main criterion, a few very large projects clearly stand out as megaprojects. These include the space station (total estimated capital cost, $38 billion[7]), ITER (total estimated construction cost, $8 billion to $10 billion), CERN's Large Hadron Collider (current estimated cost, $2.3 billion[8]), and the proposed neutron spallation source[9] (estimates begin at $1 billion). All of these projects are in the billion-dollar (plus) class, and all—with the exception of the neutron spallation source—involve significant international collaboration. The failure to attract international support was a principal factor in the decision to terminate the multibillion dollar Superconducting Super Collider (see finding below). Table 1-1 shows estimated completion dates and costs for selected big science projects.

---

[7] This figure is based on the following costs as reported by the National Aeronautics and Space Administration (NASA): pre-FY 1994 costs: $10.2 billion; shuttle launch costs (based on an average cost of about $500 million per flight): $14 billion. NASA reports $17.4 billion in construction costs from FY 94 through station completion. However, this figure includes $3.7 billion in operations and science costs, as identified by the General Accounting Office. This $3.7 billion has been excluded from OTA analysis. Source: NASA, Space Station Program Office, April 1995. NASA provided data to the House Committee on Science, Space, and Technology that account for the above costs, plus civil service and operations costs through the first 10 years of operations. These figures indicate that total costs for the station will be $72.3 billion. See Marcia Smith, *Space Stations* (Washington, DC: Library of Congress, Congressional Research Service, Apr. 6, 1995), p. 4; and U.S. General Accounting Office, "Space Station: Estimated Total U.S. Funding Requirements," GAO/NSIAD-95-163, June 1995, p. 4.

[8] The estimated cost for the LHC would be roughly twice as large ($4 billion to $5 billion) if it were developed on the same accounting basis as U.S. cost estimates. Also this figure does not include the detectors, which may total as much as $2 billion. CERN has asked the United States to contribute approximately $400 million to this project. This contribution could also include in-kind contributions such as equipment. The Department of Energy, however, will not be in a position to recommend any specific level of LHC funding until overall Department cost reduction goals through 2001 are developed. Harold Jaffe, Department of Energy, Office of High Energy and Nuclear Physics, personal communication, April 1995.

[9] The accelerator-based neutron spallation source has been proposed by the Clinton Administration as an alternative to the recently canceled nuclear reactor-based Advanced Neutron Source. The European Union is also in the preliminary planning stage for a spallation source, but no formal efforts have yet been made to explore the possibility of collaboration. See chapter 3.

TABLE 1-1: Total Estimated Costs of Selected Big Science Projects (Cont'd.)

Project	Year of completion (estimated)	Capital cost[a]	Participants
Space[e]			
Hubble Space Telescope	1990	$2.3 billion	U.S., Europe (ESA)
Compton Gamma Ray Observatory	1991	$957 million	U.S., Germany
Advanced X-Ray Astrophysics Facility	1998	$2.1 billion	U.S., Germany, Netherlands, U.K.
Cassini	1998	$1.9 billion	U.S., ESA, Italy
Earth Observing System	2000 (initial components)	$8 billion	U.S., ESA, Canada, Japan, France, Eumetsat
Space station	2002	$38 billion	U.S., Russia
Canadian Mobile Servicing System for the space station	1998-2002	$1 billion	Canada
Japanese Experimental Module for the space station	1998-2002	$3 billion	Japan
Proposed European Space Agency (ESA) module and equipment for the space station	1998-2002	$3 billion[f]	ESA
Ground-based astronomy and physics			
Gemini telescopes	1998-2000	$176 million[g]	U.S., U.K., Canada, Chile, Argentina, Brazil
Laser Interferometer Gravitational Wave Observatory	1999	$231 million	U.S.

[a] Figures represent construction and development, exclusive of operational expenses, which can raise project costs considerably. Figures represent dollars as spent or projected, unadjusted for inflation.

[b] The Neutron Spallation Source is being proposed to replace the canceled Advanced Neutron Source.

[c] The estimated cost for the LHC would be roughly twice as large ($4 billion to $5 billion) if it were developed on the same accounting basis as U.S. cost estimates. Also this figure does not include the detectors, which may total as much as $2 billion. The proposed U.S. contribution to the project is $400 million. U.S. scientists are already deeply involved in the design and construction of two LHC detectors.

[d] The U.S. share is currently 25 percent of the engineering design cost. Detailed cost estimates for ITER are not yet available. There has been no agreement among the parties about whether ITER will be built or what the U.S. share of construction costs would be.

[e] For U.S. space projects, figures reflect U.S. cost only.

[f] Unofficial ESA estimate.

[g] The U.S. share is $88 million.

SOURCE: U.S. Congress, Office of Technology Assessment, 1995, based on figures from: William Boesman, Congressional Research Service, "Big Science and Technology Projects: Analysis of 30 Selected U.S. Government Projects," August 1994; Genevieve J. Knezo, *Major Science and Technology Programs: Megaprojects and Presidential Initiatives, Trends Through FY 1996, Requested,* CRS Report for Congress (Washington, DC: Congressional Research Service, Mar. 27, 1995); NASA Budget Operations Office; and Tormod Riste, *Synchrotron Radiation Sources and Neutron Beams* (Paris, France: Organization for Economic Cooperation and Development, Megascience Forum, 1994).

Below the billion-dollar project level, it becomes more difficult to use funding to determine what constitutes megascience. A recent Congressional Research Service report on civilian big science and technology (S&T) projects identified 30 S&T development projects that cost more than $100 million in 1980 dollars.[10] Of these, 10 had

[10] William Boesman, *Big Science and Technology Projects: Analysis of 30 Selected U.S. Government Projects*, CRS Report for Congress, 94-687 SPR (Washington, DC: Congressional Research Service, Aug. 24, 1994).

been terminated,[11] leaving 20 projects completed or currently under way. Of these 20 projects, 16 were single-facility, basic science projects, accounting collectively for more than $50 billion of past, current, and proposed federal science spending (exclusive of operations costs). For the purposes of this report, the Office of Technology Assessment (OTA) has chosen to concentrate on the class of megaprojects that cost more than $100 million.

The budget impacts of these megaprojects have drawn considerable attention in the scientific community and Congress. In the United States, megaprojects account for about 10 percent of the federal (defense and nondefense) R&D budget[12] (see figure 1-1). Although the growth of megaprojects appears to have leveled off somewhat, this trend could be reversed as several big science projects are brought up for congressional consideration over the next few years.[13] Thus, megaprojects merit attention not just because of their extraordinary size, but also because their large and potentially growing share of federal spending poses fundamental questions about the character of the nation's R&D portfolio.

In recent years, the high costs and scientific rationale of some megaprojects have been severely criticized, especially by those who regard small science as the foundation of the nation's R&D enterprise. In some cases, however, there can be a complementary relationship between small science and big science. For example, the National High Magnetic Field Laboratory and the Advanced Photon Source (an advanced x-ray synchrotron facility) will essentially serve as platforms for small science, and thus reinforce the re-

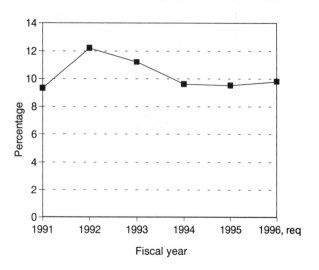

FIGURE 1-1: Civilian and Defense Megaprojects as a Percentage of Total R&D, FY 1991-FY 1996, Requested

SOURCE: Genevieve J. Knezo, *Major Science and Technology Programs, Megaprojects and Presidential Initiatives, Trends Through FY 1996, Requested*, CRS Report for Congress (Washington, DC: Congressional Research Service, Mar. 27, 1995), p. CRS-4.

search support given to individual investigators across many disciplines.[14] Telescopes provide another example of large devices or facilities that serve individual investigators. But many other large projects do not directly complement small science activities. Priority setting is therefore becoming much more of an issue because all proposed megaprojects may not be supportable without affecting the underlying national science base.

---

[11] An additional two programs (Advanced X-Ray Astrophysics Facility and Comet Rendezvous Asteroid Flyby Mission/Cassini) were partially terminated.

[12] This figure is based on a "basket" of large projects tracked by the Congressional Research Service. See Genevieve J. Knezo, *Major Science and Technology Programs: Megaprojects and Presidential Initiatives, Trends Through FY 1996, Requested*, CRS Report for Congress (Washington, DC: Congressional Research Service, Mar. 27, 1995).

[13] For example, carrying out the present development plan for a tokamak fusion reactor implies a doubling or even tripling of the annual magnetic fusion budget from its present level ($373 million in FY 1995). See chapter 3.

[14] These facilities will be used by researchers in a number of different fields, including materials science, condensed matter physics, chemistry, and molecular biology.

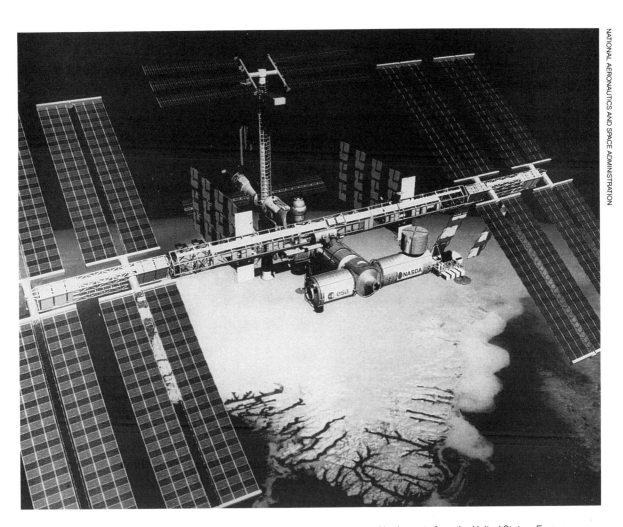

The International Space Station is depicted in its completed operational state, with elements from the United States, Europe, Canada, Japan, and Russia.

▮ Why Are Big Science Projects So Big?

The development of large projects has been driven by several factors. In some fields of inquiry, scientific projects or undertakings must be large in scale in order to advance and demonstrate the underlying science or to achieve specific technical goals. For example, probing the high-energy domains that will provide new insights into the fundamental characteristics of matter, or demonstrating the feasibility of controlled nuclear fu-

sion, will require apparatus (accelerators, detectors, reactors) of unusual size and sophistication. The International Space Station project—an effort to build and operate a permanently occupied Earth-orbiting facility—is, by its very nature, a complicated, immense undertaking. Other classes of problems, such as climate change, are truly global in nature. They require broad-based multinational, multidisciplinary initiatives to develop better scientific understanding of fundamental physical processes and to ensure the international credibility of scientific results.[15]

Other motives, less directly related to basic research questions, also underlie the development of megaprojects. Large science projects are often viewed as symbols of national prestige. They may, in addition, serve as vehicles for building up domestic capabilities in different scientific and technical fields, and thus enhancing national economic productivity.[16] Political or foreign policy imperatives confronting governments can play an important role in launching large projects, as can the desire of research institutions to sustain or enlarge their portfolio of programs.

■ Experience in International Scientific Collaboration

The United States has participated in a variety of international science undertakings, both large and small, over the past few decades. Some of these international activities have developed from U.S. domestic projects. The United States has also participated in joint research organizations and projects, and is a contributing member in still other arrangements and organizations. This scientific collaboration can take many different forms involving varying degrees of research integration, financial and legal obligations, and management oversight, as described in box 1-1. Large projects have covered a broad spectrum of activity from pure fundamental research to near-commercial demonstrations (e.g., coal gasification).

For decades, the United States has enjoyed numerous successful small-scale scientific cooperative efforts, principally through bilateral agreements. Typically, these agreements involve

NATIONAL AERONAUTICS AND SPACE ADMINISTRATION

The Ocean Topography Experiment (TOPEX)/Poseidon is a cooperative project between the United States and France to develop and operate an advanced satellite system dedicated to observing the Earth's oceans.

the exchange of information and/or scientists and provide for access to facilities. There have also been a number of small- to medium-scale collaborative efforts involving the development of specialized instrumentation sponsored by the Department of Energy (DOE), the National Science Foundation, and the National Aeronautics and Space Administration (NASA).[17]

Big science projects, however, present a different picture. Until recently, the United States has approached most megascience projects as primar-

---

[15]The worldwide global change research program, as presently conceived, could have a cumulative multinational cost approaching $100 billion by the year 2020. See President's Council of Advisors on Science and Technology, *Megaprojects in the Sciences* (Washington, DC: Office of Science and Technology Policy, Executive Office of the President, December 1992).

[16]For example, the expertise gained from the development of superconducting magnet technology for particle accelerators and for magnetic fusion could ultimately be applied to such commercially important applications as magnetic resonance imaging, electric motors, advanced materials processing, and energy storage. U.S. Congress, Office of Technology Assessment, *High-Temperature Superconductivity in Perspective*, OTA-E-440 (Washington, DC: U.S. Government Printing Office, April 1990).

[17]For example, DOE has been involved with a variety of multilateral cooperative activities under the auspices of the International Energy Agency. See chapter 3 for a discussion of NASA's long history of collaborative activity.

ily domestic ventures. Most U.S. high-energy physics, space, and fusion facilities have been designed and funded as national projects, even though there has been growing collaboration in these fields at operational levels.[18] The U.S. experience in international collaboration in science and technology R&D—where research efforts are highly interdependent and jointly funded and conducted—is actually quite limited. The United States is only now starting to participate in the joint planning, construction, and operation of large facilities or platforms (e.g., ITER and the U.S.-Russian activities associated with the space station.)[19] These represent more integrated forms of collaboration than the compartmentalized approaches in which partners work independently on discrete elements of a project, as in the case of the European and Japanese components of the space station. The United States is still discovering what particular approaches to international collaboration can lead to stable, successful execution of long-term projects.

In contrast to the United States, other industrialized countries, especially the nations of Western Europe, have had more extensive experience with scientific collaborations in projects of all sizes. Europe's long history of collaboration has been motivated and facilitated by a variety of factors including close geographic proximity, demography, high levels of nonscientific interchange among partner countries, and joint competition with the United States. In addition, the treaty establishing the European Union calls for joint research activities and programs among member states. Yet, it must also be noted that European countries collaborate extensively in large measure because they effectively have little choice. The funding requirements and technical breadth of modern science R&D—especially megaprojects—often make it necessary for European countries to join forces across a broad spectrum of projects and disciplines. This trend has strengthened in recent years. In the eyes of some observers, European scientific collaboration has now become the norm, driven by European political integration and the need to pool scientific and financial resources.

■ Why Collaborate?

Given the breadth, ingenuity, and vitality of the modern scientific enterprise, policymakers in virtually all countries are confronted with difficult choices in establishing priorities for R&D. Included in this process of priority setting and project selection is determining whether large-scale international science undertakings complement national science goals and to what extent they should be supported. At a time when all governments are sensitive to the strategic economic advantages that can accrue from knowledge-based or technology-based industries, participation in international projects is evaluated closely. Although some countries may see distinct benefits associated with multinational partnerships, others may deem participation in particular projects inconsistent with the national interest. The latter may be particularly true if a nation is attempting

---

[18]Examples of national facilities are the Fermi National Accelerator Laboratory, the Stanford Linear Accelerator Center, the National High Magnetic Field Laboratory at Florida State University, and the Advanced Photon Source at Argonne National Laboratory. Each of these facilities have open access policies that encourage collaboration with foreign scientists.

[19] Although Canadian robotics have been on the space station's critical path from the beginning, the U.S. agreement with Canada provides for all Canadian hardware, drawing, and materials to be turned over to NASA in the event Canada withdraws from the program. This gives the agency ultimate control over the contribution and its underlying technology. The same provisions governed the development of Canada's robotic arm for the space shuttle.

BOX 1-1: Forms of International Collaboration

International scientific cooperation ranges from simple exchange of information and personnel in particular areas of research to joint planning, design, and construction of equipment or facilities. As cooperative arrangements become more complex in scale or scope, the need for more formalized organizational and managerial arrangements increases. The levels of program integration, information transfer, and financial and political commitment depend on the nature of the collaborative activity. Historically, many areas of international cooperation have proceeded on the basis of mutual trust. However, big science activities involving significant expenditure of human and financial resources require well-defined agreements that delineate specific project objectives and responsibilities.

International scientific collaborative activities can be classified into four broad categories:[1]

The **joint construction and operation** of large-scale experiments and facilities is the most highly structured and interdependent form of multilateral collaboration. It involves close partnership among project participants, with each country having a roughly equal voice in project planning, financing, and management. This type of cooperation sometimes involves the creation of elaborate institutional mechanisms to facilitate project decisionmaking and execution. Examples include the European Laboratory for Particle Physics (CERN), a 17-nation consortium that pursues research in high-energy physics; the International Thermonuclear Experimental Reactor (ITER) engineering design activity being pursued by the United States, Japan, Europe, and Russia; and the European Space Agency (ESA), a 14-member organization to pursue joint European activities in space.

Lead country collaborations are a less integrated mode of collaboration. Here, one country assumes the lead in pursuing a particular project while inviting other countries to make technical and financial contributions without taking on significant management responsibilities. The space station is one example of this type of collaboration. The National Aeronautics and Space Administration retains principal decisionmaking authority over its design and planning, while integrating specific technical modules or components from Russia, Japan, and Europe. Another example is the Hadron-Electron Ring Accelerator. In this project, foreign countries are paying about 30 percent of the costs of operating this German national facility. Other illustrations of this type of cooperation include the international Ocean Drilling Program, initiated and led by the U.S. National Science Foundation; detector experiments at the Fermi National Accelerator Laboratory, to which Japan and Italy contributed key components; and the Japanese Planet-B mission to Mars, which involves five different countries.

---

to preserve or develop national expertise in a particular scientific or technological field.[20]

In the United States, the decision to collaborate rather than pursue research on a domestic basis has been determined by a set of factors specific to U.S. science goals and other interests. The goal of establishing and maintaining leadership in as many scientific fields as possible was especially important during the Cold War and dominated the

U.S. approach to collaboration through the late 1970s. However, the development of scientific ambitions and expertise abroad, the constriction of U.S. government resources at home, and the end of the Cold War may require both a redefinition of U.S. leadership and a reformulation of the U.S. approach to international scientific collaboration. In addition, other goals—including economic competitiveness, foreign policy and na-

---

[20]As an illustration, the construction of Japan's Subaru telescope in Hawaii is linked to building up its domestic astronomy program and attracting young people to the field. For this reason, Japan chose not to join the multilateral Gemini collaboration. Other examples include various national efforts to develop sophisticated capabilities in launching and deploying satellites.

BOX1-1: Cont'd.

Distributed science projects, in which countries separately design, fund, and direct portions of a larger coordinated project, are another form of collaboration. Examples of distributed science projects include data gathering under the auspices of the worldwide Global Change Research Program; harmonization efforts for human genome research under the Human Genome Organization, sponsored by the United States and Europe; and the International Solar-Terrestrial Physics Programme involving Japan, Europe, the United States, and others.

The final category of international cooperation entails specific **user group projects**, in which individual researchers or governments use the experimental facilities or capabilities of other countries, but provide the necessary equipment or financing for specific experiments. The use of another country's space capabilities to launch satellites illustrates this type of cooperation. Building instrumentation that can be used at large neutron beam or synchrotron radiation facilities is another example. When large facilities are involved, formal and informal arrangements have allowed scientists from one country "reciprocal" access to similar facilities in other countries.

Each of these collaborative forms permits, to differing degrees, the opportunity to reduce or share costs; to leverage intellectual resources and technical capabilities; and depending on the nature of the project, to address wider global concerns such as improved international stability.

---

[1]This classification has been suggested by William A. Blanpied and Jennifer S. Bond, "Megaprojects in the Sciences," *Megascience and its Background,* OECD Megascience Forum (Paris, France: Organization for Economic Cooperation and Development, 1993), pp. 43-44.

---

tional security priorities, and environmental and social considerations—increasingly affect the U.S. attitude toward collaboration.[21]

Current and recent collaborations illustrate the difficulty in deciding whether to collaborate and the challenges in clearly defining U.S. goals. OTA's review of the U.S. experience in international cooperation in high-energy physics, fusion, and space has identified several advantages and disadvantages associated with collaborative ventures.

The scope and complexity of some scientific initiatives may by their very nature require a multinational collaborative effort to ensure that research objectives are successfully achieved.[22] Indeed, collaboration has long been used to enhance the scientific and engineering capabilities in R&D projects. The pooling of intellectual and technical resources from throughout the world has led to important experimental and theoretical advances in a variety of scientific fields. Moreover,

---

[21]See, for example: William J. Clinton and Albert Gore, Jr., *Science in the National Interest* (Washington, DC: Executive Office of the President, August 1994), which sets forth broad science and technology policy goals of the Clinton Administration; and National Academy of Sciences, *Science, Technology, and the Federal Government: National Goals for a New Era* (Washington, DC: National Academy Press, June 1993), which suggests a framework for establishing science goals and priorities and rethinking the role of "scientific leadership." See also: Ralph Gomory and Hirsh Cohen, "Science: How Much Is Enough?" *Scientific American,* July 1993, p. 120; and Eugene B. Skolnikoff, *The Elusive Transformation: Science, Technology, and the Evolution of International Politics* (Princeton, NJ: Princeton University Press, 1993).

[22]For example, some scientific initiatives, such as climate change research, may require that research be carried out at several geographic locations around the world. For other initiatives that involve great technical complexity, such as the effort to harness fusion power, collaboration is viewed by many scientists as an important and even necessary vehicle for achieving project goals.

with the emergence of new centers of innovation abroad, the only way for the U.S. scientific community to extend its expertise in particular areas may be through collaboration.[23] As the scientific and technical competencies of other nations become comparable to or even surpass U.S. capabilities,[24] the United States may have to place a greater emphasis on having access to foreign facilities and participating in multilateral R&D projects if it is to remain competitive in different technical fields. In addition, the upgrading of U.S. scientific facilities may be necessary to encourage other countries to cooperate with the United States on both large and small projects.[25] These considerations underscore the need for reassessing the concept of leadership and how national scientific expertise can be most effectively advanced, as well as examining the nature of partnership and the various approaches to collaboration.

Another motivation for pursuing collaboration is economic. Concerns over the huge scale and large cost of some new projects have led scientists and policymakers in many countries to suggest sharing the burdens internationally. Collaboration is seen by some as particularly important to capital-intensive research endeavors that lack short- or medium-term commercial viability. This view has been presented to support international research projects such as ITER and the space station. Collaboration can reduce the net costs that individual nations must bear, though the aggregate cost of a multinational project may sometimes be greater than that of a project carried out by a single country. International projects may require the creation of elaborate management and logistical arrangements. For example, engineering design activities for the proposed ITER project are being carried out at three separate locations in the United States, Japan, and Germany. Also, in some cases, cost savings may not be as great as expected, because participation in international ventures still requires that investments be made in national programs. Without such investments, it may not be possible for individual countries to benefit fully from the advances coming from international projects.

Domestic and international political considerations can also be factors in pursuing collaboration. Projects are sometimes internationalized to raise their political profile and thereby ensure the continuity of funding. For instance, the formal involvement and integration of Russia in the planning and operation of the International Space Station project was to some degree motivated by the U.S. desire to support the Russian reform process and to promote Russian adherence to the Missile Technology Control Regime.[26] Political goals have also been an important aspect of European collaborative science projects.[27]

Other factors, related to changes in the nature of R&D itself, have induced both scientists and

---

[23]For example, after the cancellation of the Superconducting Super Collider, a DOE advisory panel recommended that the United States formally join the Large Hadron Collider project at CERN to ensure that U.S. scientists remain at the forefront of accelerator design and physics investigation. See U.S. Department of Energy, Office of Energy Research, Division of High Energy Physics, *High Energy Physics Advisory Panel's Subpanel on Vision for the Future of High Energy Physics*, DOE/ER-0614P (Washington, DC: May 1994).

[24]See footnote 21.

[25]Many large U.S. science facilities operate at limited capacity because of funding constraints. In addition, there is a need for upgrading equipment and instrumentation. The fiscal year 1996 budget of the Clinton Administration proposes "adding $100 million above the 1995 level to significantly enhance the usage of major DOE-operated basic research facilities." This initiative will "facilitate a more efficient use of the facilities, boost the number of users by several thousand over 1995, and improve the quality of service." See *Budget of the United States Government, Fiscal Year 1996* (Washington, DC: U.S. Government Printing Office, 1995), p. 97.

[26]See U.S. Congress, Office of Technology Assessment, *U.S.-Russian Cooperation in Space*, OTA-ISS-618 (Washington, DC: U.S. Government Printing Office, April 1995).

[27]See Antonio Ruberti and Michel Andre, "The European Model of Research Cooperation," *Issues in Science and Technology*, spring 1995, pp. 17-21.

policymakers to give greater consideration to international cooperation. The global nature of some scientific areas, such as the environment, may necessitate a more international orientation for basic research. The widespread applicability of new technologies coupled with the globalization of business may also support a more explicit international approach to scientific innovation. Increasingly, R&D activities in the private sector involve strategic alliances among companies from many different countries.[28]

■ Challenges and Limitations of International Collaboration

While international collaboration may play an increasingly prominent role in R&D, there remains a variety of challenges and limitations. Collaboration raises fundamental questions about national goals and the U.S. role in scientific and technological innovation. Efforts to increase U.S. participation in international cooperative ventures potentially conflict with the U.S. desire to maintain scientific leadership, prestige, and project control.

A number of issues associated with project financing also can make it difficult to initiate, structure, and execute international projects. The difficulty in guaranteeing long-term financial commitment by all project partners introduces an element of instability to international undertakings. In discussions with OTA, European and Japanese government officials and scientists particularly questioned the reliability of the United States in maintaining the continuity and level of funding necessary for international R&D agreements. Distributing project costs and benefits in a more or less equitable manner among partners continues to complicate collaborations. Furthermore, some projects may be so expensive or involve such a high level of technical uncertain-

ty that, even with multilateral burden sharing, the cost of U.S. or any other nation's participation could be prohibitively high. And this of course could make it difficult to generate the political support necessary to initiate and sustain such projects.

Another challenge to multinational projects is that the collaborative process itself may inhibit innovation by limiting competition among researchers. Due to the need to achieve technical consensus, collaboration that involves many partners might lead to projects that have somewhat conservative technical or scientific goals. ITER, for example, has been criticized by some observers for having a fairly conservative design because planners want to ensure that ignition of fusion fuel can actually be achieved. However, collaboration can also give rise to creative approaches or solutions because of the wider base of scientific talent that can be tapped. The success of the LHC project at CERN, for instance, is dependent on some extremely ambitious magnet and detector technologies. Moreover, it is possible to retain elements of competition within single large science projects—for example, when two or more research groups independently build and operate detectors while using the same particle accelerator. A key objective for all collaborative activities is to ensure that project objectives can be realized without suppressing innovative ideas or techniques.

Other challenges to international collaboration include the need for elaborate management and decisionmaking mechanisms and the possible loss of commercial advantage through the transfer of leading-edge national technologies. An additional issue involves striking an appropriate balance between the resources dedicated to collaboration and the need for maintaining a domestic education and R&D infrastructure to sustain and profit from a collaboration. Finally, for

---

[28]One example is the multi-billion dollar development effort of IBM, Toshiba, and Siemens to develop next-generation semiconductor memory technology. See "Computer Chip Project Brings Rivals Together, But the Cultures Clash," *Wall Street Journal*, May 3, 1994, p. A1.

some R&D projects, there may exist significant scientific and economic implications that could warrant the pursuit of purely national efforts.[29]

Policymakers within both the legislative and the executive branches have suggested various strategies to address the challenges of project selection and funding stability. Under one approach, countries would cooperate in prioritizing and selecting proposed big science projects from a variety of disciplines by placing these projects in a common "basket" where their relative costs and benefits could be traded off against each other. Others have suggested creating new international organizations to coordinate information, facilitate collaborations, or manage new international projects. Potential mechanisms for ensuring greater administrative and funding stability in multinational collaborations have also received the attention of policymakers and the scientific community. Proposals have been made that Congress adopt specific multiyear authorizations or appropriations for large projects to promote their long-term viability.

FINDINGS

The opportunities and challenges of international collaboration indicate a series of important issues to consider in structuring future large science undertakings. OTA's principal findings are presented below.

- **Big science projects cover an array of disciplines and vary considerably in form and purpose. Thus, funding and research prioritization decisions for big science projects are likely to be more effective and appropriate within their respective research fields, rather than among a group of unrelated costly projects.**

Large science projects are relatively few and highly diverse. They differ in scale, complexity, structure and the degree to which broad national or global needs are addressed. As a consequence of their differences, the scientific and social returns from big science projects tend to be incommensurate both within a particular project and among projects. For example, some projects involve the design and construction of a single large instrument such as an accelerator, while others like the Human Genome Project entail coordination of research activities that are widely dispersed. One project may have an explicit scientific rationale, while another may have broad economic, educational, or foreign policy objectives.

Although it may appear reasonable to lump big projects together for policy and budgetary reasons, in practice their disparate characteristics generally preclude concrete project-to-project comparisons. These characteristics of diversity and the difficulty in balancing costs and benefits among projects have important implications for policies addressing big science:

- Generic frameworks for setting priorities among large science projects on a national or international basis are probably not workable.
- The overall scientific merit as well as the associated costs and benefits of different projects are most effectively evaluated within the broader research and budgetary context of each specific scientific field.
- The appropriateness and extent of international collaboration in any large science project can be determined only on a case-specific basis.

While big science projects continue to draw congressional attention, they are only one example of the major budget challenges facing federal R&D efforts overall. Priority setting occurs

---

[29]For example, synchrotron radiation facilities are heavily used by U.S. academia and private industry, and thus might be regarded as essential investments in national scientific infrastructure. In the area of applied research, the federal government has spent nearly $800 million over an eight-year period in supporting the SEMATECH consortium. This consortium of U.S. semiconductor producers and suppliers was created to bolster U.S. capabilities in semiconductor processing and manufacturing to ensure a viable microelectronics commercial and defense base. U.S. member companies matched the government contributions to the project.

throughout the federal government at many different levels. At the highest level, scientific priorities are compared to other nonscience needs. Priorities are also determined within particular disciplines. However, attempts at setting priorities across different scientific fields have suffered from a lack of consensus and have been largely unsuccessful. Because large projects are not readily comparable, and their political components make each unique,[30] any attempt to develop a priority-setting scheme for big projects is likely to encounter a variety of obstacles. Consequently, the largely ad hoc funding process for big projects will be difficult to change. Still, many observers believe that some mechanism of priority setting for large projects, whether domestic or international, is essential.[31]

These observations have particular relevance to the proposed basket approach, under which major science projects in different disciplines would be identified and placed in a common group or basket for nations to select or trade off one project against another. For example, if two or more big science projects were being built contemporaneously, there hypothetically could be some trading of costs and benefits between them. Under this scenario, one nation might agree to host a new high-energy physics facility, while another might host a fusion facility. In theory, this would provide a means for different countries to share both the burdens and the benefits of international science facilities. It could also be a vehicle for building political support for projects by demonstrating that foreign partners are willing to contribute to projects in other countries, as well as those that are based at home.

In practice, however, the basket approach has a variety of limitations. The timing and development of various projects usually differ significant-

Under a bilateral agreement, the Japanese contributed to operations and upgrade of the Doublet III-D (DIII-D) tokamak at General Atomics in San Diego in exchange for "hands-on" operating experience later transferrable to their new JT-60 tokamak.

ly, and thus they cannot easily be lumped together. In addition, projects can encompass very different technologies, and consequently individual countries may be interested in participating or hosting particular projects and not participating in others. Big projects also have a variety of objectives. For example, while some large science projects may have very specific goals such as achieving controlled ignition of fusion fuel (ITER) or discovering a new class of fundamental particles (the LHC at CERN), others may have a broader set of purposes. As an illustration, neutron sources and synchrotron facilities essentially serve as platforms for small science undertakings. Although the costs of these platform facilities may be considerable,[32] they could be regarded as long-term investments that provide the underlying infrastructure for decades of research in a variety of different disciplines (e.g., materials science, sol-

---

[30]For example, some programs and projects, particularly those that are capital-intensive, have developed strong industrial constituencies.

[31]For example, see William A. Blanpied and Jennifer S. Bond, "Megascience Projects: Challenges for the 21st Century," prepared for the International Workshop on Equipping Science for the 21st Century, Amsterdam, The Netherlands, April 1992. For a discussion of possible criteria that might be used in cross-discipline priority setting see Office of Technology Assessment, *Federally Funded Research*, footnote 2.

[32]For instance, the recently terminated Advanced Neutron Source had an estimated cost of $3.2 billion, and the nearly completed Advanced Photon Source will cost approximately $800 million (including both construction and related R&D costs).

id-state physics, chemistry, and structural biology). Having ready access to such facilities could have long-term implications for scientific and industrial competitiveness.

In general, the development of proposals for scientific projects is very much a "bottom-up" process. The scientific community plays a major role in setting the scientific agenda, and years are often required for specific and detailed research proposals to take shape.[33] Depending on how the basket idea is applied, it could undermine this bottom-up process. An ad hoc procedure of apportioning projects among different countries might come into conflict with a previously agreed on national R&D strategy, or might weaken a nation's effort to develop specific scientific or technical expertise. For these reasons, the basket approach is considered by some policymakers to be infeasible.[34]

At some level, though, there must be a linking of bottom-up planning and review procedures with top-down priority setting, and thus some multilateral decisionmaking framework for large projects will probably need to evolve (see finding below). In the near term, it is possible that an informal distribution of big projects to different regions of the world will still occur.

Since future large science projects are likely to be relatively few in number, approaching them on an individual basis should not be burdensome for policymakers or scientists. For the foreseeable future, megascience projects will probably best be realized when the most interested parties simply choose to collaborate.

- **Early and explicit consideration of international collaboration in the planning and authorization process for large projects would better identify opportunities for cooperation.**

There are clear reasons to consider international collaboration in any large, complex scientific undertaking. Among them are the potential for reducing costs, sharing risks, and enhancing scientific capabilities. Indeed, some scientifically worthy but expensive projects might not be pursued at all unless carried out on a collaborative basis. A more proactive approach to international cooperation would provide the United States with a broader set of scientific and budgetary options, and would ensure more effective and mutually advantageous collaborations in the future.

A variety of benefits could result if international collaboration for large science projects were considered as an option early in the planning process. Projects can benefit from formal cooperative arrangements even in their preliminary R&D stages. Such arrangements can foster "buy-in" to later technical choices and decisions by potential partners, and can result in a more efficient project development phase as well as a more thoroughly considered final proposal. An example of this approach is in the field of high-energy physics, where the development of the underlying accelerator physics and technology for the Next Linear Collider (NLC)[35] is being coordinated and reviewed by a collaborative working group representing laboratories in the United States, Europe, Japan, and the former Soviet Union.

---

[33]The U.S. government, for example, relies extensively on expert advisory panels to review scientific project proposals and to determine the long-term agenda of particular research fields. In Europe, the newly opened European Synchrotron Radiation Facility required almost two decades of discussion and planning before it was completed.

[34]In OTA discussions with European and Japanese science policy officials, the basket approach was dismissed as being impractical. However, under certain circumstances, it may be feasible to have a "small basket" for a specific field of research. For example, the effort to develop fusion power has a variety of different requirements including the construction of an engineering reactor such as ITER, an advanced physics machine such as the Tokamak Physics Experiment, and a materials irradiation facility. Nations participating in the international fusion effort could perhaps decide to share costs and distribute benefits by building each of these facilities in different countries.

[35]The NLC is an electron-positron collider now in the concept and early development stage. It is regarded as a complementary instrument to the Large Hadron Collider at CERN.

The United States has sometimes pursued international partnerships after facing budget constraints well into a project, as in the case of the Superconducting Super Collider (SSC), the space station, and the Earth Observing System (EOS).[36] In the case of the SSC, the United States sought foreign partners as a way of sharing costs well after key scientific and engineering decisions had been made and therefore had difficulty in securing commitments. In the case of the two space projects, the United States might have saved time and money, increased program technical sophistication, and avoided tensions with partners if it had planned more extensive and integrated collaborations from the beginning (see chapter 3). In other cases, scientists and project planners gave serious consideration to collaboration only after being directed to do so by Congress. For example, this occurred when Congress directed the National Science Foundation to pursue the Gemini telescope project on an international rather than a national basis.

One approach Congress might consider is to require agencies to provide justification for pursuing or not pursuing international collaboration if projects exceed a certain monetary threshold—for example, $100 million. The specific threshold value is less important than the exercise of exploring the possible scientific and fiscal benefits of internationalizing a proposed project or elements of a project. As an alternative, policymakers might compare the projected annual peak spending for a project to the annual appropriations for the relevant overall program. For example, the SSC needed a peak appropriation of nearly $1 billion on top of a base program in high-energy physics that was being funded at a level of $600 million. Thus, from this perspective, the SSC was a strong candidate for international collaboration.

As part of the procedure for funding new projects, agencies could be required to prepare an analysis that includes the following elements:

- an assessment of whether a proposed project is too costly or technically challenging for any one party;
- the international scientific context of the project: other countries' programs, capabilities, and goals;
- the nature of U.S. discussions with other countries about collaboration;
- prospective commitments of other countries (technical and financial) to the project or to competing projects;
- national security, commercial, legal, and technology-transfer implications of international collaboration; and
- justification for seeking or avoiding such collaboration.

Such a review process would force consideration of collaboration at the start of projects, thereby better ensuring that opportunities to collaborate are not missed and that inappropriate collaborations are screened out. It should be noted that under this framework, the decision to pursue a project on a national or international basis would still depend on the specific nature of the scientific undertaking.

In each case, policymakers need to ascertain whether the greatest scientific, budgetary, and commercial leverage can be achieved by entering into partnerships or by pursuing projects domestically. In some circumstances, collaborative arrangements can enhance U.S. scientific capabilities; in others, scientific and national objectives can be met better by pursuing projects on a domestic basis. Collaboration may not always be the most desirable or efficient means for achieving

---

[36] The space station program contained collaborative elements from the beginning, but until only recently all critical aspects of the project remained firmly under U.S. control. Although the Canadian robotics contribution has been on the project's "critical path" from the beginning, the U.S.-Canadian agreement assures ultimate project control for NASA in the case of Canadian withdrawal from the program. The EOS program originally envisioned foreign technical contributions that would complement data provided by planned U.S. instruments or which, in one case, would provide unique sensor capability. Subsequent budget reductions caused NASA to downsize the program, eliminate some U.S. instruments, and greatly expand its reliance on foreign instruments for certain data.

technical goals. Moreover, if particular projects can strengthen the national skill base, or provide opportunities to improve economic productivity, collaboration might not necessarily be in the national interest.

Furthermore, in some instances, it may be beneficial to construct multiple facilities. Having parallel facilities—whether within a country or in different countries—can broaden access to facilities or instrumentation and encourage more competition and innovation in particular disciplines. For example, the United States, Europe, and Japan are each sponsoring major new x-ray synchrotron radiation facilities (see chapter 3). Although each of the projects (varying from $800 million to $1 billion in their respective construction and development costs) has similar technical characteristics, they are not necessarily redundant because of the utility of synchrotron sources to a variety of scientific fields and industries.

- **Although the United States has generally met its fiscal and performance obligations under international arrangements for scientific cooperation, and often assumed a large share of funding responsibility for projects, concerns persist among potential partners about the reliability of U.S. commitments. Future partnerships may have to be more formally structured to address these concerns.**

Questions about the reliability of U.S. commitments to international scientific collaborations were frequently raised by U.S. and foreign government officials, and other interested observers in interviews with OTA. These concerns can be traced to a few international projects canceled in the early 1980s, U.S. design changes on the International Space Station, the cancellation of the SSC, and to funding uncertainties associated with the U.S. practice of making annual appropriations for major science projects. Differences in govern-

ment structure and in approaches to science research planning, budgeting, and funding processes among the United States and its partners also contribute to the perception that the United States is less able to sustain its obligations.

Commonly cited as examples of shifting U.S. international commitments are two projects that were terminated after the United States had entered into international collaborative agreements—the Solvent Refined Coal II demonstration project canceled in 1981 (see box 1-2) and the U.S. spacecraft for the International Solar Polar Mission canceled in 1982 (see box 1-3).

Among the factors leading to the termination or rescoping of projects were changes in administrations and policies, and increasing budget pressures. These changes in U.S. priorities may not have surprised seasoned political observers, but foreign partners were in some cases dismayed by the abruptness in which the U.S. decided to withdraw from specific international endeavors. In particular, foreign scientists were largely unprepared for the sudden cancellation of the SSC and the redesigns of the space station.[37]

Although these project histories provide some basis for the widely expressed view that the United States has been an unreliable partner in science collaborations, changes in U.S. positions have generally occurred for identifiable reasons, and often involved extensive thought and debate. In some cases, projects have been terminated due to serious cost escalation or poor project management. Others have been canceled in the face of specific agency budget constraints. These decisions have tended to be exceptions to the U.S. record in international collaboration. In other instances, U.S. research agencies have given priority to support of international efforts over domestic projects in the face of unexpected budget cuts. For example, the U.S. Department of Energy

---

[37]See discussions of these projects in chapter 3 of this report.

BOX 1-2: The Solvent Refined Coal II (SRC-II) Demonstration Project

The SRC-II demonstration project was one of a number of aggressive efforts to develop commercial synthetic fuels begun in the energy crisis atmosphere of the 1970s. The SRC-II project was to be a $1.5 billion (1981 dollars) demonstration plant in Morgantown, West Virginia, that would convert 6,000 tons per day of high-sulfur, high-ash bituminous coal into a light distillate through a direct coal liquefaction process.

The project was initially begun as a phased effort between the U.S. Department of Energy (DOE) and the Gulf Oil subsidiary, Pittsburgh and Midway Coal Mining Company. The project had been jointly initiated by Congress and DOE under the Federal Non-Nuclear Energy Research and Development Act of 1974.

According to some DOE fossil energy officials, the decision to pursue the SRC-II demonstration project as an international collaboration was made after DOE agreed to construct both the SRC-II liquid fuel demonstration plant in West Virginia and the related SRC-I solid fuel demonstration plant in Kentucky. DOE had originally planned to select one of the plants for construction after completion of the design phase. To help offset the costs of building the two plants, DOE solicited participation from the Japanese and Germans who had earlier expressed interest in the direct coal liquefaction technology.

In July 1980, an agreement was signed among the governments of the United States, West Germany, and Japan to sponsor the project. A joint venture was formed with Gulf and with Japanese and German industrial firms to carry out the project. Under the agreements, DOE was to contribute about 50 percent of the total cost, Japan and Germany were to provide about 25 percent each, and corporate participants were to provide $100 million in cash and in kind.

In 1981, the Reagan Administration sought to terminate funding for SRC-II and a number of other energy demonstration and commercialization efforts. The objections were both economic and political. By 1981, oil prices were trending downward and the crisis atmosphere had abated. Concerns over federal spending were leading to increased pressure for cutting back programs of all kinds. As a policy matter, the Reagan Administration felt that such demonstration and commercialization efforts were not appropriate for funding directly through the government but rather should be done by the private sector or the Synthetic Fuels Corporation. The project was eventually terminated by a joint decision of DOE, West Germany, and Japan in June 1981. The remaining unobligated funds were transferred to energy conservation activities.

Although U.S. and German government officials were somewhat indifferent to the fate of SRC-II, Japanese government officials were dismayed by its demise, according to OTA interviews. The careers of Japanese government employees who had been instrumental in Japan's participation in SRC-II were said to have been adversely affected as a result. Still other sources suggested that Japanese participation in SRC-II had been a quid pro quo for granting them access to the General Atomics DIII-D fusion tokamak technology and had been an attempt to insulate the troubled synthetic fuels project from political attack.

Interestingly, the cancellation of SRC-II, just one of many early synthetic fuels ventures abandoned amid falling oil prices, has not been of high concern in the area of fossil fuels research, but has attained the status of legend among high-energy physicists, fusion researchers, and space scientists. Despite the rather clear rationale for its termination, foreign policymakers frequently cite the SRC-II endeavor as an example of the United States failing to honor its international obligations.

SOURCES: J. Freel et al., "Synfuels Processing: The SRC-II Demonstration Project," *Chemical Engineering Progress*, vol. 77, May 1981, pp. 86-90; William C. Boesman, *Big Science and Technology Projects: Analysis of 30 Selected U.S. Government Projects*, CRS Report to Congress, 94-687-SPR (Washington, DC: Congressional Research Service, Aug. 24, 1994), pp. 24-25; and Office of Technology Assessment, 1995.

BOX 1-3: The International Solar Polar Mission (ISPM) or Ulysses

Between 1974 and 1979, the National Aeronautics and Space Administration (NASA) and the European Space Agency (ESA) designed a highly collaborative two-satellite mission to study the poles of the Sun. In March 1979, NASA and ESA signed a Memorandum of Understanding (MOU) that planned for launch in 1983. Obtaining funding for the mission proved to be more difficult than designing the project. Although funding for the ESA satellite was not in doubt, the pressures of financing the completion of the space shuttle constrained NASA's ability to fund its $250-million ISPM budget. The ISPM received its first request of $13 million for fiscal year (FY) 1979, despite intense shuttle-related budgetary pressures. In FY 1980 and 1981, with pressures to complete the shuttle further constraining NASA's budget, ISPM survived two attempts by the House Committee on Appropriations to terminate it.

The final challenge to ISPM came in FY 1982, when the Administration cut NASA's science budget from $757.7 million to $584.2 million. NASA could meet this cut only by terminating one of its three large, scientific, satellite development programs: Galileo, Hubble, or ISPM. NASA decided to cancel the U.S. spacecraft in the ISPM and to delay launch of the European satellite until 1986.

The Europeans reacted with surprise and indignation—both at having been given no prior notice of cancellation and at the idea that an international agreement could be canceled at all. At a heated meeting between ESA and NASA officials in Washington shortly thereafter, ESA noted that it had chosen ISPM above a number of purely European missions to foster transatlantic cooperation and argued that the United States had unilaterally breached the MOU. NASA noted that the MOU had a clause allowing either partner to withdraw from its obligations if it had funding difficulties, but ESA officials said they thought that NASA would invoke this provision only in an extreme case.

The Europeans mounted intense diplomatic pressure at the Office of Management and Budget (OMB), the Office of Science and Technology Policy, the Department of State, and NASA to save the mission, proposing that NASA fly a simpler spacecraft, costing $40 million instead of the original $100 million, based on what was being built in Europe for ESA. NASA supported the new plan, but was told by OMB that no additional funding would be made available and that, if NASA wanted to keep ISPM, it would have to find the resources in its existing budget. In September 1981, NASA informed ESA that funding would not be sought for the European alternative, although the Europeans were encouraged to continue with the mission using just one spacecraft.

---

magnetic fusion energy program has consistently supported ITER design activities.[38]

Further complicating international scientific collaborations are the differences between the parliamentary government systems of our partners, in which executive and legislative authorities are merged, and the separate executive and legislative branches associated with the U.S. system of checks and balances. Ministers of parliamentary governments can effectively make and uphold long-term commitments. Under the U.S. system, executive branch officials cannot offer guarantees to the same extent. Additional action by Congress, such as support of authorizations, appropriations, treaty ratifications, or resolutions of approval, would be needed for an equivalent indication of government support.

---

[38]For a recent history of the DOE fusion energy research programs, see U.S. Congress, Office of Technology Assessment, *The Fusion Energy Program: The Role of TPX and Alternate Concepts*, OTA-BP-ETI-141 (Washington, DC: U.S. Government Printing Office, February 1995), ch. 2. DOE's decision to give priority to maintaining ITER funding over the U.S. base program was supported in reviews by U.S. fusion scientists.

BOX 1-3 Cont'd.

Cancellation of the U.S. satellite degraded the mission's scientific potential, eliminating about half of the originally planned instruments, and 80 positions for U.S. and European scientists. Cancellation also meant that the $15 million spent by European scientists on experiments for the U.S. spacecraft would be wasted. In 1982, ESA decided to proceed with a one-spacecraft mission, renamed Ulysses. Ulysses was scheduled to be launched in May 1986 but was delayed for more than four years by the Challenger accident. It was finally placed in orbit around the Sun by the Shuttle Discovery in October 1990.

Europeans contend that the ISPM cancellation deeply weakened their confidence in the reliability of U.S. commitments. According to ESA officials who participated in the ISPM negotiations with the United States: "No one can deny that the ISPM crisis had a profound and lasting effect on the attitude of ESA towards NASA and on international cooperation in general." They contrast the attitudes of the two partners to the MOU, seen as binding by ESA but a "sort of—loose—gentlemen's agreement" for NASA that was irrelevant to its internal deliberations when NASA was faced with budgetary cuts in its annual reviews. In subsequent negotiations, the Europeans have sought deeper cooperation and consultation. They contend, however, that a basic problem remains. ISPM and the negotiations over the space station (which they also describe) "show how difficult it is to conduct in a cooperative framework a space project whose funding requires yearly authorizations without a long-term commitment."[1]

U.S. analysts also lament the ISPM cancellation and the manner in which Europe was informed. However, they note that NASA did provide a nuclear power source (radioisotope thermal generator) for onboard electrical power, a space shuttle launch, and tracking and data support for the Ulysses mission. These elements translate to a U.S. financial commitment of over $500 million to the project. Moreover, as one analyst notes, ESA may have overestimated the legal status of an MOU and the strength of U.S. congressional commitment to the project from the beginning. Further, ESA has been adept at emphasizing the legacy of ISPM cancellation and using American contrition as a "bargaining chip" in subsequent negotiations.[2]

---

[1]Roger M. Bonnet and Vittorio Manno, *International Cooperation in Space: The Example of the European Space Agency* (Cambridge, MA: Harvard University Press, 1994), p. 118.

[2]Joan Johnson-Freese, *Changing Patterns of International Cooperation in Space* (Malabar, FL: Orbit Book Co.), 1990, p. 44.

Parliamentary systems, however, are not immune to changes in government and resultant shifts in policy, and under both systems, funds for research projects are subject to periodic legislative approval. But as noted later in this chapter, European and Japanese governments commonly approve multiyear scientific research programs. In contrast, the risks of periodic legislative reviews have been heightened in recent years for U.S. researchers. Specific authorizing bills for many large science research projects have not passed Congress; instead, many projects have relied on annual appropriations.

Changes in project scope and commitment, and the unpredictable nature of the U.S. budget process, continue to make foreign partners hesitant about collaborating with the United States. This is particularly true in areas where foreign programs are dependent on a U.S. program, as in human space flight operations. Since the Japanese, European, and to some extent, Russian human space flight programs are now focused around their contributions to the space station, cancellation or further major redesign could have highly disruptive consequences for these U.S. partners.[39] In contrast, in a coequal and phased collaboration such as ITER, concerns about U.S. reliability are less acute. Since ITER partners have fusion programs that are comparable in size and sophistication, a pullout by one partner or even cancellation of the entire project would likely have a less significant impact on the direction and viability of the partners' domestic fusion programs than cancellation of the space station would have on some foreign space programs.

Various mechanisms are available for addressing the concerns of potential partners about the reliability of U.S. international commitments and to meet the added challenges of multinational efforts. These include a shift in how the U.S. components of international projects are authorized and funded—from annual to multiyear approaches—and the use of explicit provisions in international agreements to enhance project stability. International scientific projects inherently bring a more complicated structure, with additional layers of decisionmaking and management, than purely domestic ventures. The success of international collaborations may require compromises and special institutional arrangements that accommodate the differences among parties in procedures and schedules for planning, approving, and funding large science projects.

There are established multiyear funding mechanisms in the U.S. budgetary, appropriations, and procurement processes that could be tapped for more predictable funding of international efforts if policymakers so choose. Among them are providing multiyear authorizations, multiyear appropriations, advance appropriations, and full funding of the total estimated project costs. For example, legislation has been introduced in the 104th Congress authorizing over $13.1 billion, in annual installments of about $2.1 billion over fiscal years 1996 to 2001, for construction of the space station.[40] This step is being taken primarily to increase the confidence of foreign partners in the U.S. commitment to the project.[41] Appropriations that remain available beyond one fiscal year are not uncommon for large defense and space construction and procurement programs. Congress can also provide specific contract authority to allow sponsoring agencies to enter into multiyear contracts to support project activities.

Although multiyear funding can provide a greater measure of assurance to foreign partners, it can raise difficult budget challenges and is not irrevocable. Upfront appropriations may limit the flexibility of both a particular project and of future federal budgets. It is important to remember that unexpended appropriations may be rescinded by Congress and subsequent Congresses are not required to appropriate funds to meet full authorized levels. Given recent experiences with some large science projects, management reforms to assure more accurate project cost estimates and improved project planning, may be necessary to boost congressional confidence in such multiyear commitments (see finding below).

Greater care in structuring the processes by which the United States enters into international partnerships and in the terms of those agreements can also enhance stability. Early consideration of the possibility for international collaboration on large science projects and continuing consultation with prospective partners could help avoid the problems encountered when partners were sought late in project design. In negotiating agreements, the partners can include provisions that detail re-

---

[39]In interviews with OTA, Japanese space officials indicated that cancellation of the space station could have "catastrophic" consequences for their space program.

[40]H.R. 1601, International Space Station Authorization Act of 1995, was introduced May 10, 1995. The cap of $2.1 billion per year is designed to impose spending discipline.

[41]Robert S. Walker, Chairman, House Committee on Science, comments at media briefing, Apr. 6, 1995.

sponsibilities in case a partner is forced to withdraw or cannot fulfill financial commitments. In projects where there are substantial uncertainties about technical feasibility and costs, a phased approach to project commitments can aid collaboration.[42] Encouraging opportunities for collaboration will have to be balanced against the need to ensure that U.S. agencies and Congress fully understand and support the financial and other commitments needed to carry the project to completion.

Some have suggested that the use of treaties might be effective in formalizing collaborative commitments in cases where projects are of strategic importance to the United States and its foreign partners. Since treaty commitments require the approval of the Senate, proponents of this approach reason that such agreements could effectively insulate key projects from changing budget priorities and improve the confidence of our partners. On closer examination, use of treaty arrangements for large international science projects is not attractive. Due to the inevitable changes associated with long-term scientific and technological undertakings, treaties are a rather inflexible and process-intensive vehicle for structuring scientific collaborations. No single U.S. science project has ever been subject to the treaty ratification process. Few, if any, collaborations are likely to require such a high level of government commitment or the associated institutional structures characteristic of treaties. Moreover, the existence of treaty obligations has not prevented Congress from refusing to fund the U.S. contributions under these arrangements, and there are generally few mechanisms available to enforce such requirements. Treaty obligations have in the past been used to sanction U.S. participation in multinational organizations such as the International Atomic Energy Agency (IAEA), which does facilitate some international research efforts in addition to its responsibilities for nuclear arms control. Treaty agreements among European nations form the basis for CERN, the European Space Agency (ESA), and collaborative research on fusion.[43]

Even if there is a deeply held belief that the United States can be unreliable, it seems not to have outweighed the benefits to other nations of including the United States in projects. There continues to be no shortage of international interest in having the United States as a partner in collaborative science projects. Among the current examples, all at various stages of planning, are: the LHC, the NLC, and ITER. In certain areas, such as space, countries such as Japan and Russia have tied their own national efforts directly to U.S. activities and goals. As new areas of scientific inquiry and new types of problems emerge (e.g., global climate change), the United States will no doubt continue to be regarded as an indispensable partner, if not the principal leader in addressing such issues.

- **To assure long-term political and funding support of large science projects, early and thorough project cost and performance analyses are essential. However, improvements in project planning and cost estimation alone will not be sufficient to ensure project stability or greater reliability on the part of the United States in fulfilling its international commitments.**

The withdrawal of the United States from particular international and domestic projects has been precipitated by a variety of factors including: changing national goals and budgetary priorities, steep cost overruns following submission of unrealistic cost estimates to secure initial political approval of projects, inadequate project planning, and the difficulties of dealing with unforeseen

---

[42]Such a phased approach is being used in the ITER collaboration with separate agreements for conceptual design, engineering design activities, and construction and operations. The parties are now in the midst of the engineering design activities and will negotiate a new arrangement on whether and how to support construction and operation.

[43]In addition, the space station agreement was treated as an intergovernmental compact by European nations, as it was discussed and approved by the parliaments of all ESA member states.

technical challenges. All of these played a role in eroding support for megaprojects that initially had strong backing in both the legislative and executive branches.

Although more detailed engineering and cost estimation procedures could enhance the viability of large and complex scientific undertakings, such improvements still might not be enough to ensure the ultimate completion of projects. For example, in early 1995, after almost a decade of rigorous planning and review costing nearly $100 million, the Advanced Neutron Source was terminated before entering the construction phase, principally because of its high cost of $2.9 billion (see chapter 3). In other cases, projects entailing particularly risky technological aspects could encounter cost escalations, despite the thoroughness of the planning and management procedures.

Nevertheless, extensive and careful preliminary work on the technical and economic feasibility of a project is essential to sustained commitment and success. As an illustration, the original EOS plans were restructured and rescoped due to questions about the initial design concept and overall project implementation (see table 1-2). The first EOS plan was criticized for its cost, the long period of time before the system could provide policy-relevant data, and its dependence on just two platforms to carry the program's instruments. Difficulties also plagued the SSC project and eroded congressional support. Changes in magnet design led to increased project costs, which in turn raised questions about SSC management and performance.[44] The United States sought foreign partners as a way of sharing costs, but only after key engineering and siting de-

TABLE 1-2: Earth Observing System Program History	
Phase	**Year**
Mission planning	1982-1987
Announcement of opportunity	1988
Peer review process	
Letter review	
(academia/government)	
Panel review	
(academia/government)	
Prioritization panel (government)	1988-1989
Announcement of selection	1989
Definition phase	1989-1990
New start	1990
Execution phase	1990 on
Restructuring process	1991-1992
Restructuring confirmation	1992
Rescoping process	1992
National Space Policy Directive 7	1992
Rescoping confirmation	1993

SOURCE: National Aeronautics and Space Administration, "EOS Program Chronology," *1993 EOS Reference Handbook* (Washington, DC: 1993), p. 9.

cisions had been made. When the desired $2 billion in foreign commitments did not materialize, support for the project diminished further, which ultimately led to its termination in 1993.

Changes in the way U.S. science projects are selected, funded, structured, and managed could aid the success of international collaborations. Given the role that unexpected cost escalations have played in the termination or redefinition of several big science projects, improvements in the planning and cost estimation of megaprojects

---

[44]Initially, the project was estimated to cost about $4.4 billion (in 1988 dollars without an allowance for contingencies); but by 1993, cost estimates had escalated to over $11 billion. At the time of termination, 15 miles (out of a total of 54) of tunnel had been dug, magnets had been tested, and $2.2 billion spent, mostly on salaries. Some observers argue that the management of the SSC was politicized and taken out of the hands of DOE technical managers who had a good record in overseeing the planning and execution of large projects. As a consequence, the various problems that developed over the course of the SSC endeavor might have been either avoided or addressed in a more effective manner.

would have several benefits.[45] More rigorous information about project costs and performance and about the potential for international collaboration could be useful in the authorization and appropriations processes and could lead to more stable project decisions. Better mechanisms for planning, engineering analysis, and cost estimation would permit policymakers to weigh more accurately the technical and financial tradeoffs of large scientific endeavors.[46] This is beneficial—and perhaps essential—regardless of whether other mechanisms, such as multiyear budgeting, are adopted to enhance project stability or to assure foreign partners.

Different modalities of funding may also be needed to address technical risks. If, for example, certain elements of a large project entail particularly high technical risks, a sequential development approach might be used to deal with such uncertainties. This could limit the cost of an undertaking by requiring that extensive prototyping or modeling be completed before commitment to the next phase of the full project can be made. For instance, if elaborate prototyping of magnets had been carried out before the entire project was approved, some of the cost overruns that plagued the SSC might have been avoided. Although a staged approach to large projects could provide a means for managing risk, such a strategy might require that project schedules be extended. In some cases, however, excessive conservatism could prevent promising or creative initiatives from ever being realized.

It may be desirable to make the initiation of large projects more difficult. However, the need for project stability may require the adoption of mechanisms that also make it more difficult to terminate such projects after they are approved. The challenge for policymakers is to develop a funding approach that ensures long-term commitment but simultaneously affords some elasticity in project design and execution.

- **Many nations have decisionmaking processes quite dissimilar to those in the United States. These may lead to greater stability, but less flexibility, in project decisions. There are signs, however, that increased budgetary pressures are also affecting the ability of other countries to sustain their international commitments.**

Other countries have elaborate planning and cost estimation procedures, as well as a phased approach to project implementation. The United States might draw on this experience in project planning and funding. In Japan, for example, the project planning process is a highly interactive, consensus-building exercise that evolves over a long period of time. The outgrowth of this consensus building has been commitment and stability. Carefully conceived project proposals with well-defined scientific and technical objectives and detailed cost breakdowns emanate from the bottom up. These proposals move through a hierarchy of administrative channels from the laboratory level through the bureau responsible for the laboratory, to the ministry in which the bureau is located,[47] and ultimately to the Ministry of Finance. Throughout the planning process, a tremendous amount of feedback is elicited. The larger the project, the more individuals are included in delibera-

---

[45]It should be noted that several projects ($500 million or less) have been completed on time and on budget. Examples of successfully completed domestic projects include the Continuous Electron Beam Accelerator Facility ($513 million), the Stanford Linear Collider ($115 million), and the Advanced Light Source ($100 million).

[46]For example, large projects like ITER require a clear strategy for funding and managing R&D and construction activities. Issues related to the site, host country regulations, contingency funding, and contract methods can directly affect cost estimates. Frequently, these factors are not well-defined during the conceptual and preliminary engineering stages when cost estimates are initially developed. Charles Baker, Leader, U.S. ITER Home Team Leader, personal communication, April 1995.

[47]For large science projects, the relevant ministries are the Science and Technology Agency and the Ministry of Education, Science, and Culture.

tions and the longer it takes for a consensus to be reached.

This process establishes accountability for overall project feasibility at the research level and also ensures administrative support until the project is completed.[48] In particular, the long planning process strengthens cost estimations. The high level of interaction among researchers and government administrators during the planning process reduces the possibility of "low-ball" estimates being made merely to secure funding.[49] These commitments are crucial to Japanese funding stability and stand in contrast to the funding and planning mechanisms of the United States. Project planning and funding by the Commission of the European Community and individual European countries is also quite interactive in nature. Proposed projects in Europe undergo a great deal of technical and financial scrutiny.

Furthermore, in Europe and Japan, scientific priorities are usually determined for fixed periods (five-year projects or programs are typical), thus insulating projects from year-to-year changes in the political and economic climate. Decisions to fund a project or program cannot be easily reversed or funding easily changed. Historically, projects have been funded with the clear intention of seeing them through to completion. In contrast, even long-term projects in the United States are subject to annual review and can be sharply reduced or terminated by Congress or a new administration.

Although multiyear budgets have been an integral part of project planning and have promoted project stability in Japan and Europe, this does not mean that long-term budgets are approved and appropriated at the same time. A staged approach is used to fund multiyear projects. The project budget is divided into segments, which are appro-

priated in given years. For very large projects such as fusion and space, obligations are made to fund a portion of the budget in each fiscal year.

However, whether these processes can withstand growing budgetary pressures is open to question. Europe and Japan are now experiencing some of the same budgetary constraints and political pressures that the United States has confronted in recent years. The Japanese Ministry of Education, Science, and Culture, which is the principal supporter of university research in Japan, has adopted a zero-growth budget for the next fiscal year. It is possible that in the future our overseas partners will have to adopt a more flexible decisionmaking process that is closer to the U.S. model. They may also experience the unexpected project changes that have been criticized in the U.S. system.

As an illustration, the prospective European commitment to the space station has changed markedly in the past few years and is still uncertain. Originally, ESA planned to participate in the station through the development of an attached pressurized laboratory facility and a Man-Tended Free Flyer (MTFF) that could dock with the station or operate independently. ESA also coupled its station-related activities to the development of its Hermes reusable spacecraft. This placed station participation within a larger plan to develop independent European human space capabilities. However, in the past few years, due in large part to funding pressures, both the MTFF and Hermes were canceled. Cancellation of these programs has produced sharp disagreements within ESA over how to allocate limited funds, how to structure European space station participation, and whether ESA should make additional contributions to the station program. As a result, plans to build a downsized version of the European at-

---

[48]For a detailed discussion of this process, see Kenneth Pechter, "Assessment of Japanese Attitudes Toward International Collaboration in Big Science," contractor report prepared for the Office of Technology Assessment, December 1994.

[49]There have been cases, though, where project cost projections in Japan proved to be unrealistic. For example, the H2 rocket launch vehicle program experienced a $700 million cost overrun because of needed engine design changes. An accelerator project at Japan's Institute of Radiological Sciences doubled in cost from $200 million to $400 million. Masakazu Murakami, Director, Policy Planning for International Programs, Science and Technology Agency, personal communication, November 1994.

tached pressurized laboratory—the sole remaining European commitment to the station—have yet to be approved.

It is important to note, that the European and Japanese approaches to project selection and planning, while more stable, might sometimes result in projects that have more conservative technical objectives than comparable U.S. projects. The additional levels of approval required to initiate a project in Europe or Japan could serve to minimize technical and financial risk or to narrow overall program goals. Historically, the sheer size and scope of U.S. research efforts have allowed a much broader portfolio of projects to be pursued, including those that are more speculative or risky in nature. This approach allowed the United States to achieve leadership positions in a variety of different disciplines.

However, as Europe and Japan have developed leading-edge scientific capabilities, their research projects have increasingly set aggressive scientific and technological goals. The magnet and detector technologies being developed for the LHC project at CERN are in some respects much more technically challenging than those planned for the SSC. The Joint European Torus (JET) was the first tokamak to produce significant quantities of fusion power using a deuterium-tritium fuel mix. Also, the Japanese decision to develop an indigenous rocket-launching capability has by its very nature required a technology development effort that involves considerable programmatic risk.

- **Developing approaches for allocating project costs and benefits in an equitable manner will continue to present challenges to all participants in international cooperative ventures. This especially will be the case in scientific collaborations involving technologies with potentially high industrial or commercial returns. The two issues that are** likely to be a source of contention in almost all future negotiations are technology transfer and facility siting.

The United States can study the experiences of international science organizations, such as CERN and ESA, that have established approaches for apportioning costs and benefits in collaborative efforts. However, the lessons learned by these organizations in bringing a number of smaller countries together for joint scientific and industrial development may prove of limited relevance to U.S. concerns and goals.

CERN and ESA policies on basic membership contributions and voting illustrate the difficulty of applying their procedures to U.S. participation in international science projects. CERN and ESA determine basic membership contributions as a share of each member's gross national product and assign each member country an equal vote in decisionmaking.[50] This method of allocating costs would be unrealistic for the United States, as it would result in a gross imbalance between the magnitude of U.S. contributions and its say in decisionmaking.

European science organizations have also developed industrial return policies to ensure that project contributions are channeled back to companies and research institutions in member countries. ESA, for example, has attempted to satisfy member demands for equity in contract apportionment by instituting a system of "equitable geographic return," whereby each country receives a percentage of project contracts proportionate to its funding contribution, both for mandatory and optional projects. ESA's system of fair return appeared to work well in the past when contracts were distributed over several years and over a series of projects. But political and budget pressures in member countries in recent years have led to demands for equitable returns on each project, re-

---

[50]At ESA, basic membership contributions are used to fund mandatory science programs. Member governments may contribute additional funds to finance optional programs outside the agency's mandatory science budget. In these optional programs, countries receive project contracts proportionate to their financial contribution.

ducing the organization's flexibility and possibly increasing costs.[51] CERN and the European Synchrotron Radiation Facility (ESRF) employ somewhat looser industrial return rules to ensure that prices of contracts come close to the lowest bid.

Rather than adopting such prearranged formulas for collaboration, it appears more consistent with U.S. national interest to continue to negotiate the allocation of costs and benefits on a case-by-case basis. The formula and procedures for distributing costs and benefits will depend on the origin and national sponsorship of each project, the science goals and priorities of the participants, and the resources each nation is willing to commit. These resources might involve not only funds, but also in-kind contributions such as expertise, instrumentation, or materials. Since the United States has joined few international scientific organizations or "umbrella" agreements in the past,[52] this approach may be the most practical path for U.S. policymakers to pursue.

Technology Transfer

Given increased domestic political pressures to link basic science research more closely to national economic development, and the increasing globalization of R&D, an international project's potential for technology transfer (from or to the United States) is likely to receive closer scrutiny in the future. Historically, U.S. policymakers have attempted to safeguard areas in which the United States has developed a clear lead or a significant commercial/industrial advantage (e.g., space technologies). Meanwhile, a more open approach has been pursued in areas where the United States

is less dominant or where the industrial return is less certain (e.g., fusion research and some areas of high-energy physics). As the global community becomes increasingly integrated, scientific and technological knowledge will no doubt diffuse more rapidly. Over the past several decades, this process of knowledge diffusion has stimulated advances in many fields (e.g., biotechnology and computer and communications technology). Thus, preventing technological leakage to other countries or preserving U.S. dominance in particular fields will be an increasingly difficult task. In certain cases, the national interest may dictate that the United States closely control leading-edge technologies as part of a collaborative arrangement.

It should be noted, though, that multilateral collaborations may also be a source of new knowledge and technology, and thus participation in such ventures will likely have a number of benefits for the United States and other nations. In addition, the involvement of developing countries in collaborative projects can serve to improve international political stability as well as transfer vital skills and technologies to other parts of the world. Technology transfer should therefore not necessarily be viewed as being at odds with national goals.

Siting

Decisions over siting have also been a source of tension in international collaborations and could exacerbate competitive pressures in the future. The right to host an international science project has been a highly sought-after prize—a source of economic benefit and political and scientific

---

[51] ESA increased its overall country-by-country fair return goal to 95 percent in 1993 and is trying to reach 96 percent by 1996, with a goal of 90 percent within each of its programs. See John Krige, "ESA and CERN as International Collaborative Science Organizations," contractor report prepared for the Office of Technology Assessment, December 1994.

[52] The most significant exception to this rule is U.S. participation in ITER, which is an equal partnership dedicated to a specific project, but is not an institution. The United States has signed international agreements to coordinate and participate in international Earth observation activities. However, these Earth observation agreements have been established between independent national programs rather than through a joint organization.

Aerial view of the European Laboratory for Particle Physics.

prestige. One study found that between 40 and 70 percent of the funds used to operate large international facilities are spent in the host nation.[53] However, the types of economic benefits accruing to the host may be in areas of low technology (e.g., construction, materials, chemicals, and services) rather than high technology (project design and components). Still, local companies that provide technical support or equipment to facilities can enhance their underlying scientific or engineering expertise. A large facility can also attract new companies and thereby raise the skill base of a region's population.

In most cases, though, contracts for the most knowledge-intensive components of large projects are typically assigned to companies in many different countries. The distribution of key project components among international partners may di-

minish the economic return to the country hosting the project. Thus, it may be more advantageous for the United States in future projects to forego opportunities to host a facility, in exchange for the opportunity to develop technologies and expertise that will advance the leading sectors of U.S. science and industry.[54]

Moreover, development of the "information superhighway" will enable scientists all over the world to gain access to a project's data or even to operate an instrument remotely. Thus, access to the site itself may be less important in future years than it has been in the past.

Also, although siting a facility in a country may result in a net economic or technical benefit to that country, it may have drawbacks or cause domestic political concerns for the host nation. For example, hosting ITER may be attractive to the national science community and to industry, but the prospect of hosting a research facility that uses radioactive materials may arouse political opposition in the locality chosen as host.

Siting should therefore be considered in a comparative context. Although the siting decision is important, it is not necessarily in the U.S. interest to treat siting as a paramount issue. Policymakers should compare the economic, technical, and political advantages of hosting a project with the benefits offered by taking responsibility for other parts of the project, especially the development of high value-added knowledge-intensive components and processes. These opportunities suggest that U.S. policymakers adopt a broader perspective on siting issues.

- **U.S. science and technology goals and priorities may have to be reevaluated as international collaboration becomes a more integral component of R&D activities.**

---

[53]This analysis was based on the spending patterns of CERN, located on the Swiss-French border; the JET fusion experiment in England; and the ESRF and the Institute Laue-Langevin for neutron research, both in France. See "International Facilities Said To Boost National Economy," *Nature*, vol. 363, May 6, 1993.

[54]For example, even if ITER was built in Japan or Europe, U.S. industry could still participate in the design and construction of the reactor and support facilities, as well as reactor components such as superconducting magnets and associated computational and electronic systems.

The benefits and challenges presented by international collaboration raise basic questions about how U.S. scientific capabilities can be most effectively advanced.

The chief goal of U.S. R&D programs is to maintain or develop leading-edge capabilities across a broad spectrum of scientific fields. Other science goals are linked to economic competitiveness, foreign policy initiatives, and national security concerns. These goals influence decisions about whether to participate in international collaborative projects. Historically, the United States has collaborated only when its participation did not affect domestic science activities or when leadership could be maintained.

Some U.S. science goals are difficult to reconcile with international collaboration. Notably, the goal of U.S. leadership in science poses a potential conflict with the very nature of collaboration. This may be especially true if leadership is defined as "dominance" in any particular field. Thus, future U.S. participation in large-scale collaborative projects may necessitate a redefinition of what constitutes scientific leadership. For example, if leadership means the development of world-class capabilities in any particular scientific or technical field, then expanded international collaboration may not necessarily diminish—and may even enhance—underlying U.S. scientific prowess. Building up national scientific capabilities and joining international partnerships are not necessarily mutually exclusive strategies. In many cases, having access to scientific facilities in other countries or participating in the planning and operation of particular projects may strengthen and diversify the U.S. science base. Moreover, participation in collaborative endeavors can allow nations to avoid duplication of major facilities and thereby permit a broader array of R&D projects to

be pursued. The ITER collaboration and the many cooperative ventures of NASA are good examples of this.

Furthermore, an emphasis on leadership can strain alliances with other nations because it appears to ignore the many achievements of the European and Japanese science communities, particularly in high-energy physics, space exploration, and fusion. As other nations continue to develop and refine their science programs and facilities, it will become increasingly difficult for the United States to exercise sole control over projects. Other nations will demand recognition of their achievements as well as a voice in key technical and administrative decisions.

The goal of promoting national economic competitiveness provides little guidance in deciding whether projects should be internationalized. Because pure science research is curiosity driven, it is often difficult to assess its short-term impact, even though over the long term, its benefits to society can be substantial.[55] Basic scientific discoveries in and of themselves usually possess little intrinsic value without further investments.[56] In those cases where commercial spinoffs are possible (e.g., advanced-materials development resulting from neutron-scattering research), economic competitiveness could play a role in shaping specific policies related to international collaboration. Whether large scientific projects can be used effectively to facilitate the development and deployment of new commercial technologies is an open question. As a general proposition, however, it is difficult to demonstrate that large science projects or specific aspects of large projects can be efficiently utilized for this purpose.

---

[55]One study concluded that rates of return for R&D in particular industries and from university research can be 30 percent or more. See Edwin Mansfield, "Estimates of the Social Returns from Research and Development," *AAAS Science and Technology Policy Yearbook, 1991*, Margaret O. Meredith et al. (eds.) (Washington, DC: American Association for the Advancement of Science, 1991). Also see Edwin Mansfield, "Academic Research and Industrial Innovation," *Research Policy*, vol. 20, 1991, pp. 1-12.

[56]See Paul David et al., Center for Economic Policy Research, Stanford University, "The Economic Analysis of Payoffs from Basic Research—An Examination of the Case of Particle Physics Research," CEPR Publication No. 122, January 1988.

The support of foreign policy goals has also shaped decisions about whether to participate in collaborative science projects. As noted earlier, the United States uses scientific agreements to help forge and reinforce alliances and friendships. Most recently, the United States has used scientific agreements to support Russia's science base. In some instances, however, political goals can have a negative impact on scientific research objectives and must be weighed against foreign policy benefits.

Overall, U.S. science goals provide little guidance to policymakers in developing a policy framework for future collaborations. In particular, the goal of leadership, as understood in the past, does not provide a clear basis for developing fundamental policies that address whether international collaboration should be pursued or what level of funding is appropriate. Reconciling U.S. goals with the benefits of collaboration will be a critical first step in this process.

- **More formal mechanisms for information exchange among science policymakers could enhance opportunities for effective international collaborations.**

An important need of decisionmakers is to have effective mechanisms for exchanging information about emerging scientific priorities and projects in various disciplines. OTA discussions with U.S., European, and Japanese science officials indicate that new intergovernmental mechanisms for information exchange could be beneficial.

There are advantages to having more formal information-sharing arrangements among governments. In some scientific fields, several countries have facilities that are complementary or parallel to those found in the United States. Better usage of some national facilities and resources could be achieved by identifying how similar facilities around the world are utilized. Although there is growing demand for access to many domestic and foreign scientific facilities, they often operate for limited time periods because of funding constraints. In some fields, there is a need for greater intergovernmental coordination in both

Section of the CERN tunnel showing a model of the Large Hadron Collider on top of the Large Electron-Positron Collider.

the use of existing facilities and the construction of new facilities. This could permit nations to consolidate and improve the efficiency of various R&D programs.

In some cases, essential U.S. scientific capabilities could be maintained or even extended in a particular field of inquiry by participating in existing ventures overseas (e.g., by joining the LHC project at CERN or the Institute Laue-Langevin European neutron facility). In specific fields of research, such as high-energy physics, U.S. and foreign programs might be designed to take advantage of existing infrastructure and expertise around the globe.

Since 1992, member countries of the Organization for Economic Cooperation and Development (OECD) have exchanged information and explored opportunities for international scientific cooperation under the auspices of the OECD Megascience Forum (see box 1-4). Before establishment of the Megascience Forum, science policymakers from different nations had limited opportunities to discuss R&D priorities as well as ideas and plans for future large projects. The Forum has sponsored both meetings for senior government officials and expert meetings where scientists and science policymakers can explore the needs of various scientific fields and proposals for new experiments or facilities. Although some major scientific fields such as high-energy phys-

BOX 1-4: The Organization for Economic Cooperation and Development (OECD) Megascience Forum

The OECD[1] Council created the Megascience Forum in June 1992 primarily as a means for information exchange and open discussion on existing and future large science projects and programs, and to facilitate international scientific cooperation among member governments. The Forum does not set priorities or conduct scientific research; it has no decisionmaking authority. Twenty-three out of the 25 OECD member countries participate in the Forum, which has a mandate of three years.

Several factors prompted the creation of the Megascience Forum. For countries with large research programs, much of the impetus came from the rising costs of big science projects and increasing budget constraints. For others, especially smaller countries, ensuring or expanding access to facilities and data was the primary concern. For all countries, the new opportunities for scientific cooperation presented by the end of the Cold War provided an additional impetus.

To facilitate discussion, the Forum has organized expert meetings in six specific scientific disciplines or broad research areas, excluding near-term commercial areas and national defense. Leading scientists in a particular field from all member and observer countries, and occasionally from other scientifically important countries (for example, China and India), are invited to attend, along with government policymakers. Discussions focus on identifying opportunities for international collaboration and mechanisms to ensure the success of cooperative projects. Meetings have been held on astronomy, deep drilling, global climate change research, oceanography, advanced neutron and synchrotron radiation sources, and particle physics. The results of each meeting are conveyed to the Forum as a basis for further discussion. The Forum has approved publication of the results of the expert meetings and its own deliberations for all six research areas.

---

[1] OECD is an intergovernmental organization founded in 1960. Its primary aim is to promote economic policies that stimulate growth, employment, and the expansion of world trade throughout the OECD area. The organization's 25 members are Australia, Austria, Belgium, Canada, Denmark, Finland, France, Germany, Greece, Iceland, Ireland, Italy, Japan, Luxembourg, Mexico, the Netherlands, New Zealand, Norway, Portugal, Spain, Sweden, Switzerland, Turkey, the United Kingdom, and the United States. Iceland and Luxembourg do not participate in the Forum. Forum observer status has been granted to the European Union, Russia, Hungary, Poland, the Czech Republic, and Korea.

ics already have international scientific organizations in which ideas and plans for future experiments are discussed, the Megascience Forum is viewed by policymakers as being complementary to these organizations. The Forum is essentially designed to facilitate communication among governments.

OTA discovered a broad range of opinion regarding the usefulness of the OECD Megascience Forum. Whereas some participants found OECD's activities beneficial (e.g., the forums on astronomy, deep-sea drilling, and neutron sources were viewed by some government policymakers as quite useful), others, particularly scientists, have questioned its utility. Nevertheless, there has been foreign support for a U.S. proposal to establish a follow-on activity to the Forum that would continue to provide an intergovernmental venue for discussion and information exchange. In addition, proposals for the development of improved

---

BOX 1-4 Cont'd.

With the Forum's three-year term due to expire in fall 1995, the United States proposed a follow-on activity. Based on extensive discussions with OECD member government officials, the U.S. proposal was modified and formally adopted by the Forum at its January 1995 meeting. The proposal will be fine tuned and a specific workplan developed at the final meeting of the Forum in June 1995. The proposal and workplan will be submitted for the consideration of the Ministers of Science of the OECD countries at their meeting in September 1995.

Under terms of this proposal, a new organization, tentatively called the Group on Large Scientific Projects (GLSP), would provide a venue for government science policy officials to explore generic issues related to megascience projects and make recommendations to member governments. The new organization would also have the authority to establish ad hoc working groups in selected scientific disciplines where adequate mechanisms for intergovernmental discussion are lacking. The working groups would exchange information on each country's domestic research plans and projects, compare project priorities, and explore prospects for international cooperation. If the working group identifies opportunities for cooperation, interested governments could enter into discussions leading to the negotiation and implementation of an international project. The responsibility for negotiating final agreements and administering projects would reside with the participating governments rather than with OECD.

Senior science policy-level officials from OECD member governments will be delegates to GLSP. Delegates to the working group meetings will include senior government program officials and, at the discretion of each government, nongovernment scientists. Working groups would meet as frequently as required and would be authorized to invite nonmember countries to participate on a case-by-case basis.

SOURCES: Organization for Economic Cooperation and Development, *What Is the OECD Megascience Forum?* (Paris, France: 1995); "The Dawn of Global Scientific Co-operation, *The OECD Megascience Observer,* No. 187, April/May 1994; and Office of Science and Technology Policy, "The OECD Megascience Forum: Past Activities and Proposed Future Plans," informational material, n.d.

---

coordination mechanisms among G-7[57] countries have recently been offered.[58]

Despite the acknowledged usefulness of information exchange, there is little support among U.S., European, and Japanese policymakers for the creation of international operational entities that would organize and supervise collaborations. Regardless of the consultation mechanisms created, the disparate characteristics of big science projects will still probably necessitate that each

international endeavor be evaluated on a case-specific basis.

- **The different levels of scale and complexity of large collaborative projects require distinct management structures.**

Management frameworks for different projects must necessarily vary in structure because each cooperative enterprise involves different degrees of program integration, information transfer, and

---

[57]G-7 is the term applied to the group of large industrial economics (United States, Canada, Japan, France, Germany, United Kingdom, and Italy) that meet regularly to consider the state of the global economy.

[58]In order to have more focused discussions about large projects among key industrialized nations, U.S., German, and Japanese officials are exploring the possibility of creating formal consultation mechanisms at the G-7 level.

STEVE BROWN, U.S. NEWS & WORLD REPORT

The impetus for the ITER collaboration originated at the 1985 Geneva summit between President Reagan and Soviet General Secretary Gorbachev.

financial or political commitment. For example, distributed science activities such as data gathering on global climate conditions may have only informal or limited project coordination requirements.[59] Scientific facilities that offer particular services, such as neutron or synchrotron sources, have a more developed, but rather straightforward, management organization.[60] Projects that involve the design and construction of large, sophisticated apparatus or instrumentation usually require more elaborate institutional mechanisms for overseeing project planning and execution.

In reviewing the experience of past and ongoing international projects, it becomes apparent that careful balance must be struck between the need for integrated project planning and oversight and the flexibility that is often necessary to successfully design project subsystems and components. For some types of projects it is fairly easy to develop modular designs that allow the different collaborators to each focus on very specific goals and essentially be concerned only with the interfaces between their subsystems and the over-

all system. The European and Japanese components of the International Space Station serve as an example of such a compartmentalized management approach. In other cases, however, a greater level of integration may be required. The several hundred researchers who are now developing the technical specifications for the LHC particle detectors at CERN must work closely with LHC accelerator experts to ensure that the ultimate physics objectives of the project can be met. As a result of this requirement, specific management review processes have been created to guarantee that overall technical and financial targets of the LHC project are being achieved. The strong institutional structure provided by the CERN organization provides additional support to project planners and designers.

The ITER fusion project presents perhaps some of the most significant management challenges in terms of the way in which technical decisions are made, and how human or financial resources are deployed. At present, engineering design activities for the proposed ITER reactor are being carried out at three separate locations in the United States, Japan, and Germany.

At each site, a "joint central team" consisting of American, European, Russian, and Japanese researchers specifies R&D tasks that have to be completed. "Home teams" for each of the four partners provide additional technical support to the joint central teams, and coordinate the work of local researchers and contractors. Specific assignments and tasks are being defined as the overall design and engineering specifications of the fusion reactor are being developed. Responsibility for the overall reactor design and project management is in the hands of the ITER director based in San Diego, California, who reports to the ITER

---

[59]For example, data-collection and storage standards might have to be developed, and entities for data sharing and analysis might need to be organized.

[60]For instance, the European Synchrotron Radiation Facility in France is a 12-nation private consortium that offers researchers access to high-intensity x-rays. This and similar facilities in the United States provide researchers in a variety of disciplines access to powerful experimental tools and thus are managed primarily as user-support organizations. Traditionally, such facilities have reciprocal access policies that allow scientists from different countries to take advantage of the unique capabilities of each installation.

council.[61] Because the reactor subsystems are integrally linked to each other, the ITER project does not especially lend itself to decentralization. Even after a reactor site is chosen, a geographically diffuse management operation will still be required to work with researchers and industrial contractors in different countries. This will necessitate a management structure that is capable of devolving responsibility, but also of developing strong oversight capabilities and effective communications channels. These requirements represent a formidable challenge. If ITER's management principle were to be characterized, it might be defined as "decentralization with coordination." The ITER experience will no doubt provide important lessons for other large-scale multinational projects that give each participating nation an equal role in project planning, financing, and decisionmaking.

A portion of the Advanced Photon Source storage ring shows the electromagnetic devices used to guide the 7 GeV positron around the 0.7 mile circumference.

CONCLUSION

As budget pressures in all countries mount and as the complexity and scale of scientific projects increase, international scientific collaboration, whether on an institutional or an informal level, will become increasingly common. Policymakers will therefore be required to carefully assess R&D projects to determine whether it is critical to the national interest that they be conducted by the United States alone, or whether they can and should be internationalized.

Although large science projects continue to draw congressional attention, they represent only a subset of a larger domain of issues relating to national R&D goals and national well-being. In the current difficult fiscal climate, one can at best expect moderately increasing R&D budgets, especially for big science. Flat or declining budgets are more likely. Because of these pressures, some scientifically worthy but expensive projects might not be pursued at all unless carried out on a col-

laborative basis. Yet, despite the burden sharing that collaboration can provide, it still may be difficult to generate the political support necessary to initiate and sustain large projects. This study identifies several major issues relevant to congressional consideration of U.S. participation in international collaborative science undertakings.

First, since large projects are not readily comparable, attempts to develop a priority-setting scheme for big projects are likely to encounter a variety of obstacles. The relatively small number of such projects should allow policymakers to rely on "bottom-up" scientific review processes to determine which projects should be pursued. The scientific community plays a major role in setting the scientific agenda, and years are often required for specific and detailed research proposals to take shape. Although there must inevitably be some linking of bottom-up planning and review with overall government R&D priority setting, selection and funding of large projects will most probably remain ad hoc. The development of

---

[61]The ITER Council has eight members, two from each of the four partners: the United States, the European Atomic Energy Community (Euratom), Japan, and the Russian Federation. Euratom is represented by officials from the European Commission, the executive Agency of the European Union.

intergovernmental mechanisms to identify scientifically worthy projects and to explore opportunities for collaboration could bring greater coherence to the process of project selection and siting. Proposals for the creation of improved coordination mechanisms are now under consideration by OECD countries.

Second, questions about U.S. reliability in international collaborations are somewhat overstated. The United States has generally fulfilled its international obligations, except in a few cases. Nevertheless, these few instances of U.S. withdrawal from international ventures and the uncertainties associated with the U.S. practice of making annual appropriations for major science projects have made foreign partners hesitant about collaborating with the United States. International collaboration can require special institutional arrangements or concessions that are not needed for domestic projects. Although multiyear funding mechanisms and improved project planning and cost estimation procedures can enhance project stability and provide additional assurance to U.S. partners, Congress can always reevaluate and even terminate projects (as can U.S. partners). The use of treaties to formalize U.S. commitments is too cumbersome a vehicle for structuring scientific projects, and will not necessarily guarantee funding stability. Despite these uncertainties, other countries continue to seek U.S. participation in a variety of scientific projects.

Third, active consideration of international cooperation before projects are authorized could provide the United States with a broader set of scientific and budgetary options. For big projects that exceed a certain monetary threshold (e.g., $100 million), or make up a large fraction of a program budget, Congress might consider requiring agencies to provide a formal justification for seeking or avoiding international collaboration. This strategy could ensure that important opportunities to collaborate are not missed and that inappropriate collaborations are screened out.

Finally, the opportunities and challenges of international partnerships raise fundamental questions about the concept of scientific leadership, of the nature of partnership, of what constitutes the national interest, and how scientific capabilities can be most effectively advanced. Traditional U.S. science goals potentially conflict with the requirements of collaboration or are too ambiguous to provide useful guidance for policymakers in deciding whether or how to collaborate. Congressional review of U.S. science goals and U.S. relations with the global scientific community in the post-Cold War era could provide guidance about where and how the nation should engage in future international partnerships.

The Changing Nature of Science | 2

This chapter provides an overview of the fundamental changes that are occurring in scientific research, including the rapid diffusion of information, new areas of scientific inquiry, and the role of large projects. These changes, the link between science and economic competitiveness, and growing budget constraints have spurred U.S. and other nations' interest in international collaboration.

DIFFUSION OF KNOWLEDGE

Over the past century, the pace of scientific and technical innovation has expanded at historically unprecedented rates. Currently, the scope and rate of human inquiry are leading to a doubling of scientific information roughly every 12 years.[1] It is estimated, for example, that nearly half of the roughly one million publications in the field of mathematics have been published in the past decade alone.[2] The sheer velocity of this scientific and technological change has transformed the very fabric of daily life, affecting the course of economic and social development as well as the relationship between human society and the natural world.

Yet, the modern scientific enterprise cannot be characterized simply by the speed at which information is generated or exchanged, but also by its breadth, creativity, and degree of sophistication. The very character of research and development (R&D) activities is experiencing fundamental change as greater interaction across disciplines is giving rise to new fields of investigation and new methods for defining, measuring, and understanding

---

[1]Gary Stix, "The Speed of Write," *Scientific American*, December 1994, p. 107.

[2]Ibid.

physical, biological, and ecological phenomena. Increasingly, advances in one field are accelerating developments in others.[3] Successive advances in underlying scientific knowledge and technology have an enabling or multiplier effect in that they permit deeper examination of more complex scientific problems. From understanding and manipulating essential genetic processes, to discovering new classes of materials, to exploring the fundamental aspects of natural law, modern science is laying the foundation for even more profound discoveries and novel applications. On many fronts, new areas of study and innovation are emerging that will no doubt have important social and economic consequences.

With the rapid development and diffusion of information and communications technologies, the extraordinary pace of scientific discovery is undergoing further acceleration. By effectively removing barriers of time and distance, new electronic networks are fundamentally altering traditional patterns of R&D. These networks have greatly expedited the exchange of information among researchers and promoted new possibilities for international collaboration within and across disciplines.

The emergence of these new tools of communication is serving to reinforce the international dimension of basic scientific research.[4] Even if science projects and investigations have been essentially national in character, the resulting scientific knowledge has, in most disciplines,

High-performance computers and high-speed electronic communications networks are essential tools for ITER fusion collaborators located around the world.

spread globally. This diffusion of information has taken on a dramatically different character in recent years. Both formal and informal global research networks now exist in practically every major domain of science. Leading scientific journals increasingly publish the work of multinational research teams. With access to the Internet and other forms of communication, the manner in which scientists design experiments, analyze data, and interact with each other is undergoing major change. In virtually every scientific field, researchers throughout the globe have daily communications in which data are exchanged, preliminary experimental findings are discussed, and new concepts and theories are debated.[5] In addi-

---

[3]For example, the tremendous advances in the field of microelectronics have been a result of advances in such disparate fields as condensed matter physics, optics, metallurgy, plasma chemistry, accelerator physics, electronic circuit theory, and software architecture. These developments in microelectronics have, in turn, affected virtually every scientific and technical discipline from aeronautics to molecular biology.

[4]The globalization of business is also strengthening the international character of scientific research. Elaborate webs of production now span the globe. These production networks often include R&D centers in many parts of the world. Multinational companies increasingly draw on the intellectual resources of a variety of different countries in both basic research and product development. In addition, corporations from different countries are increasingly forming strategic relationships to jointly carry out research and introduce new products.

[5]There is thus far limited empirical research on how communication technology is affecting the social or organizational aspects of collaboration. As communications capabilities advance, the need for face-to-face interaction could to a certain degree be supplanted by sophisticated interactive multimedia networking. However, such networking will obviously have limits, such as the need to oversee and operate complicated instrumentation. For a discussion of these issues see Bruce V. Lewenstein, "The Changing Culture of Research: Processes of Knowledge Transfer," contractor report prepared for the Office of Technology Assessment, Sept. 21, 1992; and Lisa Heinz, Coates & Jarratt, Inc., "Consequences of New Electronic Communications Technologies for Knowledge Transfer in Science: Policy Implications," contractor report prepared for the Office of Technology Assessment, August 1992.

BOX 2-1: Earth Observing System Data and Information System

As part of the U.S. Global Change Research Program to monitor global ecosystems, the National Aeronautics and Space Administration (NASA) is now constructing one of the most sophisticated and ambitious data storage and distribution systems ever developed. The Earth Observing System Data and Information System (EOSDIS), the centerpiece of NASA's Mission to Planet Earth, is designed to provide continuous, high-quality data to support better scientific understanding of the Earth's oceans, land, and atmosphere. When the multisatellite Earth Observing System (EOS) becomes fully operational, sensors aboard EOS instruments will generate immense quantities of data. EOS satellites could produce as much as 300 trillion bytes of information per year, an amount roughly comparable to 250 million, 1.2 megabyte floppy disks. In addition to gathering and processing data, EOSDIS will calibrate satellite instruments, control EOS spacecraft, and schedule the observation periods of remote sensors. EOSDIS will also integrate data from non-EOS spacecraft and non-NASA space systems, as well as key data from land-based and ocean-based sensors from around the planet. Moreover, the EOS data system is being designed to detect subtle changes in ecosystem behavior over long periods of time.

In order to facilitate interdisciplinary global change research, NASA plans to make these large quantities of experimental data easily available to a wide body of researchers at locations throughout the world. More than 10,000 physical scientists and as many as 200,000 other researchers could become regular users of the EOSDIS data repositories. This will create considerable data management and networking challenges. Having readily accessible, user-friendly data retrieval and management tools could be an important step for promoting online collaboration among researchers who are geographically dispersed. To meet these challenges, NASA is implementing a "distributed architecture" for EOSDIS rather than having a single central processing facility. Distributed Active Archive Centers, located at regional sites across the country, will each process, store, and distribute data related to specific scientific disciplines. For instance, the EROS Data Center in South Dakota will archive and distribute satellite and aircraft data, the Jet Propulsion Laboratory in California will store data on ocean circulation and atmospheric-oceanic interactions. However, researchers throughout the U.S. and the globe will have routine access to the EOSDIS data archives.

SOURCE: U.S. Congress, Office of Technology Assessment, *Remotely Sensed Data*: Technology, Management, and Markets, OTA-ISS-604 (Washington, DC: U.S. Government Printing Office, September 1994.)

---

tion, network-based scientific communications can broaden the base of research by opening up data sources and publications to researchers who previously did not have access to such information. Small institutions, in particular, can strengthen their R&D activities by accessing data provided by larger, well-established institutions.[6]

Scientists can now use sophisticated information search tools that effectively link databases in different countries to a single integrated data repository. For example, a number of biological databases are now linked together. This is particularly useful for researchers in the areas of biotechnology and molecular biology. Another illustration of sophisticated data management is the Earth Observing System Data and Information System now being developed by the National Aeronautics and Space Admimistration (NASA) (see box 2-1).

---

[6]There is some evidence that scientists who are geographically or institutionally isolated can improve their scientific productivity through the usage of electronic network resources and communications. See Heinz, ibid.

Other potentially important developments include the emergence of electronic publications, or so-called multimedia journals, that do not simply present experimental results and analysis, but may also contain interactive computer simulations that illustrate the behavior of physical phenomena.[7] "Virtual" experimental communities or "collaboratories" that permit real-time interaction among researchers have also begun to appear.[8] In some cases, experimental data are transmitted immediately from instruments to investigators throughout the world.[9] Yet, perhaps a more significant development is the ability of researchers in far-flung locations to actually witness and participate in experiments as they occur. For example, neuroscience investigators in Tennessee and Scotland recently controlled an electron microscope in California to study various tissue specimens.[10] In the future, remote access to telescopes, meteorological instrumentation, and other computer-controlled apparatus will likely be common.

These trends have a number of implications for big science projects. With the advent of new communications and data transfer tools, design and engineering activities can be decentralized more readily. For example, the development of engineering parameters and specifications for the International Thermonuclear Experimental Reactor (ITER) has been divided among teams working in the United States, Europe, and Japan. These teams frequently exchange detailed engineering analyses and documentation. In addition, distributed science activities such as the Human Genome Project and global change research, which involve the coordination of thousands of individual investigators, can be managed more effectively. Whether working in conjunction with a large group of investigators, or independently, scientists at particular geographic sites can now draw on the expertise of a much wider technical community. Thus, the existence of new information networks and technologies can serve to reduce some of the practical obstacles associated with large collaborative undertakings (see chapter 4).

NEW AREAS OF SCIENTIFIC INQUIRY

▮ The Environment

Although the scientific and technological progress of the past century undoubtedly represents a new phase in human creativity and intellectual accomplishment, these advances have given rise to a new set of challenges. In particular, the large-scale expansion of economic and industrial activities over the past several decades has raised concerns about the impact of such activities on local and global ecosystems.[11] For the first time in history, humankind can potentially alter the basic biophysical cycles of the Earth. Human activities are now resulting in materials flows commensurate with those of nature. Human releases of elements such as mercury, nickel, arsenic, and vanadium are now several times those of nature, and the amount of lead released is nearly 300 times as great as natural processes.[12] Concentrations of carbon dioxide in the atmosphere are increasing 30 to 100 times faster than the rate observed in the climatic record; methane con-

---

[7] A recent paper placed on the Internet by IBM researchers included a computer simulation of how cracks propagate in materials. Stix, see footnote 1.

[8] See "Scientists Predict Internet Will Revolutionize Research," *The Scientist*, May 2, 1994, pp. 1, 8-9.

[9] For example, data from high-energy physics and fusion laboratories are routinely disseminated to researchers in different parts of the world either during or immediately following experiments.

[10] See "New Internet Capabilities Fueling Innovative Science," *The Scientist*, May 16, 1994, p. 9.

[11] The world economy is consuming resources and generating wastes at unprecedented rates. In the past 100 years, the world's industrial production increased more than fiftyfold. See W.W. Rostow, *The World Economy: History and Prospects* (Austin, TX: University of Texas Press, 1978), pp. 48-49.

[12] See James Galloway et al., *Atmospheric Environment*, vol. 16, No. 7, 1982, p. 1678. Also see Robert U. Ayres, "Toxic Heavy Metals: Materials Cycle Optimization," *Proceedings of the National Academy of Sciences*, vol. 89, No. 3, Feb. 1, 1992, pp. 815-820.

centrations are increasing 400 times faster than previously recorded.[13]

Understanding and addressing the impacts of global climate change are likely to require unprecedented levels of global coordination and cooperation across a broad spectrum of disciplines. Gaining a predictive understanding of the Earth's physical, chemical, and biological processes will require collaboration among ecologists, microbiologists, atmospheric chemists and physicists, oceanographers, botanists, space scientists, geologists, economists, and researchers from many other fields. The challenges are indeed formidable. For example, decoupling the effects of natural change from human-induced change is an extremely difficult task. Decades of continuous monitoring of the Earth's oceans, land, and atmosphere will be necessary to document possible climate and ecosystem changes.

The United States is spending billions of dollars in a multidisciplinary, multiyear effort to measure, understand, and ultimately predict the extent and underlying mechanisms of global environmental change.[14] However, given that these environmental questions are inherently transnational in character, the efforts of the United States or a few other countries will likely not be sufficient. Any credible global environmental monitoring program will require thousands of strategically located, ground-based instruments around the planet, as well as satellite and aircraft-based instruments.[15] Systematic and carefully calibrated measurements over many decades will be necessary to develop even a limited predictive understanding of climatological and ecosystem processes. The involvement of many if not all nations will be necessary to design and implement an effective monitoring effort. Moreover, developing the appropriate tools—whether technical, behavioral, or institutional—for adaptation to widespread ecological change will also require considerable global coordination. Thus, in the environmental area, international collaborative undertakings will likely increase in both number and complexity.[16]

■ Biotechology

Another significant revolution in scientific inquiry is in the field of biological sciences.[17] Since the early 1970s, considerable progress has been made in research in genetics, cellular and molecular biology, virology, and biochemistry. This progress has led to the creation of biotechnologies, which are defined as tools or techniques used in research and product development, and to the growth of related industries. Biotechnologies have enabled the diagnosis of human genetic disorders that would not have been detected by conventional methods; they have led to increases in food production and to the discovery of new drugs and vaccines. Biotechnologies also have several potential environmental applications, such as pollution remediation and pest control. The potential to improve human health and environmental

---

[13]See U.S. Congress, Office of Technology Assessment, *Changing by Degrees: Steps To Reduce Greenhouse Gases*, OTA-O-482 (Washington, DC: U.S. Government Printing Office, February 1991), p. 45.

[14]This effort, designated the U.S. Global Change Research Program (USGCRP), consists of a number of existing and new programs. The largest element of USGCRP is the National Aeronautic and Space Administration's (NASA) Mission to Planet Earth, a program that uses space- and ground-based instruments to observe changes in Earth's ecosystems. NASA's Earth Observing System is the principal component of the Mission to Planet Earth effort. See U.S. Congress, Office of Technology Assessment, *Global Change Research and NASA's Earth Observing System*, OTA-BP-ISC-122 (Washington, DC: U.S. Government Printing Office, November 1993).

[15]Ibid.

[16]For a detailed discussion of how natural and human systems may be affected by climate change and what tools are available to adjust to such change, see U.S. Congress, Office of Technology Assessment, *Preparing for an Uncertain Climate*, OTA-O-563 (Washington, DC: U.S. Government Printing Office, September 1993).

[17]For an indepth discussion of biotechnologies, see U.S. Congress, Office of Technology Assessment, *Biotechnology in a Global Economy*, OTA-BA-494 (Washington DC: U.S. Government Printing Office, October 1991).

quality is truly global in nature and requires that the best ideas be sought out, regardless of the nation in which they originated.

Because of the strong biological science research base and entrepreneurial spirit that exist in this country, commercial development of biotechnologies has been strongest in the United States. A multiyear, research initiative is now under way to maintain and extend U.S. leadership in biotechnology and to spur economic growth. The Biotechnology Research Initiative is supported by 12 federal agencies. Another initiative, the Human Genome Project, is a 15-year, $3-billion, distributed effort to locate and characterize human genes for biomedical research in the 21st century.

In recent years, many nations have focused increasing attention on developing and/or expanding biotechnology research programs and the capacity to convert research into new products. The link between biotechnology R&D and future economic competitiveness is a primary motivation for funding these programs. This link is likely to continue to grow in the future. However, the increasing internationalization of scientific research may be a challenge to the pursuit of strictly national biotechnology programs.

■ Other Trends in Science

In recent years, there has been a marked increase in the level of interaction among researchers from different disciplines. The availability of satellite imagery of the Earth's oceans and land masses, for example, has led to research initiatives that explore the linkages among agriculture, meteorology, geology, and ecology. Materials scientists and molecular biologists are collaborating in the synthesis of new classes of high-performance materials that are biocompatible and biodegradable;

chemists, physicists, and electrical engineers have joined forces to create innovative optical and computational devices. Psychologists, mathematicians, and linguists are developing software concepts that emulate natural language structures. Social and physical scientists are exploring the applications of complexity and chaos theory to human behavior. As the barriers between disciplines become more porous, previous trends toward specialization may be supplanted by a broader movement toward interdisciplinary research. The ease with which researchers from far-flung locations around the globe can now exchange and debate ideas is likely to reinforce this trend toward cross-disciplinary interaction.

Finally, with the end of the Cold War, a fundamental shift in the focus of R&D activities is occurring in the United States and abroad. Public and private expenditures on R&D now reflect a greater emphasis on civilian applications. Yet, comparable levels of spending for civilian and defense R&D activities will probably come about only over the long term, and will be subject to changing national security requirements. In fiscal year 1993, spending on defense R&D still represented about 60 percent of total federal support for R&D activities. In contrast, the national expenditure on civilian basic research amounted to about 25 percent of total government R&D spending.[18]

SCIENCE AND COMPETITIVENESS

Scientific and technological innovation have been closely linked to economic growth since the Middle Ages.[19] In the 20th century, efforts to harness the benefits of science have resulted in a highly structured and institutionalized approach to both basic and applied research. The essential premise underlying public support of fundamen-

[18]William J. Clinton and Albert Gore, Jr., *Science in the National Interest* (Washington, DC: Executive Office of the President, Office of Science and Technology Policy, August 1994).

[19]See N. Rosenberg and L.E. Birdzell, *How the West Grew Rich: The Economic Transformation of the Industrial World* (New York, NY: Basic Books, 1986).

tal scientific research is that it expands the base of human knowledge and thereby opens new possibilities for improving societal well-being.[20]

Although it is often difficult to assess the near-term impact of basic scientific research, its benefits to society over the long term, can be substantial.[21] For example, fundamental research in solid-state physics in the early decades of this century ultimately laid the groundwork for the modern electronics and computer industries. The emerging biotechnology industry can trace its origin directly to discoveries in the fields of molecular biology and biochemistry. Frequently, discoveries or insights from disparate fields of research can lead to fundamental advances. For instance, magnetic resonance imaging, a noninvasive medical diagnostic tool now in wide use, resulted from nuclear physics research dealing with the magnetic behavior of atomic nuclei. Even with a more structured approach to basic research, many significant technological developments have originated from research that was driven principally by curiosity. As an illustration, the study of bacteria that live in hot springs led to a new technique for rapidly cloning DNA (deoxyribonucleic acid), a discovery of potentially great scientific and commercial importance.[22] The process of understanding and harnessing natural phenomena has often been a serendipitous affair.

Although basic research can provide the essential inputs for commercial innovation, it alone is not sufficient to bring about improvements in national economic well-being. This is illustrated in one way by the lack of correlation between the number of Nobel prizes awarded to a particular nation and its overall economic and technological prowess.[23] Basic scientific discoveries in and of themselves usually possess little intrinsic value without further investments.[24] These investments might include more focused applications of research, the development of organizational and educational capabilities,[25] or greater awareness of how discoveries in different disciplines can improve existing manufacturing processes and products.

With the diffusion of knowledge throughout the world, many countries have developed comparable technical capabilities in a variety of industries. This has given rise to a highly competitive global arena that, in turn, has created an underlying tension between basic and applied research. Increasingly, policymakers are calling for national research efforts that are tied more directly to

---

[20]For some categories of R&D, particularly those that explore the frontiers of scientific understanding or entail significant risk, government support may be required if socially optimal levels of investment are to be realized. Government involvement may be particularly crucial when fundamental scientific or technological barriers need to be overcome in a short time. The challenge for policymakers is to determine where government can best use its R&D resources to complement, rather than replicate, the activities of the private sector. Government support of R&D activities can take many forms, including tax credits; direct financing of R&D through government labs, university research grants, or private contracts; or joint public-private partnerships.

[21]One study concluded that rates of return for R&D in particular industries and from university research can be 30 percent or more. See Edwin Mansfield, "Estimates of the Social Returns from Research and Development," *AAAS Science and Technology Policy Yearbook, 1991*, Margaret O. Meredith et al., (eds.) (Washington, DC: American Association for the Advancement of Science, 1991). Also see Edwin Mansfield, "Academic Research and Industrial Innovation," *Research Policy*, vol. 20, 1991, pp. 1-12.

[22]The polymerase chain reaction method for cloning DNA is now being used in a number of applications ranging from "DNA fingerprinting" to the production of genetically engineered drugs.

[23]For example, from 1960 to 1992, the Japanese received only four Nobel Prizes in science but had over 22,000 patents issued by the U.S. Patent Office. See Center for Science, Trade and Technology Policy, George Mason University, "Large Science Priorities of Selected Countries," contractor report prepared for the Office of Technology Assessment, Jan. 23, 1995.

[24]See Paul David et al., Center for Economic Policy Research, Stanford University "The Economic Analysis of Payoffs from Basic Research—An Examination of the Case of Particle Physics Research," CEPR Publication No. 122, January 1988.

[25]The world's fastest growing economies have placed an extraordinary emphasis on primary and secondary education. This investment in education has often been complemented by investments in science and technology.

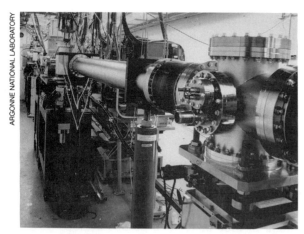

ARGONNE NATIONAL LABORATORY

X-ray beams originating from the Advanced Photon Source storage ring are directed through a beamline (as shown) to an experimental station.

ment report *Federally Funded Research: Decisions for a Decade* concluded:

> Given the extraordinary strength of the U.S. research system and the character of scientific research, there will always be more opportunities than can be funded, more researchers competing than can be sustained, and more institutions seeking to expand than the prime sponsor—the Federal Government—can fund. The objective, then, is to ensure that the best research continues to be funded, that a full portfolio of research is maintained, and that there is a sufficient research work force of the highest caliber to do the job.[28]

At a time when all governments are sensitive to the strategic economic advantages that can accrue from knowledge-based or technologically based industries, participation in large-scale international science projects is carefully scrutinized. Whereas some countries may see distinct benefits associated with multinational collaboration, others may deem participation in particular projects as militating against the national interest. This can be especially true if a nation is attempting to develop its expertise in a particular scientific or technological field.

Yet, building up national scientific capabilities and joining international collaborations are not necessarily mutually exclusive strategies. In many cases, having access to scientific facilities in other countries or participating in the planning and operation of particular projects may strengthen and diversify a nation's science base. Over the past several decades, the diffusion of scientific and technological knowledge has, in fact, accelerated progress in many fields (e.g., biotechnology,

meeting the needs of society.[26] In both government and the private sector, there has been an inclination to shift funding priorities to the applied research area, where returns on investment can be more immediately realized. What is not clear, however, is whether there is an ideal mix of basic and applied research programs, or whether a major shift to applied programs will limit the range of new discoveries and innovations.[27] Regardless of the way in which national science priorities are set, it is important to recognize that there is not necessarily a linear relationship between basic and applied research. Rather, a complex interaction exists that cannot easily be characterized. Although additional funding for both basic and applied research would permit the pursuit of a broader range of scientific opportunities and possible commercial applications, enlarging the U.S. research system could lead to additional problems in the future. As the Office of Technology Assess-

---

[26]See, for example, George E. Brown, "New Ways of Looking at U.S. Science and Technology," *Physics Today*, September 1994. Also see Chancellor of the Duchy of Lancaster, *Realising Our Potential, A Strategy for Science, Engineering and Technology*, presented to Parliament by Command of Her Majesty (London, England: Her Majesty's Science Office, May 1993).

[27]Currently, total nondefense U.S. support of R&D is about 1.9 percent of the gross domestic product (GDP). The major portion of that funding is industrially sponsored applied R&D. The portion of funding directed toward basic research is 0.42 percent of the GDP, two-thirds of which comes from the federal government. See footnote 18.

[28]U.S. Congress, Office of Technology Assessment, *Federally Funded Research: Decisions for a Decade*, OTA-SET-490 (Washington, DC: U.S. Government Printing Office, May 1991).

computer and communications technology). Also, as many Asian nations have demonstrated, long-term investments in education or science and technology can be particularly productive when linked to international networks of research. Increased global cooperation in science will no doubt provide economic and social benefits for many nations. The challenge for policymakers is to ensure that the costs and benefits of collaborative activities are shared more or less equitably.

ROLE OF LARGE PROJECTS

Large projects have been a key component of our nation's science portfolio for several decades. Although small science is the backbone of the modern scientific enterprise, big science has steadily encroached onto the scene. Unlike small science projects, almost no knowledge can be generated from a megaproject in the area of direct inquiry until some large-scale investment has occurred. However, significant indirect benefits can be realized throughout the course of a project. For example, ITER research may produce major indirect benefits in the areas of materials science and magnet design even if the ITER project is not brought to completion.

Over the past few years, expenditures on large projects and facilities have essentially leveled off at about 10 percent of the total federal (defense and nondefense) R&D budget, but this situation could change as several big science projects are brought up for congressional approval.[29] Although some large undertakings such as the National High Magnetic Field Laboratory and the Advanced Photon Source (an advanced x-ray synchrotron facility) provide platforms for small science, and thus reinforce the research support given to individual investigators across many disciplines, many other projects do not complement small science programs.

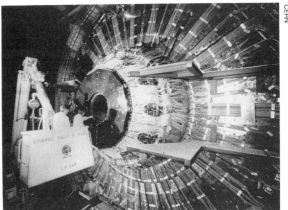

Scientists making adjustments to DELPHI particle detector.

In recent years, the role of large, costly projects has stimulated considerable debate in Congress and the science community. Priority setting is becoming much more of an issue because all proposed megaprojects may not be supportable without eroding the underlying national science base. The Superconducting Super Collider (SSC), the International Space Station, the Earth Observing System (EOS), and ITER are just a few examples of recent megaprojects.

There are several reasons for engaging in large scientific ventures. In some fields of inquiry, scientific projects must be large in scale in order to advance and demonstrate the underlying science or to achieve specific technical goals. For example, probing the energy domains that will provide new insights into the fundamental characteristics of matter, or demonstrating the feasibility of controlled nuclear fusion, will require apparatus (accelerators, detectors, reactors) of unusual size and sophistication. The International Space Station project—an effort to build and operate a permanently inhabited Earth-orbiting facility—is by its very nature, a complicated, immense undertaking. Other classes of problems, such as climate change, are truly global in nature and require

---

[29]This figure is based on a "basket" of large projects tracked by the Congressional Research Service. See Genevieve J. Knezo, *Major Science and Technology Programs: Megaprojects and Presidential Initiatives, Trends Through FY 1996 Requested*, CRS Report for Congress (Washington, DC: Congressional Research Service, Mar. 27, 1995).

broad-based multinational, multidisciplinary initiatives to develop a better scientific understanding of fundamental physical processes and to ensure the international credibility of scientific results.

Although large science projects are often symbols of national prestige, their principal justification is that they serve as a means for strengthening essential national capabilities in different scientific fields. For example, the U.S. high-energy physics program has, over the course of several decades, led to the development of leading-edge capabilities in the areas of accelerator design and detector methods. Other examples are Japan's Subaru telescope project, which is being used to strengthen the Japanese research base in astronomy, and strategic programs such as the various national efforts to develop sophisticated capabilities in launching and deploying satellites. Admittedly, some projects have strong scientific rationales, whereas others are being pursued less for science and more for broad social, economic, and technological reasons.

In addition, there is sometimes a strong political rationale for pursuing large collaborative undertakings. For instance, European governments support a number of extensive research programs through the European Union Research Commissariat. In addition, separate facilities and institutions have been created including the European Laboratory for Particle Physics (CERN), the European Synchrotron Radiation Facility (ESRF), and the European Space Agency (ESA). The governments involved believe that promoting scientific cooperation among scientists throughout Europe will strengthen the political processes associated with the unification of Europe. Coordinated small science projects have had a unifying effect as well.

Finally, if pursued in a multidisciplinary or multilateral fashion, large science projects permit, to differing degrees, the opportunity to leverage intellectual resources and technical capabilities. Synergies can often be achieved simply by bringing individual investigators or research groups together. Depending on the nature of the undertaking, large projects may also provide op-

portunities for addressing scientific questions that will benefit humankind (e.g., human genome research).

INDUSTRIAL IMPLICATIONS OF LARGE PROJECTS

Although the principal purpose underlying large scientific endeavors centers on the pursuit of basic research and engineering goals, some megascience activities have been used to varying degrees as a means for developing industrial capabilities in certain spheres of technology (e.g., rocket-launching capabilities, satellite design, superconducting magnets, advanced materials). As a consequence, some programs and projects, particularly those that are capital-intensive, have developed strong industrial constituencies. In the United States, Europe, and Japan, for example, major industrial enterprises perform key system and component development work for national space agencies. ESA has, in fact, evolved a contracting system that is designed to return a significant proportion of member-state contributions to national companies. Thus, in certain cases, large science undertakings have been used by governments as an instrument of industrial policy.

Whether large scientific projects can be effectively used to facilitate the development and deployment of new commercial technologies is an open question. As a general proposition, though, it is difficult to demonstrate that large projects or specific aspects of large projects can be efficiently utilized for this purpose. There have been varying results in different fields.

Although over the course of many decades there has been considerable transferability of advances in high-energy and nuclear physics to the commercial sector, such spin-off technologies have developed in a rather unpredictable and discontinuous fashion. These spin-offs include ion implantation in the semiconductor industry, accelerator-based cancer therapy, CAT (computerized axial tomography) scanner systems, positron emission tomography, free electron lasers, and synchrotron generated x-ray beams. None of these technologies were conceived in a deliberate or direct manner; rather they were unanticipated off-shoots of basic experimental research. Moreover, these transfers from high-energy and nuclear physics research to the marketplace have taken place over a considerably long time.

In contrast, the development of rocket-launching systems, satellites, and space platforms has been a direct and integral objective of different national space programs. Unlike the basic research focus of high-energy physics projects, some space activities have an explicit technological orientation and can be more naturally geared to achieving the specific engineering or performance goals necessary for commercial applications.

Other programs have objectives that require progress both in basic scientific understanding and in certain underlying technologies. In pursuing nuclear fusion as a commercial power source, which is primarily a basic research undertaking, there are certain technological imperatives that must be met before further fusion advances can occur. The attainment of these technical goals could also provide opportunities for spin-offs to other fields. In particular, the goals of demonstrating the technical and economic feasibility of fusion power using magnetic confinement schemes envision the development of advanced materials and greater use of superconducting magnet technologies. Proposed advanced tokamak fusion reactor designs, for example, call for extremely powerful superconducting magnets. Research on high-performance, low-activation materials and on the design and fabrication of superconducting magnetic coils for fusion reactors have become critical elements of all major fusion programs, and major industrial companies in Japan, Europe, and the United States have emerged as key project par-

The European Spacelab module in the cargo bay of the orbiting space shuttle Columbia.

ticipants.[30] These companies could be well positioned to apply their expertise with magnets to areas outside fusion, such as magnetic resonance imaging, free electron lasers, electric motors, advanced materials separation processing, and energy storage.[31]

Apart from the development of technological systems or components for projects, large scientific facilities themselves can also provide benefits to national economies. One study found that between 40 and 70 percent of the funds used to operate large international facilities are spent in the

---

[30]For example, in Japan, Toshiba, Hitachi, and Mitsubishi have contracts to advance superconducting magnet technology. In the United States, Westinghouse and Lockheed-Martin are active in fusion-relevant superconducting magnet technology development.

[31]See U.S. Congress, Office of Technology Assessment, *High Temperature Superconductivity in Perspective,* OTA-E-440 (Washington, DC: U.S. Government Printing Office, April 1990). See also U.S. Department of Energy, Office of Energy Research, *The U.S. Fusion Program as a Source of Technology Transfer* (Washington, DC: September 1993).

host nation.[32] Although substantial portions of these funds are used to provide basic services such as construction, materials, chemicals, or food, local companies that provide technical support or equipment can enhance their underlying scientific or engineering expertise. A large facility can also attract new companies and thereby raise the skill base of a region's population. However, contracts for the most knowledge-intensive components of large projects are typically assigned to companies in many different countries. Thus, in most cases, the particular location of a facility is generally not of strategic economic importance.

---

[32]This analysis was based on the spending patterns of CERN, located on the Swiss-French border; the Joint European Torus fusion experiment in England; and the ESRF and the Institute Laue-Langevin for neutron research, both in France. See "International Facilities Said To Boost National Economy," *Nature*, vol. 363, May 6, 1993.

U.S. Experience in International Collaboration 3

T he United States has a long history of collaboration in science dating back to the 1940s. Scientific cooperation is conducted primarily through informal agreements among scientists and institutions and through bilateral agreements between governments. High-energy physics, fusion, and space-related science activities are rich with examples of this type of cooperation. U.S. experience is more limited in large-scale collaborative projects where research efforts are highly interdependent and jointly funded and constructed. The International Thermonuclear Experimental Reactor (ITER) and U.S.-Russian activities associated with the space station are examples of large-scale collaborative efforts that involve close participation among nations. Although experience with this type of collaboration has been limited, valuable lessons have been learned.

National science goals influence whether the United States participates in scientific collaborative efforts; these goals provide the context for establishing national science programs and for developing government agency policy. In this chapter, our nation's overarching science goals are described briefly, followed by a discussion of the U.S. experience with collaborative projects in science and their implications for future activities. Several research areas are discussed: high-energy physics, fusion, scientific activities in space, and neutron sources and synchrotrons.

U.S. GOALS IN SCIENTIFIC COLLABORATION

A review of the literature suggests that since World War II, the overriding goal of U.S. megascience projects has been to establish and maintain leadership in as many scientific fields as possible. The view that maintaining scientific leadership is important

has been reaffirmed in a recent White House report, *Science in the National Interest*.[1]

The significance assigned to this primary goal of leadership may have to be reevaluated, however, given the development of sophisticated science programs and facilities worldwide, the increasing costs of science, and the rapid diffusion of information. The United States is no longer the clear leader in all scientific disciplines. Other industrialized countries have developed comparable or competitive capabilities in many technical fields. Europe and Japan, for example, have leading-edge, high-energy physics and fusion programs and facilities. The ambiguous nature of the goal of maintaining scientific leadership also raises fundamental questions about what projects to fund and what level of commitment is most appropriate. Resolving these questions is the challenge that lies ahead for U.S. policymakers and for the scientific community.

Even so, leadership in science can be a source of national prestige. A classic illustration of the relation of megaprojects to national prestige is the Apollo mission to the Moon more than 25 years ago. The unexpected Soviet launching of two Sputnik satellites had rocked the foundations of the U.S. science community and its assumed technological superiority. Putting a man on the Moon was the culmination of a massive U.S. commitment to meet the Soviet challenge and win the space race. National prestige has also been cited as one of the reasons for justifying U.S. commitment to the space station.

Scientific leadership can also provide intellectual benefits to the United States by attracting top-notch foreign scientists to conduct research here. For decades, foreign scientists have made significant contributions to U.S. science efforts and have enriched its scientific community.

Other U.S. science goals are linked to economic productivity, foreign policy, national security imperatives, and environmental and social considerations. Scientific research can provide the foundation for innovation and technological development, which contributes to national economic well-being. Technological development in some fields, such as biotechnology and computers, relies on advances in basic science research. For example, research done on particle colliders and synchrotron radiation has stimulated the development of magnet technologies that have important medical and industrial applications. Likewise, basic research in solid-state physics in the 1950s laid the foundation for U.S. dominance in computer technologies today. These and other new products and processes fuel U.S. economic growth here and contribute to its competitiveness abroad.

As economic activities become more global, competition will continue to get tougher: new countries will join the competition, and new markets will emerge. It is in this context that the United States may rely even more on the results yielded by basic scientific research. In the words of Frank Press, former President of the National Academy of Sciences, "Basic research is our comparative advantage in the world. In time, a lot of countries will be able to manufacture as well as the Japanese. We're different in being able to create wealth with science."[2]

It is important to note, however, that other countries are leaders in technology development, yet they devote fewer relative resources to basic science research than the United States. Both Germany and Japan promote applications-oriented research with a view to developing products and processes for new markets. Based on the successes of the German and Japanese models, ensuring the proper mix of applied and basic research may be key to economic development.

---

[1] William J. Clinton and Albert Gore, Jr., *Science in the National Interest* (Washington, DC: Executive Office of the President, Office of Science and Technology Policy, August 1994).

[2] Lee Smith, "What the U.S. Can Do About R&D," *Fortune*, Oct. 19, 1992, p. 75.

U.S. scientific preeminence and expertise have also contributed to foreign policy success and in the achievement of American goals around the world. Bilateral scientific research agreements, for example, have been used for years to build and strengthen alliances or signal displeasure. In the 1960s, bilateral science and technology (S&T) agreements between the United States and the Peoples Republic of China encouraged contact among scientists as well as government officials. As a symbolic message, the United States scaled back its S&T agreements with the Soviet Union after the Soviet invasion of Afghanistan.

Scientific agreements may also provide incentives to observe and maintain other treaties or agreements. For example, Russia's invitation to participate in the Space Station Project was, in part, contingent on its adherence to the Missile Technology Control Regime, an informal, voluntary agreement among suppliers of space technology to restrict the export of systems and components used for ballistic missiles. Moreover, bilateral scientific agreements may play a role in sustaining the science base of the former Soviet Union, promoting its stability, and preventing the proliferation of weapons-related expertise. With the end of the Cold War, however, S&T agreements may be less important as foreign policy tools.

Science has contributed in significant ways to national security goals as well. Our military technological superiority is the result of advances in fundamental science and engineering. As our national security goals are redefined by the end of the Cold War, basic science will continue to figure prominently. One of the most troublesome security challenges now facing the United States is the proliferation of nuclear weapons. New and improved technologies, particularly in arms monitoring and verification, will be required to meet this challenge.

Over the years, scientific research has enjoyed the strong support of different administrations and Congress. However, funding priorities have shifted in response to international events and domestic politics (see box 3-1).

Recently, complex and costly science projects, such as the Superconducting Super Collider (SSC), the Advanced Neutron Source, and the Tokamak Physics Experiment,[3] have motivated debate in the Administration and Congress about national research goals and the capacity of the U.S. government to fund basic research. In this context, there has been much discussion about the potential for international collaboration in large science projects. Collaborative efforts are now under way in space, fusion, and high-energy physics.

HIGH-ENERGY PHYSICS

High-energy physics is a field of basic scientific inquiry that explores the fundamental characteristics of matter and the basic forces that govern all physical phenomena. To gain insights about elementary particles and their interactions, physicists probe energy domains far removed from those encountered in daily life.[4] In its attempt to extend the frontiers of human knowledge about underlying natural processes and laws, and to answer questions about the origin of the universe, the high-energy physics field has especially defined itself by drawing on the intellectual resources of scientists throughout the world.

---

[3]The TPX is a fusion device proposed to be built at the Princeton Plasma Physics Laboratory. Congress has not yet authorized funds to begin construction of the approximately $700 million TPX. For an indepth discussion on the TPX, see the recent report, U.S. Congress, Office of Technology Assessment, *The Fusion Energy Program: The Role of TPX and Alternate Concepts,* OTA-BP-ETI-141 (Washington, DC: U.S. Government Printing Office, February 1995).

[4]Existing and new particle accelerators operate at energies in the billion electron volt (GeV) to trillion electron volt range (TeV). By comparison, the thermal combustion of a single carbon atom contained in coal releases about four electron volts. Thus, a single particle (e.g., a proton or electron) being accelerated to 1 TeV would have an energy about a trillion times greater than that associated with the burning of a carbon atom.

BOX 3–1: Funding Priorities

Broad-based federal support for scientific research has spanned five decades. During this period, the ability of the United States to conduct research has grown considerably and so, too, has the demand for funding. Today, there are far more opportunities for research than there are funds to support projects. Consequently, research funding decisions have been challenging and sometimes contentious for Congress, the Administration, and the scientific community.

Since federal support began in the mid-1940s, a key consideration in allocating federal funds has been the need to maintain a diverse portfolio of large and small science projects. Other considerations have included enhancing the U.S. science base in specific research areas, and training scientists and engineers. In recent years, budgetary considerations have focused increased attention on the need for more explicit priority setting as a way to help allocate federal resources and strengthen the nation's portfolio. Currently, priority setting is distributed throughout the federal government at many different levels. At the highest level, scientific priorities are compared to other nonscience needs. Priorities are also determined across research fields and within particular disciplines. The OTA report, *Federally Funded Research: Decisions for a Decade*, identified priority setting as a pressing challenge for the U.S. research system in the 1990s.[1]

A snapshot of historical funding priorities reveals that during World War II, federal investment focused on military and atomic energy-related projects. In the 1950s and 1960s, Soviet achievements in space and expanded military spending prompted the United States to increase funding for its own space initiatives and defense programs. By the late 1960s, however, research funding had declined due, in part, to the enormous costs of the Vietnam War and the expansion of domestic social programs. The decade of the 1970s brought renewed interest in space projects, the expansion of funding for energy and health research, and cuts in defense research and development (R&D). In the 1980s, during the Reagan Administration, defense projects regained top funding priority, and energy and health research funding declined. At the same time, basic science funding also increased. Big science and technology projects, such as the space station, the Superconducting Super Collider, the Strategic Defense Initiative, and the Human Genome Project figured prominently on the national agenda. Finally, the belt-tightening of the early 1990s brought yet more changes, including termination of the SSC project, redesign of the space station, and the addition of Russia as a space station partner in 1994.

Despite the vicissitudes of funding during this period, megascience projects, including presidential science initiatives, have continued to command a noticeable portion (about 10 percent) of total federal R&D expenditures.[2] However, because of the disparate characteristics of large projects, comparisons and priority setting have proven difficult, resulting in a funding process for large projects that remains largely ad hoc.

---

[1] See U.S. Congress, Office of Technology Assessment, *Federally Funded Research: Decisions for a Decade*, OTA-SET-490 (Washington, DC: U.S. Government Printing Office, May 1991).

[2] Genevieve J. Knezo, *Major Science and Technology Programs: Megaprojects and Presidential Initiatives, Trends Through the FY 1996*, CRS Report for Congress, 95-490 SPR (Washington, DC: Congressional Research Service, Mar. 27, 1995.

The principal scientific tool of this field of research is the particle accelerator. By accelerating particles to extremely high energies and bringing them together in collisions, researchers are able to develop greater understanding of the innermost structure of matter. This is done by observing the debris from collisions using extremely sophisticated detectors. Because energy and mass are interchangeable, high-energy particle collisions essentially redistribute mass and energy to create

TABLE 3-1: Elementary Particles and Force Carriers		
First-generation family	**Second-generation family**	**Third-generation family**
Electron	Muon	Tau neutrino
Electron neutrino	Muon neutrino	Tau lepton
Up quark	Charm quark	Top quark
Down quark	Strange quark	Bottom quark
Force carriers	**Force**	
Photon	Electromagnetic force	
W boson	Weak nuclear force	
Z boson	Weak nuclear force	
Gluons	Strong nuclear force	

SOURCE: U.S. Department of Energy, Office of Energy Research, Division of High Energy Physics, *High Energy Physics Advisory Panel's Subpanel on Vision for the Future of High Energy Physics,* DOE/ER-0614P (Washington, DC: May 1994).

new particles.[5] The higher the impact energy, the more massive these new particles can be, thus revealing hitherto unknown or *hidden* properties of matter. As a consequence of the need for higher energies, accelerators have increased considerably in size over the years. Accelerators and detectors are large, elaborate, expensive devices, and experiments typically involve the collaboration of hundreds of scientists and engineers.

Over the past 50 years, the experimental discoveries and theoretical insights of researchers worldwide have led to the construction of a remarkably successful model that describes the types of particles that exist in nature and how they interact with each other. This so-called Standard Model depicts all matter as consisting of only

three families of fundamental particles. (See table 3-1.) Each family contains two types of *quarks*[6] and two types of *leptons*.[7] The protons and neutrons that form atomic nuclei are combinations of two different types of quarks, and the electrons that surround atomic nuclei are leptons. The remaining quarks and leptons are not found in ordinary matter and can only be studied in high-energy processes. The forces that operate among quarks and leptons are mediated by additional particles.[8]

Although the Standard Model has proved a successful predictive and explanatory tool, physicists believe that it cannot answer a number of questions. For example, why are there so many elementary particles and why do they appear as three

---

[5]This phenomenon is described by Einstein's formula $E = mc^2$. The process by which new heavy particles are created from the collisions of lighter particles is akin to a bowling ball emerging from the collision of two tennis balls. For example, the recently discovered *top quark*, the heaviest of known elementary particles, has a mass equivalent to that of a gold atom. Evidence for the existence of the top quark, the last quark to be identified, was announced in March 1995 by two independent teams of researchers at the Fermi National Accelerator Laboratory.

[6]The names given to these six quarks are: up, down, strange, charm, bottom, and top. They each have different masses and charges. The proton consists of two up quarks and one down, while a neutron consists of two downs and one up. For further information see Daniel Morgan, *High-Energy Physics Accelerator Facilities*, CRS Report for Congress (Washington, DC: Congressional Research Service, Sept. 17, 1993), appendix, pp. CRS-22 to CRS-23.

[7]Each elementary particle also has a corresponding *antiparticle* with identical mass but opposite charge. For example, the antiparticle of the electron is the positron. Positrons are produced in accelerator collisions and have found important use as a medical diagnostic tool, a technique called positron emission tomography. Combinations of quarks and antiquarks can account for the roughly 200 known particles or *hadrons* that have been discovered.

[8]Quarks and leptons interact by exchanging particles known as force carriers. The strong force that holds quarks together to form protons and neutrons is mediated by gluon particles; the weak force is mediated by W and Z bosons, and the electromagnetic force is mediated by photons. It is speculated that the force of gravity is also mediated by a particle carrier, but no such carrier has been discovered.

families as opposed to any other number? What is the origin of mass and why do the fundamental particles exhibit no regularity in their masses?[9] Why is the universe made primarily of matter when the Big Bang theory would predict the creation of equal amounts of matter and antimatter?[10] Can the missing mass of the universe be explained by an as-yet undiscovered class of super-heavy particles?[11] The high-energy physics community believes that experimental clues to these questions could be provided by the next generation of high-energy particle accelerators. With the termination of the SSC, the Large Hadron Collider at CERN is the only currently approved project that will be capable of addressing most of these issues.[12]

∎ U.S. Goals

Since World War II, the United States has been a global leader in both the experimental and the theoretical domains of high-energy physics. U.S. high-energy physics facilities are among the best in the world and have provided unique opportunities to conduct research and to advance scientific understanding.[13] In addition, these facilities have stimulated interest in science among the nation's

young and have served as an important component of graduate-level education and training. Although establishing and maintaining a leadership position in high-energy physics research has been a major goal of U.S. programs, a policy of open access has also encouraged many researchers from Europe, Japan, and other parts of the world to participate in U.S. projects. Indeed, several prominent foreign scientists have received their training at U.S. facilities.

In recent years, U.S. leadership in high-energy physics has been challenged by scientific developments in Europe and Japan. Additionally, domestic budget constraints have limited various experimental endeavors, and some new or existing projects have been either deferred or canceled. The recent termination of the SSC project was a major blow to the U.S. program.[14] In the early 1980s, the U.S. high-energy physics community embraced the construction of the SSC as its top priority. The project was expected to open new windows of discovery and thereby solidify the leadership position of the United States well into the next century. Questions about its management, performance, and spiraling cost estimates,

---

[9]One theory suggests that particles acquire mass through interaction with a ubiquitous force field known as the Higgs field. Confirmation that such a field exists would come from the discovery of very heavy particles known as Higgs particles. Theory predicts that Higgs particles would have masses in the 1 TeV range, energies that cannot be produced by any existing accelerator. The Large Hadron Collider (LHC) device at CERN (as well as the canceled SSC) is designed to explore the energy range where Higgs particles might exist if the Standard Model is correct.

[10]This particular question is being addressed specifically by the *B-factory* projects being carried out at the Stanford Linear Accelerator Center and at the KEK facility in Japan.

[11]A central problem of modern astronomy is that most of the mass of the universe (90 percent) cannot be seen (so-called *dark* matter), but can be inferred from the gravitational behavior of galaxies. One possible theory accounts for this missing mass by positing the existence of neutral, stable particles that have not yet been detected. Such *supersymmetric* particles might be seen at the energies provided by the LHC facility now under construction at CERN.

[12]Although the LHC will have a combined beam energy roughly three times lower than the SSC, the luminosity or beam intensity of the LHC will be 10 times greater than that of the SSC. The LHC will be able to probe energies up to about 2 TeV. However, because of its higher luminosity, there will be a greater number of undesired collisions (so-called *noise*) that must be filtered by sophisticated detectors. The detector technologies that will be deployed at the LHC will be much more complex than those planned for the SSC.

[13]The Department of Energy operates several high-energy physics and related nuclear physics facilities. They include the Alternating Gradient Synchrotron and the Relativistic Heavy Ion Collider at Brookhaven National Laboratory, the Tevatron at Fermilab, the electron linac at the Stanford Linear Accelerator Center, and the Continuous Beam Accelerator Facility (CEBAF) in Newport News, Virginia. The National Science Foundation funds the Cornell Electron Storage Ring.

[14]Murray Gell-Mann, a recipient of the Nobel Prize for his work in particle physics, described the termination of the SSC as a "conspicuous setback for human civilization." "Physicists Ponder Life After the Demise of the Supercollider," *New York Times,* Aug. 9, 1994, p. C5.

The ALEPH detector at CERN.

upgrading existing facilities and participating in international efforts.

In 1994, a subpanel of the Department of Energy High Energy Physics Advisory Panel (HEPAP) presented options for the future U.S. program. The HEPAP subpanel noted the importance of international collaboration in preserving U.S. scientific and technological capabilities. U.S. scientists already participate in experiments at several laboratories in Europe and Japan. For example, several hundred American physicists and engineers are now involved with various experiments at the DESY (Deutches Elektronen-Synchrotron) facility in Germany and at CERN in Switzerland. As a specific measure to ensure that U.S. scientists remain at the forefront of accelerator design and physics investigation, the subpanel recommended that the United States also join the LHC project at CERN.[16] However, the subpanel concluded that the long-term future of U.S. high-energy physics will depend on the research and development (R&D) foundation built here, not in Europe or Japan.

While many important technical innovations have resulted from high-energy physics research and related areas of nuclear physics research, these spinoffs have invariably been unanticipated, have occurred over a period of decades, and have often resulted from scientists from many countries working together.[17] In light of this history and the somewhat esoteric character of high-energy physics research, it is difficult to argue that participa-

however, severely damaged support for the project.[15] Because of its cancellation, the United States is now exploring ways to maintain a presence at the high-energy frontier by utilizing and

---

[15]Initially, the project was estimated to cost about $4.4 billion (in 1988 dollars without an allowance for contingencies), but by 1993, cost estimates had escalated to more than $11 billion. At the time of termination, 15 miles (of a total of 54) of tunnel had been dug, magnets had been tested, and $2.2 billion spent, mostly on salaries. Some observers argue that the management of the SSC was politicized and taken out of the hands of Department of Energy technical managers who had a good record in overseeing the planning and execution of large projects. As a consequence, the various problems that developed over the course of the SSC endeavor might have been either avoided or addressed in a more effective manner.

[16]U.S. Department of Energy, Office of Energy Research, Division of High Energy Physics, *High Energy Physics Advisory Panel's Subpanel on Vision for the Future of High Energy Physics,* DOE/ER-0614P (Washington, DC: May 1994).

[17]Some examples of spinoffs from high-energy physics and nuclear physics research include ion implantation in the semiconductor industry, accelerator-based cancer therapy, computerized axial tomography (the CAT scanner), positron emission tomography, free electron lasers, synchrotron generated x-ray beams, and large data-handling and transfer software. See Paul David et al., Stanford University, Center for Economic Policy Research, "The Economic Analysis of Payoffs from Basic Research—An Examination of the Case of Particle Physics Research," CEPR Publication No. 122, January 1988.

TABLE 3-2: Escalation of Costs in High-Energy Physics and Related Areas of Nuclear Physics

Project	Decade	Nominal capital cost
Bevatron (U.S.)	1950s	$10 million
Stanford Linear Accelerator (U.S.)	1960s	$115 million
Fermilab Tevatron (U.S.)	1970s	$250 million
Continuous Electron Beam Accelerator Facility (U.S.)	1980s-1990s	$510[a] million
Relativistic Heavy Ion Collider (U.S.)	1990s	$595[a] million
Superconducting Super Collider (U.S.)	1980s-1990s[b]	$8 billion-$11 billion[a]
Large Hadron Collider (Europe)	1990s[c]	$2.3 billion[d]

[a] Estimated total project cost.

[b] Project terminated, 1993.

[c] Completion planned 2005 to 2008.

[d] The estimated cost for the Large Hadron Collider would be roughly twice as large ($4 to $5 billion) if it were developed on the same accounting basis as U.S. cost estimates. Also this figure does not include the detectors, which may total as much as $2 billion.

SOURCE: Organization for Economic Cooperation and Development, *Megascience and Its Background* (Paris, France: 1993), p. 19; Congressional Research Service, "Big Science and Technology Projects: Analysis of 30 Selected U.S. Government Projects," August 24, 1994; and Harold Jaffe, Department of Energy, Office of High Energy and Nuclear Physics, personal communication, April 1995.

tion in multinational particle physics projects could undermine a country's technological competitiveness (see chapter 2).

■ Role of International Collaboration

High-energy physics research is a particularly good candidate for international collaboration for two reasons: 1) research in this field is essentially curiosity driven with little or no expectation of short-term commercial returns, and 2) the knowledge generated from particle physics experiments is more of a global than a national asset. Indeed, the most exciting advances in particle physics have resulted from the pooling of intellectual resources throughout the world. In light of the great expense required to build new accelerators (see table 3-2), collaboration among nations is likely to deepen in coming years.

The most recent accomplishment of researchers—the experimental verification of the existence of the top quark[18]—provides a compelling illustration of the universal character of the high-energy physics enterprise. More than 800 scientists from Brazil, Canada, Colombia, France, India, Italy, Japan, Korea, Mexico, Russia, Taiwan, and the United States collaborated on the two colliding beam experiments at Fermilab (CDF and DZero) that discovered the top quark. Moreover, about one-third of the funds for the 5,000-ton, $100 million CDF detector were provided by the Japanese and Italian governments. Over its entire history, 151 foreign institutions from 34 nations have been actively involved in research at Fermilab. Similar collaborative efforts have also occurred at Stanford Linear Accelerator Center (SLAC), the National Laboratory for High-Energy Physics (KEK) facility in Japan, and CERN. Because the high-energy physics community has evolved into a tightly linked network in which researchers from throughout the world communicate almost daily, collaboration has become an integral feature of nearly all empirical and theoretical undertakings.

Even with greater collaboration, innovation and competition in high-energy physics can be achieved by having multiple detectors at a single facility. For example, evidence for the discovery of the top quark was reinforced by the fact that two

---

[18] See S. Abachi et al. (The D0 Collaboration), "Observation of the Top Quark," Fermilab preprint, February 1995; and F. Abe et al. (The CDF Collaboration), "Observation of Top Quark Production in [proton-antiproton] Collisions," Fermilab preprint, February 1995.

TABLE 3-3: High-Energy Physics Facilities					
Electron-positron collider			Hadron collider and fixed target machines		
Name	Institution	Country	Name	Institution	Country
LEP	CERN	European Consortium	Tevatron	FNAL	United States
SLC	SLAC	United States	SPS	CERN	European Consortium
CESR	Cornell University	United States	AGS	BNL	United States
TRISTAN	KEK	Japan	UNK 600		Russia
BEPC		China	PS	KEK	Japan
VEPP-4M		Russia	HERA	DESY	Germany
			LHC	CERN	European Consortium
			CEBAF		United States

KEY: AGS = Alternating Gradient Synchrotron; BEPC = Beijing Electron-Positron Collider; BNL = Brookhaven National Laboratory; CEBAF = Continuous Electron Beam Accelerator Facility; CERN = European Laboratory for Particle Physics; CESR = Cornell Electron Storage Ring; DESY = Deutches Elektronen Synchrotron; FNAL = Fermi National Accelerator Laboratory; HERA = Hadron Elektron Ring Anlage; KEK = National Laboratory for High Energy Physics; LEP = Large Electron-Positron Collider; LHC = Large Hadron Collider; PS = Proton Synchrotron; SLAC = Stanford Linear Accelerator Center; SLC = Stanford Linear Collider; SPS = Super Proton Synchrotron; TRISTAN = Transposable Ring Intersecting Storage Accelerator in Nippon; UNK 600 = Accelerating and Storage Complex; VEPP = Very Large Electron-Positron Project

SOURCE: OECD Megascience Forum.

independent detector teams—the CDF and DZero groups—provided empirical findings. The LHC will also have two detector groups using different approaches—the ATLAS and CMS detectors.

In some cases, having parallel facilities—whether within a country or in different countries—is desirable. For example, both the United States and Japan are constructing *B-meson factories* as a means to understand the fundamental differences between matter and antimatter.[19] Even though the ultimate goals of the two projects are similar, they will employ different underlying technologies. This diversity of approach could lead to the development of new accelerator designs. In this particular case, construction of the B-factory in Japan was an integral component of its long-term strategy to develop expertise in the construction of advanced linear colliders.[20] As in the case of the top quark, having parallel efforts can provide important experimental verification of newly observed phenomena.

Although the design and management of future experimental facilities will likely involve many nations, existing high-energy physics facilities around the world (see table 3-3), with the exception of CERN, are currently funded and operated on a national basis. This is due principally to the fact that planning for most high-energy physics projects started 20 years ago or more. In addition, at various points in the past, high-energy physics research was regarded as a possible source of defense-related information. Even during the Cold War, however, scientists from Western countries

---

[19]A B-factory produces pairs of B mesons and anti-B mesons for the purpose of studying the phenomenon known as *charge-parity (CP)* violation. CP violation, which could explain why the universe appears to contain much more matter than antimatter, is an important concept in the Standard Model of particle physics. The U.S. B-factory is being built at the SLAC at a cost of $293 million. A similar factory is also being constructed at the KEK facility in Japan for about $350 million. Relative to other projects such as the LHC ($2.3 billion), the B-factory costs are low enough to be pursued on a noncollaborative basis. Some observers, however, argue that only one B-factory was necessary.

[20]Hirotaka Sugawara, Director, KEK National Laboratory for High Energy Physics, personal communication, Nov. 16, 1994.

were invited to work at the U.S.S.R.'s high-energy physics facilities on well-defined programs.[21]

■ Implications for the Future

In light of its many achievements over the past several decades, the U.S. high-energy physics program has been generally regarded as quite successful. U.S. capabilities are world class, and policies that encourage collaboration through open access arrangements have advanced the underlying science and strengthened ties with the international high-energy physics community. Because of the sophisticated nature of experimental work and the significant capital investments required, the level of this multinational interaction can be expected to intensify in coming years.

The history of the U.S. high-energy physics program, along with tightening budgets, suggests some important issues for consideration by policymakers and scientists alike:

- If it is determined that future high-energy physics projects should be carried out on an international basis, such initiatives will most likely fare better if they are truly collaborative from the outset: in planning, financing, construction, and operation. In the SSC project, the United States sought foreign partners as a way of sharing costs well after key engineering decisions had been made. This did not prove to be a good formula for successful development of an international venture.

- U.S. participation in the LHC project at CERN could lay the foundation for future cooperative efforts in high-energy physics. Regardless of the particular form of the U.S. contribution to the LHC—whether knowledge, dollars, or equipment—an important precedent is being set in the area of international collaboration.[22] Participation in the LHC could maintain and perhaps even extend American capabilities in the design of accelerator and detector systems and components (e.g., superconducting magnets). The HEPAP subpanel concluded that participation in the LHC project could also "strengthen our [U.S.] credibility as a capable host for such [large] projects in all fields of science."[23] The Department of Energy (DOE) is expected to recommend that U.S. contributions to the LHC project be roughly $40 million annually over the next decade.[24]

- Government decisionmakers from countries with major high-energy physics programs could benefit from the creation of mechanisms that facilitate multilateral planning of future large high-energy physics facilities. This would apply to hadron colliders that succeed the LHC[25] and to proposed electron-positron colliders such as the Next Linear Collider

---

[21]See Center for Science, Trade and Technology Policy, George Mason University, "Large Science Project Priorities of Selected Countries," report prepared for the Office of Technology Assessment, December 1994.

[22]CERN's member states contribute both to the infrastructure costs of the laboratory in proportion to their gross domestic product, and to the costs of their experimental teams who build and use detectors. Nonmember states, including the United States, need bear only the second of these financial burdens. However, because nearly 500 American physicists are involved with the two LHC detectors, the CERN Council is seeking U.S. contributions to the LHC accelerator project itself. John Krige, "ESA and CERN as International Collaborative Science Organizations," contractor report prepared for the Office of Technology Assessment, January 1995.

[23]U.S. Department of Energy, see footnote 16.

[24]See testimony of Martha Krebs, Director of DOE's Office of Energy Research, before the Subcommittee on Energy and Water Development, House Committee on Appropriations, Mar. 9, 1995. DOE, however, will not be in a position to recommend any specific level of LHC funding until overall Department cost reduction goals through 2001 are developed.

[25]The HEPAP subpanel (chaired by Sidney Drell) points out that "preliminary examination indicates that it may become practical to build a proton collider with beams of up to 10 times the energies of the LHC, using technology that could be developed in the next decade." Such a collider could be used to search for so-called *supersymmetric* or superheavy particles that may lie beyond the energy range of the LHC. U.S. Department of Energy, see footnote 16.

(NLC).[26] The NLC is already a multinational grass roots effort among scientists from more than 20 nations (preliminary experiments involve researchers from the United States, Japan, and Russia). Some scientists believe that the NLC should be set up as an international organization similar to CERN.[27] Even though it is only at an early concept stage, this embryonic collaboration could receive greater attention from relevant governments.

- Policymakers could explore opportunities for consolidation of high-energy physics research activities, as well as the possible elimination of duplicative programs and facilities. Strategies for efficiently utilizing existing high-energy physics facilities could also be developed. This could mean closing down some facilities and using the funds to extend operations at others. The DOE budget for fiscal year (FY) 1996 takes a step in this direction by providing funds to increase the effectiveness of high-energy physics facilities at Fermilab, SLAC, and Brookhaven. Cost-effectiveness can also be achieved by upgrading existing facilities. The construction of the new Main Injector[28] at Fermilab is one such undertaking. The United States could also examine where high-energy physics objectives might be met by using facilities in other nations. U.S. and foreign high-energy physics programs could be designed to take advantage of existing expertise and infrastructure throughout the world.

- Greater attention and possibly higher levels of funding could be given to nonconventional (e.g., nonaccelerator) approaches to high-energy physics. In light of the extraordinary costs of state-of-the-art accelerator facilities, support of novel approaches to particle acceleration could ultimately provide a fundamentally different and less costly means for probing the high-energy frontier. Although work in this area is now quite speculative, some interesting nonconventional approaches have emerged.[29]

- Given the success of the U.S. high-energy physics program over the past several decades, policies of *open* and *reciprocal* access for foreign scientists to national installations should be maintained. However, at a time of tightening budgets in virtually all industrial countries, strategies for ensuring equitable sharing of high-energy physics facility costs and benefits should also be explored.

FUSION ENERGY RESEARCH

For more than four decades, researchers in the United States and elsewhere have been working to understand and control nuclear fusion, the reac-

---

[26]Hadron colliders and electron-positron colliders are complementary experimental approaches. Hadron colliders provide great reach in energy, while electron-positron colliders provide a precise method to search for new phenomena in finer detail. The Large Hadron Collider at CERN and the Tevatron at Fermilab are designed to collide particles (hadrons) that are comprised of quarks. These collisions result in considerable debris, which makes it difficult to analyze data. In electron-positron collisions, however, the colliding particles (electrons and positrons, which are fundamental particles like quarks) annihilate each other; thus the only particles remaining after the collision are those created by the energy released. This makes it relatively easy to identify collision products. David Burke, Stanford Linear Accelerator Center, personal communication, Sept. 13, 1994.

[27]Japanese physicists are quite interested in taking a lead role in constructing the NLC facility. However, the Japanese government has taken no official position on this matter. Sugawara, see footnote 20; and Wataru Iwamoto, Ministry of Education, Science, and Culture, Research Institute Division, personal communication, Nov. 15, 1994.

[28]The new Main Injector at Fermilab, which is scheduled to begin operating in 1999, will greatly increase the number of high-energy collisions that experimenters can observe, and thus provide the opportunity for new discoveries. The Main Injector will be the most powerful proton accelerator in operation until the completion of the LHC in about 2004.

[29]For example, some researchers are exploring how particles can be accelerated by plasma waves. Some preliminary work suggests that in just one meter, plasma wave accelerators could reach energies around 30 GeV—about one-third of the energy that can be attained by the 27-kilometer circular electron-positron collider at CERN. A variety of serious technical hurdles must be surmounted before such a plasma wave scheme becomes workable. See Jonathan Wurtele, "Advanced Accelerator Concepts," *Physics Today,* July 1994, pp. 33-40.

BOX 3–2: Fusion Reactions

A fusion reaction occurs when the nuclei of atoms of two light elements fuse to form an atom of a heavier element and additional particles, releasing energy. Scientists have found it easiest to produce fusion reactions using isotopes of hydrogen, the lightest element. The reaction illustrated in figure 3-1 shows the fusion of deuterium (D) and tritium (T) nuclei to produce a helium nucleus and a free neutron. The reaction releases a total of 17.6 million electron volts (MeV) of energy.[1] The neutron carries 14.1 MeV or four-fifths of the energy. In a fusion power reactor, the 14-MeV neutrons would be captured in the material surrounding the reaction chamber and converted into heat. The helium nuclei carrying 3.5 MeV would remain in the chamber, heating the fuel and making more reactions possible.

For the reaction to occur, certain conditions of temperature, density, and confinement time must be met simultaneously. Theoretically, there are a broad range of approaches that could be used to create fusion reactions.[2] In the laboratory, scientists have heated fusion fuels to over 100 million degrees Centigrade to form a *plasma*, a state in which individual atoms are broken down or ionized into their constituent electrons and nuclei. At these extremely high temperatures, the positively charged nuclei are able to overcome their natural repulsion and fuse. However, the plasma must be kept together long enough for enough of the nuclei to fuse to be a net producer of energy.

Several approaches to confining the plasma have been explored. In *magnetic confinement*, strong magnetic fields are used to control and shape the charged particles making up the plasma. These fields prevent the plasma from touching the reaction chamber walls, which would instantly cool and stop the reaction. The most technically successful magnetic confinement concept is the *tokamak*, which confines the plasma in a toroidal or donut-shaped vessel.

Inertial confinement fusion, the process used on a much larger scale in the hydrogen bomb, represents another approach under investigation. In this process (shown in figure 3-2), a pellet of fusion fuel is rapidly heated and compressed by intense lasers or heavy-ion drivers to such high densities that the fuel's own inertia is sufficient to contain it for the very short time necessary for the reaction to occur. Gravitational fields are sufficient to confine the fusion reactions in the Sun and other stars, but this approach cannot be duplicated on Earth.

---

[1]For comparison, burning a single atom of the carbon contained in coal produces about 4 electron volts. A fusion reaction therefore releases more than 4 million times as much energy per atom as coal combustion. An electron volt is the amount of energy that a single electron can pick up from a 1-volt battery. One electron volt equals 1.52×10^{-22} Btu (British Thermal Unit), or 4.45×10^{-26} kilowatt-hours, or 1.6×10^{-19} joules.

[2]For more detail on fusion science and the history of magnetic fusion research, see U.S. Congress, Office of Technology Assessment, *Starpower: The U.S. and the International Quest for Fusion Power*, OTA-E-338 (Washington, DC: U.S. Government Printing Office, October 1987). See also, U.S. Congress, Office of Technology Assessment, *The Fusion Energy Program: The Role of TPX and Alternate Concepts*, OTA-BP-ETI-141 (Washington, DC: U.S. Government Printing Office, February 1995), pp. 65-80, for recent developments and more on the state of research into other fusion concepts.

---

tion that powers our Sun, the stars, and the hydrogen bomb, in the hopes of one day tapping that process as a safe, environmentally attractive, and economical energy source. Fusion reactions occur when the nuclei of two lightweight atoms combine, or fuse, releasing energy (see box 3-2). Fusion research gave birth to and nourished the new field of plasma physics, which explores the behavior of plasmas, the fourth state of matter.

Among the advantages cited by fusion supporters are a virtually limitless fuel supply and potentially less serious environmental impacts than competing fossil or nuclear fission technologies. Developing fusion power requires first demonstrating its scientific and technical feasibility and then establishing it as a commercially attractive (i.e., economically competitive and publicly acceptable) power source. Significant domestic and

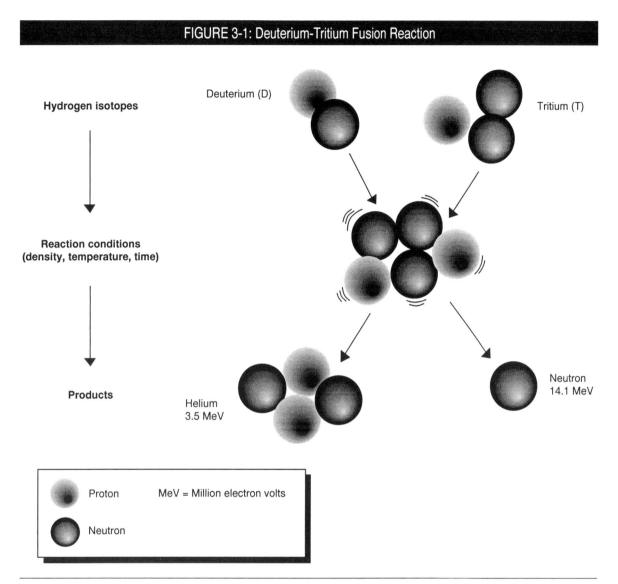

FIGURE 3-1: Deuterium-Tritium Fusion Reaction

Hydrogen isotopes

Deuterium (D)

Tritium (T)

Reaction conditions
(density, temperature, time)

Products

Helium
3.5 MeV

Neutron
14.1 MeV

Proton   MeV = Million electron volts

Neutron

SOURCE: Office of Technology Assessment 1995, based on figure from U.S. Department of Energy, Office of Fusion Energy.

international resources have been devoted to achieving this goal, and substantial scientific and technical achievements have been realized to date. Most experts, however, readily concede the world is still several decades and several tens of billions of dollars away from realizing commercially relevant fusion-generated electricity.

Notable progress has been made in addressing the scientific and technical challenges to fusion power development. Researchers at the Princeton Plasma Physics Laboratory attained a world record in fusion energy production of 10.7 mega-watts (MW) in experiments on the Tokamak Fusion Test Reactor (TFTR) in 1994. This marked an increase in fusion power production by a factor of about 100 million over that achievable 20 years ago. Fusion temperatures of 400 million degrees Centigrade have also been attained in experiments.

Among the scientific challenges remaining to be met in fusion research include achieving high-energy gain (energy output that is many times higher than energy input to create the reaction) and ignition (the point at which a reaction is self-sus-

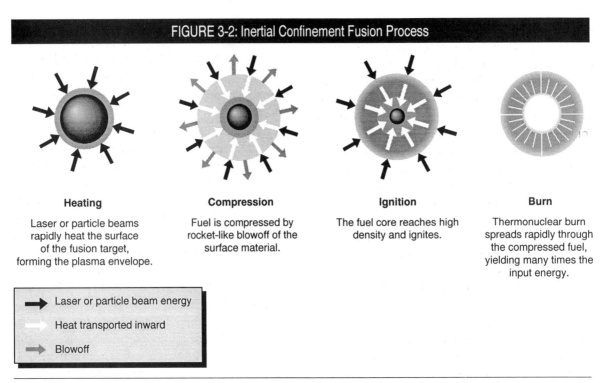

FIGURE 3-2: Inertial Confinement Fusion Process

Heating

Laser or particle beams rapidly heat the surface of the fusion target, forming the plasma envelope.

Compression

Fuel is compressed by rocket-like blowoff of the surface material.

Ignition

The fuel core reaches high density and ignites.

Burn

Thermonuclear burn spreads rapidly through the compressed fuel, yielding many times the input energy.

→ Laser or particle beam energy

→ Heat transported inward

→ Blowoff

SOURCE: Lawrence Livermore National Laboratory.

taining even when external heating is turned off). To develop a magnetic fusion powerplant, scientists must also be able to achieve high-energy gain in a steady state (continuous, rather than intermittent, operation). Reaching the critical milestone of breakeven (the point at which the energy produced by fusion reactions equals the energy input to heat the plasma) remains beyond the reach of current facilities. The TFTR experiments reached just over one-quarter of breakeven for a few moments. The proposed ITER is being designed to reach ignition and to operate for long pulses of several hundred to more than 1,000 seconds. If successful, ITER would accomplish several critical milestones in the development of a fusion power reactor. Substantial engineering challenges in developing materials, components, and systems for operating fusion reactors also remain and will have to be met through a broad-based program of scientific, technical, and industrial R&D.

Under plans established a few years ago, tens of billions of dollars and about three decades of continued successful R&D are expected to be required before the science and technology are sufficiently advanced to enable construction of a demonstration commercial fusion power reactor. This facility (dubbed DEMO) is scheduled to follow ITER in about 2025. An actual commercial prototype is anticipated to be operational around 2040 under this schedule.

DOE sponsors two fusion research programs: the Magnetic Fusion Energy (MFE) program of the Office of Fusion Energy under the Office of Energy Research, and the Inertial Confinement Fusion (ICF) program in the Office of Defense Programs. The Office of Fusion Energy has responsibility for research on the energy aspects of both magnetic and inertial confinement fusion. Work on ICF science and technology in defense programs advances eventual energy applications of inertial fusion energy. DOE-sponsored fusion research activities are carried out at national laboratories, universities, private companies, and international research centers.

■ Program Goals and Funding

Fusion research program goals have been established by legislation and by presidential and secretarial decisions.[30] The overarching goal of the program is to demonstrate that fusion energy is a technically and economically viable energy source, specifically by developing an operating demonstration fusion power reactor by about 2025 to be followed by an operating commercial prototype reactor by about 2040. Other goals include the development of fusion technologies, the education and training of fusion scientists and engineers, and the encouragement of industrial participation and international collaboration. Budget realities, however, have tempered the expectations for achieving this optimistic development schedule.[31] Civilian energy goals for the ICF energy program are directed at the development of components for fusion energy systems that can take advantage of the target physics developed by the Defense Programs ICF research. Underlying both the MFE and the ICF research programs is a desire to maintain the U.S. position in the forefront of fusion research internationally and to preserve U.S. capability to participate in any future fusion technology advances.

Legislative authority for fusion energy research is found in the Atomic Energy Commission Act of 1954 (AEC Act);[32] the Magnetic Fusion Energy Engineering Act of 1980 (MFEEA);[33] and the Energy Policy Act of 1992 (EPACT).[34] Further legislative direction has been provided in committee reports accompanying the annual appropriations acts.[35]

EPACT calls for: support of a broad-based fusion energy program; participation in ITER engineering design activities and related efforts; development of fusion power technologies; industrial participation in technology; the development, design and construction of a major new U.S. machine for fusion research and technology development;[36] ICF energy R&D; and the development of a heavy-ion ICF experiment. EPACT builds on the framework established by MFEEA for a broad-based fusion research and technology development program, including support of research on alternative confinement concepts and fuel cycles. The 1980 act marked a shift in the program from a focus on fundamental fusion science and plasma physics to technology development.

The AEC Act is another source for DOE support for fusion-related nuclear physics (including plasma physics) and engineering education and training missions. Fusion research activities advance the general purposes of the AEC Act to: "encourage maximum scientific and industrial

---

[30]For more on the goals and structure of the DOE fusion energy programs see Office of Technology Assessment, *The Fusion Energy Program*, see footnote 3.

[31]DOE's FY 1995 budget request candidly admits that "budgetary constraints over the past few years may mean that the schedule for meeting such objectives is delayed." U.S. Department of Energy, Office of the Chief Financial Officer, *FY 1995 Congressional Budget Request: Energy, Vol. 2, Supply Research and Development,* DOE/CR-0021 (Washington, DC: February 1994), p. 425.

[32]Act of Aug. 30, 1954, ch. 1073, 60 Stat. 921, as amended, 42 U.S.C. 2011 et seq.

[33]Public Law 96-386, Oct. 7, 1980, 94 Stat. 1539, 42 U.S.C. 9301.

[34]Public Law 102-486, Oct. 24, 1992, sec. 2114, 106 Stat. 3073-3074 (codified at 42 U.S.C. 13474).

[35]See, for example, Conference Report on H.R. 2445, H. Rept 103-292, 103d Cong., 1st sess., at 139 Cong. Rec. H7948, Oct. 14, 1993 (daily ed.). The conferees directed DOE to give highest priority to participation in ITER and supporting TFTR experiments.

[36]The language in EPACT referring to a major new machine has been interpreted by some as authorization for the proposed TPX, and as others as referring to ITER, still others maintain that federal expenditures for construction of either facility have yet to be authorized specifically. In any case, the appropriations bills have deferred spending on TPX construction pending review, while allowing procurement for long lead-time component technologies to continue.

progress"; aid education and training; promote widespread participation in the development of peaceful uses for atomic energy;[37] and encourage international cooperation.[38] The act authorizes a broad range of research on nuclear processes, atomic energy theory and production, and the use of nuclear energy or materials for the generation of usable energy and for commercial and industrial applications.

Over the past two decades, fusion energy programs have been the subject of extensive reviews.[39] Most of these reviews have complimented the steady technical and scientific progress that has been achieved. Over the past decade, however, reviewers have expressed concern about increased risk to the success of the program from what many have seen as a premature narrowing of magnetic fusion research to a single focus on the tokamak path and curtailment of research on alternative confinement concepts in response to budget constraints. Even so, the reviewers strongly endorsed pursuit of further critical advances in fusion science relying on the tokamak as the most developed (and successful) concept available. Reviewers have also raised concerns that existing budget levels will not be adequate to carry out even the narrowed program objectives on the scales and schedules proposed.

Funding for the fusion programs in FY 1995 is $362 million for magnetic fusion energy and $177 million for inertial fusion. About $157 million of the MFE funds are allocated for activities that directly or indirectly support the ITER collaboration. Funds supporting ITER are spent on U.S. research activities designated as advancing ITER-related R&D. Only about $600,000 is for direct support of joint ITER administrative activities. The FY 1996 budget request for magnetic fusion is $366 million and includes support of the ongoing ITER collaboration and initial construction funds for the proposed new Tokamak Physics Experiment (TPX) at the Princeton Plasma Physics Laboratory. The $257 million, FY 1996 budget request for ICF activities includes construction funds for the National Ignition Facility (NIF)—the next major facility required for advancement of inertial confinement fusion.[40]

■ International Collaboration in Fusion Research

International cooperation and collaboration in fusion research date from the late 1950s, when much fusion research was declassified for the Second Geneva Convention on the Peaceful Uses of Atomic Energy. Since then, cooperation among researchers in the United States, the Soviet Union, Europe, and Japan has grown from informal exchanges between research laboratories, to formal bilateral collaborative agreements between gov-

---

[37]Atomic energy is defined as all forms of energy released in the course of nuclear fission or nuclear transformation. 42 U.S.C. 2014. Transformation is interpreted to include fusion.

[38]42 U.S.C. 2013.

[39] See: U.S. Department of Energy, Fusion Policy Advisory Committee (FPAC), *Report of the Technical Panel on Magnetic Fusion of the Energy Research Advisory Board, Final Report,* DOE/S-0081 (Washington, DC: September 1990); Fusion Energy Advisory Committee, *Report on Program Strategy for U.S. Magnetic Fusion Energy Program,* DOE\ER-0572T (Washington, DC: U.S. Department of Energy, Office of Energy Research, September 1992); Fusion Energy Advisory Committee, *Advice and Recommendations to the U.S. Department of Energy in Response to the Charge Letter of September 18, 1992,* DOE/ER-0594T (Washington, DC: U.S. Department of Energy, Office of Energy Research, June 1993); Fusion Energy Advisory Committee, *Advice and Recommendations to the Department of Energy in Partial Response to the Charge Letter of September 24, 1991: Part D,* DOE\ER-0555T (Washington, DC: U.S. Department of Energy, Office of Energy Research, June 1992). For a more detailed summary of these reviews, see Office of Technology Assessment, *The Fusion Energy Program,* see footnote 3. For more on prior reviews, see U.S. Congress, Office of Technology Assessment, *Starpower: The U.S. and the International Quest for Fusion Power,* OTA-E-338 (Washington, DC: U.S. Government Printing Office, October 1987).

[40]NIF is primarily motivated by the desire to maintain technological expertise in areas of nuclear weapons design as a component of the DOE's *Stockpile Stewardship* program. NIF's contribution to the development of fusion energy and other scientific applications are adjunct functions of the project.

ernments, to the ongoing collaboration on the ITER design.

The ITER Collaboration

The United States, the European Atomic Energy Community (Euratom), Japan, and the Russian Federation are engaged in an unprecedented collaboration on the engineering design of the proposed International Thermonuclear Experimental Reactor. This collaboration has its roots in discussions among the leaders of the European Community, Japan, the Soviet Union, and the United States in the mid-1980s. The impetus for the start of the ITER collaboration came from the discussions between President Ronald Reagan and Soviet General Secretary Mikhail Gorbachev at the 1985 Geneva Summit.

ITER's purpose is: 1) to establish the scientific and technological feasibility of magnetic fusion energy as a source of electric power by demonstrating controlled ignition and extended burn of deuterium-tritium (D-T) plasmas; and 2) to demonstrate and test technologies, materials, and nuclear components essential to development of fusion energy for practical purposes. It would not be equipped, however, to actually generate electricity. Demonstrating the production of electricity in a magnetic fusion energy powerplant would be left to the DEMO reactor, a device anticipated for construction no sooner than 2025.

If built, ITER would be by far the largest, most capable, and costliest fusion experiment in the world. ITER uses a tokamak design; it would be more than eight stories tall and 30 meters in diameter. The device is intended to sustain controlled fusion reactions in a pulsed mode for periods of at least 15 minutes. ITER is expected to be capable of producing more than 1,000 MW of thermal fusion power. Plasma temperatures inside the confinement chamber would be more than 150 million degrees Centigrade. Due to the radioactivity that will be generated, maintenance and monitoring of the reactor vessel will have to be carried out by remote methods. The impressive scale of ITER is dictated by the physical requirements of heating and containing a plasma to fusion conditions on a steady-state basis using available technology and materials.

ITER offers not only great scientific challenges, but practical technological challenges as well. For example, ITER's superconducting magnetic coils will be the largest ever manufactured. Each coil will weigh more than 400 tons. The amount of superconducting materials required to make them exceeds the currently available manufacturing capabilities of any one party; therefore, a cooperative effort is under way to coordinate the materials manufacture, fabrication, and assembly.

ITER is being conducted in four phases under formal intergovernmental agreements among the parties: 1) the now-completed conceptual design activities (CDA); 2) the ongoing engineering design activities (EDA); 3) the possible, future construction phase; and 4) the operations phase. Each phase is governed by a separate agreement among the parties. To date the costs of ITER activities have been shared equally among the four parties.

The CDA phase ran from January 1988 to December 1990 under the auspices of the International Atomic Energy Agency (IAEA).[41] All four parties contributed personnel and support to the ITER team for development of a conceptual design, scope, and mission for the project.

The EDA phase is being conducted under an intergovernmental agreement concluded in July 1992 and extending to July 1998.[42] Each of the parties has committed the equivalent of $300 million (1993 dollars) worth of personnel and equipment to the design effort over that period. The

---

[41]The CDA was conducted under a set of Terms of Reference developed by the ITER Parties, but formally transmitted by the IAEA Director General to the Parties for their individual acceptance. The ITER CDA agreement was in actuality a set of four acceptances of the same letter from the IAEA Director General.

[42]The ITER EDA agreement was executed on behalf of the U.S. government by Secretary of Energy Admiral James Watkins.

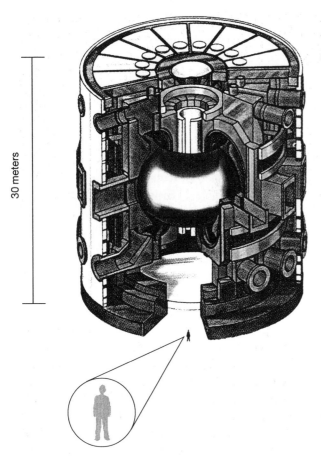

The Proposed International
Thermonuclear Experimental Reactor
SOURCE: U.S. Department of Energy.

30 meters

*Inside the vacuum vessel of the TFTR at the
Princeton Plasma Physics Laboratory.
Graphite and graphite composite tiles
protect the inner wall of the vessel.*

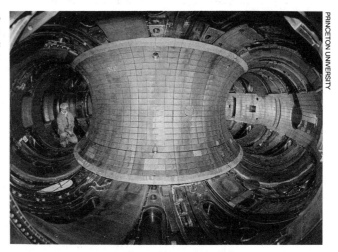

PRINCETON UNIVERSITY

The ITER Engineeering Design Activities agreement was formally signed by the United States, Euratom, Japan, and the Russian Federation in July 1992.

purpose of the EDA phase is to produce a "detailed, complete, and fully integrated engineering design of ITER and all technical data necessary for future decisions on the construction of ITER." On completion, the design and technical data will be available for each of the parties to use either as part of an international collaborative program or in its own domestic program. Other objectives of the EDA phase are to conduct validating R&D supporting the engineering design of ITER, to establish siting requirements, to perform environmental and safety analyses related to the site, and to establish a program for ITER operation and decommissioning.

EDA activities are overseen by an ITER Council composed of two representatives of each party and the ITER Director who is responsible for coordinating the activities of the Joint Central Team (JCT) and other R&D in support of ITER. The JCT is an international design team composed of scientists, engineers, and other professionals assigned to the project by the parties. The formal seat of the Council is in Moscow. JCT activities are carried out by the parties and the four home teams at three joint work sites—Garching, Germany; Naka, Japan; and San Diego, California. Each work site is responsible for a different aspect of ITER design. In consultation with the ITER Council, the JCT, and each party's designated *Home-Team* Leader, the ITER Director assigns and coordinates R&D activities by the four *home country* fusion programs that support the JCT.

The next major step in ITER development will be the negotiation of a process for deciding on a host site. Exploratory discussions on a site selection process are currently under way. Site selection will have to be completed before specific site-related safety, environmental, and economic analyses and design work for the ITER facility can be finalized. A decision on a site and whether to proceed to ITER construction and operations phases is scheduled to be made before 1998. These subsequent phases would require a new international agreement. None of the parties is committed to proceed beyond the EDA phase.

The ITER construction phase is tentatively planned to start in 1998 and to be completed by 2005. Initial estimates of ITER construction costs were about $6.9 billion in 1993 dollars. More recently, some analysts have projected ITER costs of between $8 billion and $10 billion. Detailed cost estimates for this one-of-a kind research facility await completion of ITER engineering design work. Interim design and cost analyses are expected in mid-1995. Final design and cost estimates are due in January 1998, if site selection has been completed.

The fourth or operating phase of ITER is proposed to begin in 2005 and run through approximately 2025. The early years would be dominated by a focus on the physics issues relating to achieving and sustaining an ignited plasma. A more intense engineering phase will follow. As an engineering test facility, ITER will be designed to allow researchers to install, test, and remove numerous ITER components, experimental packages, and test modules to examine materials properties, component characteristics, performance, and lifetimes in an environment approximating the conditions of an operating fusion powerplant. This experience will aid efforts in the design and development of a demonstration fusion powerplant.

Other Fusion Collaborations

Although they are not on the scale of the ongoing ITER collaboration, other precedents exist for cooperation in fusion research under various bilateral and international agreements. Among the most recent examples are the Large Coil Task (LCT) test facility at Oak Ridge National Laboratory, and collaboration on the DIII-D tokamak at General Atomics with the Japanese Atomic Energy Research Institute.[43] Positive experiences on the LCT experiments contributed to the confidence of the parties in entering into the ITER collaboration. Contributions from the Japanese in exchange for access to and operating time on the DIII-D helped pay for upgrades to the device. Efforts are ongoing to negotiate an agreement for collaboration among the ITER parties on a conceptual design for a 14-MeV (million electron volt) neutron materials test facility.

The 14 MeV neutron source would be an accelerator-based materials testing facility that would be used to expose fusion reactor materials to intense bombardment by high-energy 14 MeV neutron beams to approximate over a few short years the effects of a lifetime of exposure in an operating fusion reactor. The availability of a 14 MeV materials testing facility is considered by all world fusion programs to be essential to the development of low-activation alloys and other materials for use in fusion powerplants.

There is experience with international collaboration in the operation of a major fusion facility. The joint European fusion research program is carried out under the Euratom Treaty. The European fusion community consists of the magnetic fusion programs of member states of the Euratom Treaty plus Sweden and Switzerland. Research projects and funding levels are established under successive, but overlapping five-year research programs developed by the European Commission (EC) in consultation with fusion researchers and government ministers of member countries. The research programs are approved by the Council of the European Union (EU). Member-nation fusion programs carry out the research and receive contributions of up to 80 percent for projects included in the EC research program.

The Joint European Torus (JET), a large tokamak facility near Culham, England, is jointly funded and staffed by the Euratom fusion program and 14 European countries. JET was established as an independent collaborative undertaking that is separate from, but cooperates with, member-state fusion programs. The goal of JET is to confirm fusion's scientific theories and to demonstrate the scientific feasibility of nuclear fusion for power generation. JET is currently the world's largest tokamak; it hosts about 370 staff scientists and an equal number of contractors. In 1991, JET was the first tokamak to produce significant quantities of fusion power using a D-T fuel mix, reaching a record plasma current of 7.1 million amperes. JET researchers have been able to achieve, individually, all the required conditions (i.e., plasma temperature, density, and confinement time), for a fusion power reactor, but the JET is too small to achieve them all simultaneously. In 1996, JET is scheduled to begin a final phase of experiments involving fusion power production with D-T plasmas, using a recently installed pumped divertor. These experiments are intended to support ITER design activities.

Negotiations to establish JET were begun in 1973 and concluded in 1978. Several years of negotiation were necessary to concur on an appropriate site following completion of the design in

---

[43]These collaborations are discussed in Office of Technology Assessment, *Starpower*, see footnote 39.

1975. JET is operated under statutes adopted by the European Community (now the European Union) and governed by the JET Council, which includes representatives of the member countries. The EC fusion program provides 80 percent of JET funding; the 14 participating countries provide 20 percent, with the United Kingdom paying a 10-percent host premium on its share.

■ Implications for Future Collaborations

Early successes in international cooperation in fusion led to today's unprecedented ITER collaboration in which four equal parties are working together in an effort to design and construct the world's largest tokamak to achieve the critical goal of an ignited plasma. The earlier efforts created relationships among fusion researchers internationally and laid the groundwork for a more formal partnership in ITER. Budgetary strains facing science research also contributed to the desire for international collaborative efforts to continue progress in fusion and plasma science. The ITER team has been progressing in its design efforts supported by R&D and technology development activities in the parties' home-team fusion programs. The level of cooperation and success in ITER to date has led analysts to suggest that this collaboration could prove to be a model for future international efforts.

The ITER project and other international collaborative efforts in fusion, such as the proposed 14-MeV neutron source materials testing facility, still face a number of scientific, technical, political, and budgetary hurdles. Many difficult issues concerning funding, technology transfer, siting, intellectual property rights, project management,

and allocation of benefits and costs remain to be negotiated before ITER can proceed to the next and considerably more expensive construction phase. The United States and its ITER partners are currently engaged in preliminary discussions concerning the form that such future negotiations will take.[44]

The U.S. fusion program faces substantial budgetary challenges and has come under increasing scrutiny as Congress is confronted by tough choices about the future of fusion energy research and other megascience activities. Carrying out the present development plan for a tokamak fusion reactor, currently the most technically advanced magnetic fusion concept, implies a doubling, or even tripling of the annual magnetic fusion budget ($373 million in FY 1995). This amount assumes that the United States will continue to pay an equal one-quarter share of the cost of ITER, with the other three parties international partners picking up the other shares (see figure 3-3). However, no agreements on ITER construction have yet been negotiated, including how much each of the participating parties will pay.[45]

The most immediate decision is whether to fund construction of the TPX, an approximately $700 million superconducting, steady-state advanced tokamak intended to replace the existing TFTR when the reactor is decommissioned after the current round of experiments. If the TPX is not built, the United States will soon be left without a new domestic leading-edge magnetic fusion device. In the view of many in the fusion research community, U.S. researchers and industry will also be deprived of vital experience that could

---

[44] On November 21, 1994, Secretary of Energy Hazel O' Leary transmitted the "Interim Report to the Congress on Planning for International Thermonuclear Experimental Reactor Siting and Construction Decisions," to several congressional committees in partial response to requests for a detailed ITER siting and development plan in the FY 1993 and FY 1994 Energy and Water Development Appropriations conference reports. The Secretary advised the committees that a more complete response could not be provided until the ITER Interim Design Report is completed and accepted by the parties.

[45] Some at DOE and in the fusion research community are exploring what role, if any, the U.S. fusion program could play in a future ITER collaboration if U.S. fusion program budgets remain flat as projected, or are reduced. Some have suggested that the United States might attempt to negotiate a role as a junior partner in ITER to preserve access to the facility and the technology for the U.S. fusion program. But it is not at all clear whether the other parties would react favorably to this approach.

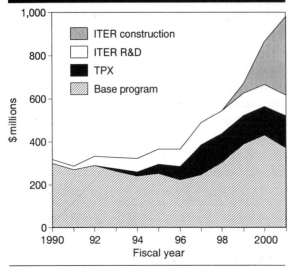

FIGURE 3-3: Estimated Funding Levels Required for the U.S. Magnetic Fusion Energy Program for TPX, ITER, and 2025 DEMO in FY 1990-2001
($ in millions as spent)

NOTE: This figure is based on internal Office of Fusion Energy planning estimates and the funding levels shown are not reflected in FY 1995 budget request documentation. The increase in base program funding in FY 1997-2001 reflects increased activity in support of TPX and ITER and for a proposed fusion materials test facility.

SOURCE: Office of Technology Assessment 1995, based on information from the U.S. Department of Energy.

position them to compete for ITER contracts and take advantage of ITER technology.

If Congress or the executive branch decides not to increase fusion budgets to the extent that would be needed to pursue expensive new devices at this time, or even to reduce fusion budgets, a dramatic rethinking of the structure and priorities of the U.S. fusion effort will be required.[46] At a minimum, a flat or reduced budget will mean that continuing to support ITER collaboration at currently projected levels will cut even more deeply into the

U.S. base program and constrain any efforts to expand investigation of alternative concepts.

A decision to reduce U.S. commitment to the ITER collaboration would pose difficult problems not only for us, but also for our partners. The United States has committed to provide resources to support its one-quarter share of the ITER EDA through 1998 in an international agreement signed on behalf of the Government by Energy Secretary James Watkins.[47] Changes to the EDA agreement require consent of all parties. The United States and any other party can freely elect not to participate in the next and more expensive ITER construction phase. Pulling back from the existing EDA commitment would certainly prove disruptive to the successful completion of ITER since the collaborative efforts of the parties are highly integrated and interdependent. The decision would have profound consequences not only for fusion research, but also for the future of U.S. involvement in international collaborative efforts on large science facilities. U.S. withdrawal from ITER would trigger an extensive reexamination of the U.S. fusion program, in which ITER participation has had a central role, backed by EPACT and directives from congressional appropriators. U.S. withdrawal from ITER would also require our partners to reexamine and possibly restructure their fusion research programs because ITER R&D activities now occupy a dominant role in those programs. It is by no means clear that the governments of the remaining parties would be willing to fund ITER design completion and construction on the scale and schedule currently envisioned.

The United States is not alone in pondering whether it is ready to take the next ambitious and highly expensive step in the development of fu-

---

[46]Office of Technology Assessment, *The Fusion Energy Research Program,* see footnote 3; and Robin K. Roy, Project Director, Office of Technology Assessment, testimony at hearings before the Subcommittee on Energy and Environment, House Committee on Science, Feb. 15, 1995.

[47]As is typical in such agreements, the ITER EDA Agreement and Protocol provides that the parties agree "subject to their laws and regulations" to carry out the collaboration. The agreement may be amended or terminated only by written agreement of the parties. International Atomic Energy Agency, "International Thermonuclear Experimental Reactor (ITER) Engineering Design Activities (EDA) Agreement and Protocol 2," ITER EDA Documentation Series No. 5, 1994.

sion as an energy source for the future. In 1990, a review panel for the EC fusion program also expressed some reservations about the pace of progress and, in calling for a reevaluation of the EC fusion program in 1995, noted:

> The Board wishes to advise the European fusion community that, while prospects and results may by then be so encouraging as to justify pressing ahead, either independently or in the ambit of a convincing international agreement, one possible outcome of such an evaluation would be to redirect the whole European Programme should the 1995 Report not favour immediately proceeding with construction of the Next Step device. Without prejudice to a possible increase in the fusion effort should conditions warrant, the Board wishes to make it clear that, in its view, the present scale of fusion spending cannot be considered an automatically assured expenditure floor unless there is clear evidence of progress toward the Programme's ultimate goal.[48]

The European review panel commented favorably on the benefits to be derived in reducing the technical and financial risks of proceeding with a next-step fusion machine by relying on an international collaboration. It also raised a suggestion that the ITER program be expanded into an extended and articulated international fusion program that would share all the main functions of fusion reactor development including the development of a neutron source for materials testing, and a major investigation of alternative fusion concepts.[49]

Japanese fusion research programs have been funded at levels comparable to U.S. and European fusion efforts and, like them, have devoted a significant share of current budgets to support of the ITER collaboration. The future of the Japanese fusion program also hinges on decisions to be made about construction of ITER. The Japanese government is deferring any decision on funding for a new large tokamak, the JT-60 Super Upgrade, proposed by the Japanese fusion research community as a successor to the Japanese JT-60U. According to OTA interviews, continued funding of the fusion program at current levels beyond the end of the existing research plan is by no means secure.

The significant integration of the major world fusion programs resulting from collaboration on ITER and other projects has created a situation in which, at present, no party supports a fully independent broadly based national fusion research program. The United States and its partners have heavily invested the future of their research programs on progress in ITER. Decisions on whether to proceed with ITER construction will mark a critical point both in the development of fusion power and in the success of international collaborations in big science. Proceeding with ITER as currently envisioned will demand an increase in the fusion budgets of all the partners and a long-term commitment to construction and operation of the facility in addition to maintaining the supporting infrastructure of domestic fusion programs. Should the United States (or any of the other partners) elect to delay or reduce its contribution, or withdraw entirely from the ITER collaboration, it would force a reevaluation and restructuring of all the partner's national fusion programs and would put the future of ITER in question. It would also heighten concerns about the risks of international collaboration and the reliability of commitments.

The U.S. fusion research program is currently facing a critical decision point on whether or not to build the TPX to explore advanced tokamak regimes in steady-state conditions as a replacement for the TFTR which is being shut down this year. TPX is intended as a national fusion research facility to be managed and used by scientists from laboratories and universities across the country. Without TFTR or a replacement such as TPX, the U.S. fusion program will not have any domestic

---

[48]Fusion Program Evaluation Board, "Report Prepared for the Commission of the European Community," July 1990, p. 56.
[49]Ibid.

large tokamaks to advance fusion research and will become even more focused on ITER.

Our ITER partners will face similar choices in a few years when their major national machines are scheduled for closure. Plans for new ambitious national fusion research devices in Europe and Japan have been deferred in favor of ITER. However, all parties eventually will have to define the appropriate roles and levels of support for domestic fusion programs in an era of expanded international collaboration.

Failure to pursue construction of ITER, or even a considerable delay in startup of construction and operations could prove disruptive to the partners' own fusion programs and could trigger a redefinition of fusion goals and priorities. One possible outcome could be that the partners might elect to build on past successful collaborations on the LCT, and ITER CDA and EDA to forge a new collaborative path on future fusion research facilities, perhaps at a less ambitious scale, schedule, and cost than originally envisioned for ITER.

SCIENTIFIC ACTIVITIES IN SPACE [50]

International collaboration has long been a vital part of U.S. scientific activities in space. The National Aeronautics and Space Administration (NASA) oversees most U.S. civilian international space activities. The National Oceanic and Atmospheric Administration, in coordination with NASA and non-U.S. partners, supports a smaller number of space-based Earth observation projects. Since its inception in 1958, NASA has concluded nearly 2,000 cooperative agreements. Virtually all of its science projects involve at least a minor international component, and collaboration has played a major role in several of NASA's largest science-related projects.[51]

NASA engages primarily in bilateral collaborations. Its most extensive collaborative relationships have been with Canada, the European Space Agency (ESA),[52] and Japan. In addition, NASA conducts major bilateral cooperative projects with individual European countries such as France, Germany, Italy, and Russia.

NASA is currently involved in 11 science-related programs that have a U.S. development cost of more than $400 million. Of these, six projects have costs more than $1 billion: the International Space Station, the Earth Observing System (EOS), the Advanced X-Ray Astrophysics Facility (AXAF), the Cassini mission to Saturn, the Hubble Space Telescope, and the Galileo mission to Jupiter. All of these projects involve significant international collaboration. Table 3-4 lists these projects, U.S. partners and their roles, the project status, and NASA's current estimates of development costs. Because of the complexity of accounting for all shuttle- and personnel-related expenses, these figures may not fully reflect each project's ultimate cost.[53]

---

[50] This discussion encompasses science and technology development activities that support NASA's Space Science program (astronomy, astrophysics, lunar and planetary exploration, solar physics, and space radiation), as well as other activities in geosciences, life sciences, and microgravity research.

[51] The National Aeronautics and Space Act of 1958 identified international collaboration as a fundamental goal. NASA's first international cooperative science project was the 1962 Alouette mission with Canada, a basic science project to investigate the ionosphere. For a list of more than 60 international cooperative ventures in space science between 1962 and 1985, many involving U.S. participation, see U.S. Congress, Office of Technology Assessment, *International Cooperation and Competition in Civilian Space Activities*, OTA-ISC-239 (Washington, DC: U.S. Government Printing Office, July 1985), pp. 379-380.

[52] ESA is a 14-member European space research organization. Its members are Austria, Belgium, Denmark, Finland, France, Germany, Ireland, Italy, the Netherlands, Norway, Spain, Sweden, Switzerland, and the United Kingdom.

[53] These figures also do not account for operations costs. Mission operations and data analysis (MO&DA) costs vary considerably and, when included in the analysis, can raise the costs for some projects significantly. For example, MO&DA costs for the Compton Gamma Ray Observatory (CGRO) through FY 1995 are $112 million, 20 percent of development costs. MO&DA costs for the Galileo program are $331 million, 37 percent of development. And MO&DA expenditures for the Hubble Space Telescope—$1.7 billion—have already reached 110 percent of the program's development costs.

TABLE 3-4: Current Large International U.S. Projects in Space (more than $400 million)			
Project	**Partners and project roles**	**Status**	**U.S. cost[a] (spent to FY 1995)**
Space station	U.S.: Project leadership, overall design, construction, launch, operations Russia: Pressurized modules, fuel resupply, "lifeboats," launch, operational expertise Japan and ESA: Pressurized modules, launch, servicing equipment Canada: Robotics	Design currently under way. Assembly planned 1997-2002, followed by 10 years of operations	$38 billion ($14.4 billion)
Earth Observing System (EOS and EOSDIS)	U.S.: Spacecraft, instruments, launch, operations Canada, Japan, France, ESA, Eumetsat: Instruments, IEOS[b] spacecraft	EOS-AM1 launch planned for 1998 EOS-PM1 launch planned for 2000 Other launches planned for 2000 and beyond	Total program: $8 billion ($2.6 billion)
Advanced X-Ray Astrophysics Facility (AXAF)	U.S.: Spacecraft, instruments, launch, operations Germany, Netherlands, UK: Instruments	AXAF-I launch planned for 1998	$2.1 billion ($1.1 billion)
Cassini	U.S.: Spacecraft, instruments, launch, operations ESA: Titan probe (Huygens) Italy: Antenna	Launch planned for 1997	$1.9 billion ($1.3 billion)
Global Geospace Science (GGS)	U.S.: Spacecraft, instruments, operations, launch Russia, France: Instruments, science support	Wind launched in 1994 In operation Polar launch planned for 1995	$583 million
Collaborative Solar Terrestrial Research Program (COSTR)	U.S.: Instruments, operations, launch ESA: Spacecraft, instruments, launch Japan: Spacecraft, instruments, operations	Geotail launched in 1992 In operation SOHO launch planned for 1995 Cluster launch planned for 1995	$511 million
Ocean Topography Experiment (TOPEX)	U.S.: Spacecraft, instruments, operations France: Launch, instruments	Launched in 1992 In operation	$407 million
Compton Gamma Ray Observatory (CGRO)	U.S.: Spacecraft, instruments, launch, operations Germany: Instruments	Launched in 1991 In operation	$957 million
Ulysses	U.S.: Power unit, launch, tracking ESA: Spacecraft, instruments, operations	Launched in 1990 Mid-mission in solar orbit	$569 million
Hubble Space Telescope (HST)	U.S.: Spacecraft, instruments, launch, operations ESA: Instrument, solar arrays, operations	Launched in 1990 In operation	$2.3 billion
Galileo	U.S.: Spacecraft, probe, instruments, launch, operations Germany: Retro-propulsion module, instruments, tracking	Launched in 1989, arrival at Jupiter planned for 1995	$1.3 billion

[a]Capital costs include development, launch, orbital assembly, and construction of facilities. National Aeronautics and Space Administration (NASA) civil service, non-program facility, and administrative support expenses are *not* included. For Space Station (27 missions), CGRO, Ulysses, Hubble (two missions) and Galileo, NASA reports average shuttle launch costs of $400 million to $500 million. Figures represent dollars as spent or projected, unadjusted for inflation.

[b]The International Earth Observing System (IEOS) includes: NASA—EOS; NASA/Japan—Tropical Rainfall Measuring Mission (TRMM); NOAA—Polar-Orbiting Operational Environmental Satellite (POES); Japan: Advanced Earth Observing Satellite (ADEOS); European Space Agency (ESA) & Eumetsat—Polar-Orbit Earth Observation Mission (POEM).

SOURCE: National Aeronautics and Space Administration—Julie Baker, Resources Analysis Division, personal communication, May 1, 1995; Office of Legislative Affairs; and Space Station Program Office.

■ Nature of International Collaboration in Space

The character of international collaboration in space differs significantly from the nature of U.S. involvement in cooperative activities in other areas of science. Large collaborative ventures in other disciplines often rely on international scientific teams working interdependently at single facilities. These international teams work on both technology development and scientific investigations. In these collaborations, the level of information transfer about technical design and fundamental science is high. For example, several hundred researchers and accelerator experts are working closely at CERN to develop technical specifications for the LHC accelerator and particle detectors to ensure that the ultimate physics objectives of the project can be met.

Cooperative scientific projects in space have been more compartmentalized, with partners working more independently of one another in highly segmented projects. NASA often competitively selects the design of instruments proposed by internationally constituted scientific teams responding to competitive notices of opportunity. But space technology development—especially for the critical infrastructure elements that constitute a large portion of the cost of space projects (launchers, satellites and platforms, and so forth) —is typically conducted without any exchange of detailed design or manufacturing information.

Compartmentalization was originally a high priority because of the need to ensure the success of collaborative projects with partners whose technical capabilities fell below those of the United States and to prevent the transfer of potential dual-use civilian-military technologies. The heightened attention to preventing technology

---

BOX 3–3: Selected NASA Guidelines for International Cooperation[1]

- Preference for project-specific agreements.
- Preference for agency-to-agency cooperation.
- Technical and scientific objectives that contribute to NASA program objectives.
- Distinct ("clean") technical and managerial interfaces.
- No or minimal exchange of funds between cooperating partners.
- No or minimal technology transfer.
- Open sharing of scientific results.

---

[1] These guidelines were developed during the 1960s and last revised in December 1991 in NASA Management Instruction (NMI) 1362.1C. For a discussion of the guidelines, see Space Policy Institute and Association of Space Explorers, "International Cooperation in Space—New Opportunities, New Approaches," *Space Policy*, vol. 8, August 1992, p. 199.

---

transfer has also been a reflection, in part, of both the much higher commercial potential of space technologies versus those in areas such as high-energy and nuclear physics, and the historical importance of maintaining U.S. leadership in space-related activities. Maintaining this leadership position is a fundamental consideration in guiding U.S. participation in international cooperative efforts.[54]

NASA long ago codified its approach to international collaboration in a set of guidelines. Among other provisions, these guidelines call for minimizing the transfer of technologies; the creation of "clean technical and managerial interfaces"; and collaboration on a project-by-project basis, rather than making the United States party to multiproject umbrella agreements (see box 3-3).

---

[54] The National Space Policy defines leadership as preeminence in areas critical to achieving national security, scientific, economic, and foreign policy objectives. But U.S. government agency efforts to pursue international projects are also guided by other broad goals, defined by the National Space Policy, which are to: 1) strengthen national security; 2) achieve scientific, technical, and economic benefits; 3) encourage private sector investment in space; 4) promote international collaboration; 5) maintain freedom of space for all activities; and 6) expand human activities beyond Earth. National Security Council, "National Space Policy," National Space Policy Directive 1, Nov. 2, 1989. This policy was formulated by the Bush Administration. The Clinton Administration, through the Office of Science and Technology Policy (OSTP), is currently undertaking a review and update of the policy.

An additional issue, NASA's dependence on other countries for technologies on a mission's critical path, has featured prominently in recent congressional debate on U.S. space policy.[55] Although NASA has no official policy on the issue of critical paths, dependence on other countries for critical-path items has been controversial because it raises questions about U.S. independence and control in collaborative space projects.

■ History of Space Collaboration

Despite NASA's longstanding and highly explicit guidelines for collaboration, its policies and approach to collaboration have changed over time. The agency's compartmentalized approach to collaboration was initially designed in the 1960s to foster space cooperation while preserving and enhancing U.S. leadership and independence in space-related science and technologies. World leadership was a primary, longstanding, and well-articulated U.S. space goal in the 1960s and 1970s. During this period, NASA was able to achieve this goal because its budget and technical capabilities far exceeded those of other Western industrialized nations. With Western partner countries eager to learn from the United States, NASA pursued collaboration largely on its own terms, creating what might be called a period of U.S. preeminence in international space cooperation. According to Vice President Quayle's Space Policy Advisory Board:

> [T]he United States . . . approached international cooperation from a position of strength, at its own initiative, largely on its own terms, and usually as a discretionary, "value-added" activity that complemented core U.S. elements of a particular mission or capability. The size of the U.S. space program and the preeminence of U.S. space capabilities made such an approach pos-

The European Spacelab module being loaded onto the space shuttle Columbia.

sible. International partners were willing to accept American dominance in cooperative undertakings as the price of associating themselves with the recognized leader in space.[56]

By the late 1970s and early 1980s, however, the situation had changed in important ways. Partly as a result of extensive cooperation with the United States, some partner nations had developed significant and sophisticated autonomous capabilities. Partner nations expressed increasing desires to participate more substantively in critical decisions about the development and operation of collaborative projects, and objected to playing junior partner to the United States. ESA, founded in 1975 to give Europe an autonomous space launch

---

[55] The term *critical path* refers to an element essential to a project's operation and success, in contrast to technologies and services that are strictly value-added in nature. For an example of discussion of the subject, see the 1994 floor debate on space station funding. *Congressional Record*, June 29, 1994, pp. H5394-5395.

[56] Vice President's Space Policy Advisory Board, *A Post Cold War Assessment of U.S. Space Policy: A Task Group Report* (Washington, DC: Office of the Vice President, December 1992), p. 9.

capability and to raise Europe's technical standard in space, has been particularly active in expressing this desire.[57]

Europeans cite their experience with the Spacelab project as a turning point in relations with NASA. In this program, Europe's first large-scale venture into human space activities, ESA developed a laboratory for use aboard the space shuttle. From NASA's point of view, the Spacelab program was successful. It provided a value-enhancing addition to the space shuttle at low cost to the United States[58] and gave the shuttle program an international dimension that increased its political prestige at home. Europe's gains from the project included valuable experience in building human-rated space equipment and access to the benefits of the shuttle program. However, ESA, which was hoping to recoup at least part of its investment (and large cost overruns) in the project through serial production of several laboratories, was disappointed that NASA bought only the two modules stipulated in the agreement. Moreover, many Europeans felt the project was a poor bargain. They asserted that Europe had built merely an accessory for the U.S. space shuttle with little practical return for European space-related science or industry. European scientists and engineers further complained that NASA treated Europe condescendingly, not as a partner.[59]

Questions about the stability of U.S. funding and periodic project redesigns also created challenges to collaboration by raising questions about U.S. reliability among potential partners. Foreign partners most frequently cite the 1981 cancellation of U.S. plans to build a spacecraft for the International Solar Polar Mission (ISPM), a joint project with ESA (see box 1-3). In 1979, NASA and ESA started a program to send two spacecraft out of the Earth's orbital plane to study the poles of the Sun. In 1981, NASA canceled plans to build the U.S. ISPM spacecraft, basing its decision on the need to close a $500 million budget shortfall in the fiscal 1982 budget. Europeans expressed surprise and dismay at the NASA decision but were unable to reverse the cancellation.

Although NASA kept its commitment to launch and track the European probe (renamed Ulysses), and provide its nuclear power source, Europeans have long cited the ISPM cancellation to illustrate their claims about the unreliability of U.S. commitments.[60] However, the real impact of the ISPM experience is less certain. Other countries may cite the ISPM example as part of a strategy to obtain more favorable terms in negotiations for joint space projects with the United States. Nevertheless, ISPM was an important milestone in the U.S.-European collaborative relationship.

As a result of these developments, in the 1980s, U.S. collaborative space policy entered an extended period of transition from the earlier era of U.S. preeminence to one in which the goal of leadership was less sustainable and more ambiguous. The ambiguity of the period was reflected in U.S. space policy documents, which moved from broad and unequivocal statements in the late 1970s and early 1980s about the need to maintain U.S. space leadership, to more opaque statements in the late 1980s and early 1990s that called for the United States to maintain leadership in certain

---

[57] ESA was formed by the merger of the European Space Research Organization and the European Launcher Development Organization, both of which were founded in 1964.

[58] An earlier OTA report noted that "Spacelab cost (ESA) in excess of $1 billion. . . . For budgetary reasons, the alternative to an ESA Spacelab was not a less capable U.S. Spacelab, but rather no Spacelab at all." Office of Technology Assessment, *International Cooperation and Competition in Civilian Space Activities*, see footnote 51, p. 409.

[59] For a description and analysis of the Spacelab experience, see Joan Johnson-Freese, *Changing Patterns of International Cooperation in Space* (Malabar, FL: Orbit Book Co.), 1990, pp. 25-30.

[60] In virtually every interview conducted with U.S. space science partners in research for the present report, questions about U.S. stability were highlighted prominently by reference to the ISPM experience.

loosely defined critical areas (usually involving space transportation and human space flight).[61]

A final development in the late 1980s and early 1990s—constrictions in the space budgets of the United States and its foreign partners—spurred further changes in the U.S. and multilateral approaches to collaboration. The result of all these developments has been a significant change in NASA space policy: a greater willingness in several projects to accept foreign contributions as critical-path elements;[62] a more active program of flying U.S. instruments on foreign spacecraft; and a NASA strategic plan that speaks of keeping the United States at the forefront of space-related science and technology, rather than maintaining world leadership.[63] Although NASA policy still leaves much ambiguity about the role of U.S. space leadership, the agency's practices over the past few years have demonstrated greater flexibility in dealing with the issue. The continuing challenges to collaboration and the U.S. experience in the largest current international collaborative projects are discussed below.

▌ Challenges to Collaboration

Although collaboration has worked well in several automated, small- and medium-scale science projects, NASA has encountered significantly more difficulty in structuring and executing collaborations in a few large programs, especially those involving human spaceflight. Instability in project financing and technical design (at NASA and, more recently, among U.S. partners) has also rendered collaboration more difficult.

The scale of large space projects—in terms of budgets and public profile—has made it difficult for NASA to structure stable, effective, and—when necessary—interdependent collaborations. This has been especially true in human space flight because of its enormous expense and its importance for U.S. leadership and prestige in space activities.

In large, high-profile projects (often involving human space flight), the pressures on the United States to maintain control over international collaborations have been greater than in smaller, automated missions. These pressures have come from NASA, as well as from outside, and were especially intense through the end of the Cold War. For example, in 1990, the Advisory Committee on

---

[61]The debate about space goals within and outside NASA was vigorous, but filled with ambiguity. Sally Ride's 1987 report, *Leadership and America's Future In Space*, strongly advocated the pursuit of space leadership. And President Reagan's February 1988 National Space Policy directive confirmed "leadership in space" as the basic goal of U.S. policy. But a new Bush Administration national space policy directive in November 1989 noted that although leadership would continue to be a fundamental objective, "Leadership in an increasingly competitive international environment does not require United States preeminence in all areas and disciplines of space enterprise. It does require United States preeminence in the key areas of space activity critical to achieving our national security, scientific, technical, economic, and foreign policy goals." Nevertheless, in 1992, Vice President Quayle's Space Advisory Board focused on the importance of international collaboration as a way "to influence the direction of future space undertakings around the world." The Clinton Administration has not yet issued a new space policy, but the first goal of the new 1994 U.S. science policy is to "maintain leadership." See National Security Council,"National Space Policy," see footnote 54; and Vice President's Space Policy Advisory Board, *A Post Cold War Assessment of U.S. Space Policy: A Task Group Report* (Washington, DC: Office of the Vice President, December 1992), p. 42; Clinton and Gore, see footnote 1, p. 7.

[62] Kenneth Pedersen notes that the U.S. preference for retaining control over critical path items will change because the increasing size and complexity of projects will produce "numerous critical paths whose upkeep costs alone will defeat U.S. efforts to control and supply them all." Moreover, Pederson argues, "It seems unrealistic today to believe that other nations possessing advanced technical capabilities and harbouring their own economic competitiveness objectives will be amenable to funding and developing only ancillary systems." Kenneth S. Pedersen, "Thoughts on International Space Cooperation and Interests in the Post-Cold War World," *Space Policy*, August 1992, p. 217.

[63] It must be noted that the United States is still the acknowledged leader in many areas. In a worldwide scientific consensus unique to space research, European and Japanese space officials acknowledge overall U.S. leadership. With a yearly space budget of $14 billion, the United States spends more than Europe and Japan combined on civilian space activities. Only the Soviet Union has pursued a space program of comparable scale and technical breadth. Since the disintegration of the U.S.S.R., Russia has continued the space program, but under severe financial constraints.

the Future of the U.S. Space Program (the Augustine Committee) recommended that international collaboration be used to demonstrate U.S. space leadership, but cautioned that the United States should retain operational control over critical-path elements in areas such as human space exploration.[64]

Pressures to maintain control have been especially strong in NASA's largest international human space project—the space station. The problems of international collaboration in the space station illustrate both the challenges of international cooperation in large projects and how the evolution of U.S. cooperative policy has affected ongoing projects. Although the space station program contained collaborative elements from the beginning, until very recently all critical aspects of the project remained firmly under U.S. control.[65] Consistent with the earlier U.S. approach to collaboration, the original station partners were not invited to assist in its basic design or construction; rather, they were invited to contribute supplementary elements. This approach to international collaboration had the advantage of adding elements to the station at no extra cost to the United States (see box 3-4.)

However, this approach to collaboration caused resentment among U.S. partners. According to one space policy analyst, the Europeans and Japanese saw the U.S. position as "arrogant and, particularly in Europe, insufficiently sensitive to a partner's ability to contribute significantly to the station program." It was further noted that the foreign partners were further dismayed by official NASA statements that the space station was critical to U.S. leadership and that international collaboration would "engage resources that otherwise might be used in support of programs competitive to the United States." This philosophy of collaboration conflicted with fundamental European and Japanese desires to achieve areas of autonomy in their space programs and more equal technical cooperation with the United States.[66] This made it more difficult to forge commitments among partners and to reach detailed agreements on management and utilization issues.[67] A 1989 NASA internal design review excluded the space station's foreign partners and caused further tension in the cooperative relationship. Since 1990, NASA has made a greater effort to include partners in station redesign activities. Despite these efforts, OTA has concluded that "the space station experience appears to have convinced the partners that they should not enter into such an asymmetrical arrangement [with the United States] again."[68]

However, with the addition of Russia as a station partner in 1993, the U.S. position on collaboration changed fundamentally. Under the new International Space Station program, the United States will rely on Russia for several critical elements, including: guidance, navigation, and con-

---

[64] Advisory Committee on the Future of the U.S. Space Program, *Report of the Advisory Committee on the Future of the U.S. Space Program* (Washington, DC: U.S Government Printing Office, December 1990), p. 8.

[65] Although the Canadian Mobile Servicing System has been on the station's critical path from the beginning, the U.S. agreement with Canada provides for all Canadian hardware, plans, and materials to be turned over to NASA in the event Canada were to withdraw from the program. As in the agreement for the shuttle's Canadarm, this gives the agency *ultimate* control over the contribution and its underlying technology, in case of default.

[66] John M. Logsdon, "Together in Orbit: The Origins of International Participation in Space Station Freedom," December 1991, pp. 139-140.

[67] The desire (or need) to maintain U.S. control may also have reduced the potential financial savings offered by collaboration by excluding opportunities to take advantage of partners' expertise in critical areas of station design, construction, and operation. For example, NASA might have capitalized on Europe's experience in building Spacelab and satisfied the European desire to use this expertise by assigning construction of all (or most) pressurized station laboratories to ESA. Instead, the United States, ESA, and Japan will each build separate pressurized facilities.

[68] U.S. Congress, Office of Technology Assessment, *U.S.-Russian Cooperation in Space*, OTA-ISS-618 (Washington, DC: U.S. Government Printing Office, April 1995), p. 65.

BOX 3-4: The Space Station

The space station is a U.S.-led international effort to build and operate a permanently occupied Earth-orbiting research facility. The station is designed to play several roles: an orbital scientific laboratory for microgravity, Earth observation, and other experiments; a facility to study and develop skills for long-term human duration in space; and a model of international cooperation.

The program began officially in January 1984, when President Reagan announced the U.S. intention to build a space station and invited international participation in the endeavor. In 1988, after almost four years of discussions and negotiations, the European Space Agency (ESA), Canada, and Japan signed cooperative agreements to participate with the United States in building and operating the station. The original plan called for a station, named *Freedom*, to be built by the early 1990s. However, several program redesigns and funding reductions delayed station construction. In 1993, the United States invited Russia to participate in the station.[1] The new International Space Station project, based on the downsized *Alpha* design, is divided into three phases and calls for 34 construction-related space flights.

- Phase 1, 1994 to 1997—Joint Space Shuttle-Mir program.
- Phase 2, 1997 to 1998—Building of station "core" using: U.S. node, lab module, central truss and control moment gyros, and interface to Shuttle; Russian propulsion, initial power system, interface to Russian vehicles, and assured crew-return vehicle; Canadian remote manipulator arm.
- Phase 3, 1998 to 2002—Station completion. Addition of U.S. modules, power system, and attitude control; and Russian, Japanese, and ESA research modules and equipment.

Russian cooperation on the station is of a different nature than European and Japanese participation. Whereas Europe and Japan are making value-added contributions of pressurized research modules, the Russians are providing several critical space station components. These include the FGB module (for guidance, navigation, and control), reboost and refueling, a service module, a power mast, and a *Soyuz*/ACRV (emergency return vehicle).

Like Russia, Canada is also on the station's critical path. Based on its experience developing the Canadarm for the space shuttle, Canada is supplying robotic systems for station assembly and maintenance. However, unlike the U.S. agreement with Russia, the agreement with Canada would provide NASA with all Canadian hardware, plans, and materials should Canada withdraw from the program.

The United States is responsible for the vast majority of the station budget. It spent about $10 billion on pre-*Alpha* station work and will have spent an additional $28 billion on design, construction, launch, and assembly to complete the station. In a unique cooperative feature, the United States anticipates spending nearly $650 million in direct payments to Russia to pay for procurement of Russian equipment for the station. The Japanese anticipate spending $3 billion on the JEM (Japanese Experimental Module). ESA is considering a $3-billion station-related program. And Canada is spending about $1 billion.

---

[1] A new intergovernmental agreement and revised Memoranda of Understanding are now being negotiated, bringing Russia into the program.

SOURCES: National Aeronautics and Space Administration; and Office of Technology Assessment, 1995.

---

trol in Phase 2; habitation until the U.S. habitation module is launched; crew-return ("lifeboat") modules through 2002; and reboost and fuel resupply. The Russian collaboration policy has evoked high levels of controversy in the United States and among the space station's foreign partners. Domestic objections to dependence on Russian technology are based on concerns about Russia's political and economic stability, questions about its technical reliability, the potential for loss of U.S. jobs, and traditional pressures to maintain U.S. control over critical mission elements.[69] Foreign partners expressed resentment over not having been consulted about Russia's sudden entry into the program.[70]

These concerns have been much less prominent in smaller and robotically operated science collaborations with Western Europe, Japan, and Russia. In these projects, NASA has for a longer time been receptive to new, more interdependent forms of collaboration. The agency has formed collaborations with European and Japanese space agencies, relying in some cases on partners for critical mission components. NASA has relied on ESA for critical solar power panels for the Hubble Space Telescope and on Germany for retro-propulsion systems and other critical components of the Galileo program. Although EOS has gone through several reorganizations and downsizings, it is extensively collaborative on both a mission and a programmatic level (see box 3-5). Out of the limelight of human space flight and without the huge price tag of the space station, these science projects have enjoyed greater flexibility and have not been burdened with carrying the full weight of U.S. leadership and prestige.

Another factor contributing to successful collaboration in science projects is financial and technical stability. This has affected both large- and medium-scale projects. Over the past decade, budgets for several NASA science projects were cut significantly while these projects were under development. Cuts have occurred both because of

The NASA Hubble Space Telescope solar panels were built by the European Space Agency. Here the Canadian-built robot arm on the space shuttle Endeavor is being used to inspect the telescope.

budget constraints and because funding requirements rose considerably above initial estimates.[71] For example, funding concerns prompted the restructuring of the space station in 1987, 1989, and 1991. The projected cost (originally $8 billion) rose considerably before it was downsized again in 1993. The program is now projected to cost $38 billion. As noted above, funding for EOS was also reduced several times within a few years, from $17 billion to $8 billion.[72] After large mid-program cost increases, AXAF and the CRAF/

---

[69] NASA reports that it is "prudently developing contingency plans to allow the program to go forward in the event an international partner is unable to fulfill its obligations. Congressional representatives have endorsed the need for such planning in the case of Russia." Beth A. Masters, Director of International Relations, National Aeronautics and Space Administration, letter to OTA, Apr. 26, 1995.

[70] The issue of Russian reliability, NASA contingency plans, the reactions of foreign partners to Russia's inclusion in the program, and the general risks and benefits of U.S.-Russian space cooperation are discussed in Office of Technology Assessment, *U.S.-Russian Cooperation in Space*, see footnote 68.

[71] For descriptions of funding cuts in large science projects, see William C. Boesman, *Big Science and Technology Projects: Analysis of 30 Selected U.S. Government Projects* (Washington, DC: Congressional Research Service), Dec. 7, 1994.

[72] This figure accounts for EOS costs only through the year 2000.

BOX 3-5: The Earth Observing System

The Earth Observing System (EOS) is a multisatellite program to provide long-term, continuous data on global climate change. The program began in 1989, with National Aeronautics and Space Administration (NASA) plans to build three copies of two 15-ton polar-orbiting platforms. However, congressional concerns about cost and the risks of concentrating resources on two large spacecraft led NASA in 1991 to reduce the original program from $17 billion to $11 billion and to spread EOS instruments among several smaller orbiters. Since 1991, further funding cuts have reduced the program's budget to $8 billion (exclusive of EOS science costs) through the end of the century. The House Committee on Science has asked the National Academy of Sciences to review the EOS program with an eye to reducing its costs even further.

EOS is a highly collaborative project, involving instruments and spacecraft from the United States, Europe, Canada, and Japan. In exchange, these countries will fly several U.S. instruments on their own missions. EOS was originally coupled to the space station agreement in 1989. The two programs were later separated, and EOS is now NASA's contribution to the International Earth Observing System (IEOS), a joint project of the United States, Europe, Canada, and Japan. In addition to EOS, the IEOS includes a joint U.S.-Japanese project, the Tropical Rainfall Measuring Mission; data from the National Oceanic and Atmospheric Administration's Polar-Orbiting Operational Environmental Satellite program; Japan's Advanced Earth Observing System program; and the Polar-Orbiting Earth Observation Mission, a joint project of the Euopean Space Agency and Eumetsat.

NASA plans to launch the first two EOS satellites (EOS AM-1 and PM-1) in 1998 and 2000. NASA has spent about $2 billion to date on the program. Although EOS has a budget of $8 billion, this will finance the program only through the year 2000. NASA has designated $2.2 billion of the current EOS budget for EOSDIS, the system to manage and distribute the enormous amounts of data generated by the project.

SOURCE: Office of Technology Assessment, 1995.

Cassini program each eliminated a proposed spacecraft.[73]

In addition to these periodic downsizings for large projects, the congressional budget review has generated annual uncertainties about the stability of funding for virtually all space projects. Uncertainty about continued or stable yearly funding has been particularly acute for the space station. The program survived by only one vote in the House of Representatives in 1993. Uncertain-

ty continues to affect other projects under analysis here, such as the Cassini mission to Saturn.

Periodic downsizings and the uncertainties of the annual appropriations process make collaboration difficult by generating questions among foreign partners about the reliability and stability of U.S. commitments. As noted earlier, cancellation of the U.S. ISPM spacecraft reverberates to this day. Yet, questions about funding stability can

---

[73] NASA originally planned the AXAF x-ray telescope as one large telescope. However, in 1992, the agency eliminated some instruments and divided the project into two telescopes—AXAF-I (x-ray imaging) and AXAF-S (x-ray spectroscopy)—to reduce costs. In 1994, further budget pressures resulted in cancellation of funding for AXAF-S. At that time, Congress instructed NASA to undertake discussions with Japan about the possibility of flying the AXAF-S spectrometer on a Japanese craft. These discussions are still under way. Cassini is a joint U.S.-ESA mission to investigate Saturn and its moon Titan. When it was initiated in 1990, the project called for two spacecraft: Cassini to fly to Saturn and a Comet Rendezvous Asteroid Flyby (CRAF) mission to rendezvous with and investigate a comet and asteroid. However, by 1992, estimated project capital costs had risen from $1.6 billion to $1.9 billion. Simultaneously, Congress reduced funding for the project. Under these constraints, CRAF was canceled the next year, leaving Cassini as the sole U.S. component of the project.

affect even projects that are successfully concluded.

In the past, analysts contrasted uncertainty about the funding of U.S. projects with the more stable budgets of its foreign partners, particularly ESA and the Japanese space agency (NASDA). During the 1970s and 1980s, funds for projects at ESA and NASDA—once approved—were less subject to the annual uncertainties of U.S budgets. However, over the past five years, ESA has experienced severe budget reductions (in its nonmandatory programs) that have necessitated the cancellation of its Hermes space plane program and Man-Tended Free Flyer (MTFF), reductions in Earth observation budgets, and substantial uncertainty about the agency's long-term plans. Like U.S. programs, ESA projects now face more rigorous and uncertain yearly budget reviews, with more frequent delays and downsizings than before. Of central concern to the United States, continued disagreements within ESA about the agency's proposed program to build a pressurized module, a Crew Rescue Vehicle (CRV), and an Autonomous Transfer Vehicle for cargo raise questions about ESA's commitment to the space station.[74] Recently, ESA dropped the CRV from its proposed contribution. France may seek to develop the CRV in a collaborative project with Russia.[75]

Canada's commitment to build the robotic Mobile Servicing System (MSS) for the station has also come into question. In early 1994, Canada decided to terminate its critical path contribution to the station, but was dissuaded from doing so by President Clinton. Instead, Canada reformulated its contribution, with the U.S. assuming financial responsibility for portions of the MSS. Canada also delayed for two years a decision on whether to build an auxiliary contribution to the MSS, the

Special Purpose Dexterous Manipulator.[76] Thus, the reliability of its partners has now become a concern for the United States.

Finally, financial stability—in both U.S. and foreign projects—also depends on the clarity of science goals and changes in project specifications that affect collaborative relationships. In this area, there is a stark contrast between human space flight and robotic space projects. In smaller and robotic projects, scientific goals have often been much clearer and less subject to dispute than in ventures involving human space flight. For example, consensus among partners about the scientific goals of planetary missions has been much stronger than about the space station. Whereas planetary and astronomical projects tend to focus clearly on scientific questions, the enormous cost of building facilities for human space programs such as the space station renders them infrastructure projects designed to satisfy a variety of goals—scientific, technical, economic, and political. These multiple goals complicate the execution of larger space projects, whether domestic or international in character.

All of these factors—NASA's history of midproject downsizing, the annual congressional budget cycle, the ISPM experience, and questions about scientific goals—make it more difficult for the United States to engage in large-scale cooperative ventures. Collaboration has been easier in smaller projects where funding has been more stable and the financial risks are lower. This greater financial stability makes it easier to build the relationships of mutual trust among partners that are crucial to effective collaboration.

■ Results of NASA Collaborations

NASA's collaborative efforts have produced significant successes for the U.S. space program and

[74] According to a NASA official, "There is a growing program downside to not knowing whether we can count on Europe in this program." See "ESA Accord Postponed," *Aviation Week and Space Technology*, Ap. 3, 1995, vol. 142, No.14, p. 29; and Craig Covault, "Station Partners Reassess ESA's Role," *Aviation Week and Space Technology*, Mar. 27, 1995, vol. 142, No. 13, pp. 27-28.

[75] See Declan Butler, "France May Break Ranks Over Space Station," *Nature*, vol. 374, Apr. 27, 1995, p. 756.

[76] For a discussion of this issue, see Marcia Smith, *Space Stations* (Washington, DC: Congressional Research Service, Apr. 6, 1995), p. 11.

served U.S. interests and goals well. NASA indicates that it has saved money and increased the scientific yield of many U.S. projects by adding instruments and expertise from partner countries without sacrificing operational control or space leadership. Spacelab and the Canadian arm for the space shuttle are good examples of this type of cooperation.[77] Collaboration in space activities has also strengthened relations with U.S. allies and served other foreign policy interests.

Yet, in part due to changes in U.S. and foreign space policy, the reduction in available resources, and monumental events in world politics, the results of space-science collaboration over the past decade, although mostly positive, have been uneven. Recent U.S. experience in collaboration on large science projects in space has been paradoxical: although NASA initially designed projects that for the most part preserved U.S. independence, leadership, and operational control, its two largest projects—the space station and EOS—have evolved into highly interdependent collaborations.

Although the current rescoped EOS program might be seen as a model of interdependence in collaboration, this was not NASA's original vision. Rather than planning an extensively integrated international project from the beginning, NASA significantly expanded the program's dependence on foreign instruments when funding restraints dictated a dramatic downsizing of the U.S. contribution to the program. The downsizing of the EOS budget was the prime motive for expanding the program's international aspect.

EOS began as a project to build three copies of two U.S. polar-orbiting platforms with contributions of instruments from Europe and Japan. Foreign instruments were intended in some cases to complement proposed U.S. instruments. For example, data from the Japanese Advanced Spaceborne Thermal Emission and Reflection Radiometer (ASTER) were originally intended to complement NASA's proposed High-Resolution Imaging Spectrometer (HIRIS). In one case, ESA's Multifrequency Imaging Microwave Radiometer, NASA chose to rely exclusively on a foreign instrument for critical measurements.

However, the original EOS plan was criticized for its cost, the long period of time before the system could provide policy-relevant data, and its dependence on two large platforms to carry all the program's instruments. As a result, it was reviewed, rescoped, and downsized several times (see table 1-2).

NASA accomplished the downsizing of EOS with little loss of capability. However, in doing so, NASA has now come to depend much more extensively on several foreign instruments as critical U.S. mission elements[78] or on foreign spacecraft for flying critical U.S. instruments.[79] NASA acknowledges that reduced funding has increased U.S. dependence on foreign instruments and flights:

At $8 billion, EOS must depend increasingly on the international partners. Failure to accomplish planned international cooperation on [Japan's] Advanced Earth Observing System (ADEOS), [ESA's] Polar-Orbit Earth Observa-

---

[77] An earlier OTA report noted that "[C]anadian expenditures (over $100 million) for the Shuttle's highly successful remote manipulator arm freed the United States from this Shuttle expense." Office of Technology Assessment, *International Cooperation and Competition in Civilian Space Activities*, see footnote 51, p. 409.

[78] The cancellation of HIRIS, for example, left NASA much more dependent on Japan's ASTER. NASA also eliminated the planned EOS synthetic aperture radar (SAR) and will now rely instead on data from European, Japanese, and Canadian SARs.

[79] NASA originally planned to fly 30 instruments on two U.S. platforms with no involvement of foreign spacecraft. In the rescoped program, NASA will fly 24 U.S. instruments on 21 U.S. and 10 non-U.S. platforms. NASA has retained all six foreign instruments originally slated for the program. National Aeronautics and Space Administration, Office of International Relations, fax communication, Jan. 27, 1995.

tion Mission (POEM), [U.S.-Japanese] Tropical Rainfall Measuring Mission (TRMM), and their follow-on missions will leave gaping holes in IEOS [International Earth Observing System].[80]

For the space station—designed as the U.S. flagship for human activities in space—NASA also designed a U.S.-controlled project with international enhancement. Although the United States sought supplementary international contributions from the inception of the station program, NASA insisted that the United States would build the station, with or without foreign participation.[81] Originally, this vision of collaboration was consistent with the goals and technical capabilities of potential partners. Although negotiations with European partners proved difficult, the United States was able to maintain operational control and to use international contributions as supplementary enhancements for two reasons: 1) no partner country or organization had the resources to mount an independent station program, and 2) U.S. partners had different priorities for human space flight.

For example, ESA initially planned to use the space station as an adjunct to its plans for achieving an autonomous human space flight capability in low Earth orbit. Its original plan therefore called for free-flying elements (such as Hermes and the MTFF) that could dock with the station or operate independently of it. This fit well with NASA's desire for "enhancing" contributions. From the beginning of their involvement with the program, the Japanese have seen the JEM (Japanese Experimental Module) as a chance to develop technologies for human space flight. Canada's contribution (robotics for station assembly and maintenance) builds on expertise developed for the shuttle program.

However, throughout the late 1980s and early 1990s—under increasingly intense funding pressures—NASA's station plans changed several times and were the subject of considerable uncertainty. Financial constraints reached a pinnacle in 1993. Simultaneously, the United States had undertaken discussions with Russia about technical cooperation. Technical cooperation with Russia was seen as an important tool for supporting U.S. foreign policy goals, which included Russian adherence to the Missile Technology Control Regime and the general goal of supporting the transition to a market-oriented democracy in Russia. This conjunction of financial, domestic political, and foreign policy imperatives resulted in a U.S.-Russian agreement to cooperate in a broad range of station design, construction, and supply activities.

Russia's inclusion in the space station program parallels the internationalization of the EOS program. Both projects originally envisioned cooperation of a mostly value-added nature, but evolved into deeply collaborative enterprises. In the case of the station, Russia's inclusion as a critical-path partner was motivated originally by both financial[82] and foreign policy considerations. The process was similar, however: contrary to its original intentions, well into each project, NASA "backed into" highly interdependent foreign collaborations.

The EOS and space station experiences demonstrate the complexity and difficulty of planning long-term collaborations on a large scale. In both cases, the original U.S. goals for international col-

---

[80]National Aeronautics and Space Administration, *EOS Reference Handbook* (Washington, DC: 1993), p. 12.

[81]"[T]he U.S. position was that the United States would develop a fully capable space station on its own, but that potential partners were welcome to suggest enhancements to that core station which would increase its capability." Logsdon, "Together in Orbit," see footnote 66, p. 137.

[82] The General Accounting Office has since reported that Russian participation will provide no significant cost savings to the United States. See U.S. General Accounting Office, *Space Station: Update on the Expanded Russian Role*, GAO/NSIAD-94-248 (Washington, DC: U.S. Government Printing Office, July 1994).

laboration changed, as a result in large measure of financial pressures and project downsizings. Given the benefit of hindsight, NASA might have saved time and money, increased program technical sophistication, and avoided tensions with partners if it had planned more integrated collaborations from the beginning. This may very well have been possible in the EOS program. Rather than undertaking a very large $17 billion U.S. project, NASA might have planned a more coordinated, international effort with a much smaller U.S. contribution.[83]

However, it is doubtful that the United States could have pursued a similar course in planning the space station. In the early 1980s, the goals and financial and technical capabilities of partner space agencies in Europe and Japan would have made a mutually interdependent collaboration less likely. Also, collaboration with the then Soviet Union was completely out of the question. Although downsizing did play a large role in forcing NASA to alter the character of its space station collaboration, the political changes that made cooperation with Russia possible were sudden and unexpected.

■ Future of Space Collaboration

There is a consensus—inside and outside NASA —that reduced budgets will necessitate expanded international collaboration on future large science projects in space. With the end of the Cold War, and the lessening of competitive pressures vis-a-vis the former Soviet space program, there will also be new opportunities to collaborate on a broad range of space-related science activities. NASA's two largest current projects—EOS and the space station—already demonstrate levels of interdependence with both Western partners and Russia that would have been impossible a decade

ago. NASA's future plans for astronomy and planetary exploration also include significant international components. The agency is already discussing joint work with Russia and/or ESA for missions to the Moon and Mars, as well as projects to study the opposite ends of the solar system: the Sun and Pluto.

If collaboration is to be effective in these future cooperative activities, the United States must first decide on its goals for space. If leadership continues to be a paramount goal of U.S. space activities, this will complicate future, more integrated collaborative efforts because:

- No space agency, including NASA, has the financial resources to maintain the type of world leadership that the United States established in the past.
- The goal of maintaining U.S. leadership through collaboration creates fundamental tensions with partners who have developed sophisticated autonomous capabilities and are pursuing independence in some areas of space-related science. These partners are unlikely to accept future collaborations on past U.S. terms.
- The experience of the space station and EOS demonstrates that maintaining U.S. control over critical mission components has proved an elusive and perhaps unattainable goal in very large projects.
- The goal of U.S. leadership in space can be ambiguous and in some cases contradictory.

Moreover, as one space policy analyst notes, the end of the Cold War may devalue the traditional goal of leadership. In this scenario, "[T]he future scope, pace and vitality of the USA's approach to space cooperation would depend on other, less political interests—principally, economic, technological and scientific in nature."[84]

---

[83] A smaller EOS with greater international collaboration planned from the beginning may also have become a different program than the present EOS. Participants in an OTA workshop on EOS noted that had the project "initially been designed as an $8 billion program, it likely would be different than today's EOS." See U.S. Congress, Office of Technology Assessment, *Global Change Research and NASA's Earth Observing System*, OTA-BP-ISC-122 (Washington, DC: U.S. Government Printing Office, November 1993), p. 31.

[84] Pedersen, "Thoughts on International Space Cooperation," see footnote 62, p. 212.

Aerial overview of the Advanced Photon Source facility under construction.

Instability and uncertainty in funding for U.S. space projects may also continue to complicate space collaboration efforts. Although the United States has thus far avoided direct harm from the ISPM cancellation, project downsizings, and the annual uncertainties of the budget process, continued lack of confidence among U.S. partners could impede future collaborative opportunities—especially those in which the United States would take a leading role. Likewise, new instabilities and uncertainties in funding for foreign space agencies pose challenges for U.S. collaboration with its traditional partners.

Nevertheless, the United States still dominates many areas of space research and has space resources matched by no other single country. This will continue to give the United States wider lati-

tude in choosing projects and collaborative opportunities.

NEUTRON SOURCES AND SYNCHROTRONS

Over the past several decades, the use of neutron and synchrotron beams has led to fundamental advances in understanding the properties of matter. These tools have opened new areas of research and application in materials science, structural biology, polymer chemistry, and solid-state physics. Neutron sources and synchrotrons are large science facilities that essentially serve as platforms for small science. They could be regarded as infrastructure investments for several fields of science and technology. Thus, having access to state-of-the-art neutron-scattering and x-ray synchrotron[85] facilities could have long-term competitive implications. For this reason, many industrial nations have supported their own independent facilities. Although the cost and complexity of neutron and synchrotron installations have escalated with advances in the underlying science, international cooperation has been limited primarily to information sharing and joint experimental work by researchers, rather than the joint development of large international facilities.

Neutron scattering and x-ray scattering are complementary techniques that have been used to elucidate much of what we understand about the structure of many important materials. X-rays interact strongly with matter and thus can provide significant information about the surface and bulk properties of a given material. Due to their electrical neutrality, neutrons can penetrate deeply into compounds to provide information about the structural and nuclear properties of materials. Neutrons can pinpoint the location of light atoms such as hydrogen and carbon, which are difficult to locate with x-rays. The identification of such light atoms is particularly important in completing the structural blueprint of organic and biological substances. When used at low energies, neutrons can be employed to study the dynamic or vibrational characteristics of matter. The use of both neutron and x-ray beams has allowed researchers to develop extraordinary precision in understanding the basic behavior of both natural and synthetic substances.[86]

■ Neutron Sources
History
The use of neutron structural probes has provided the technical foundation for the successful development of many different types of polymers (plastics), novel alloys, ceramics, liquid crystals, pharmaceuticals, catalysts, and magnetic materials. For example, the introduction of magnetic recording heads in electronic equipment directly benefited from the understanding provided by neutron-scattering studies. The widespread introduction and use of plastic materials has also been greatly facilitated by the use of neutron scattering. Properties such as flexibility, hardness, and wear resistance are determined principally by the way in which long polymer chain molecules are packed together. Developing plastics that have a greater range of properties and improved performance depends directly on the structural analysis that neutron probing provides. In addition, neutron physics has provided the means to analyze residual stress and to identify defects in metals, ceramics, and advanced composites.[87] It has allowed us to better understand the structure of viruses, as well as to profile surface impurities and irregularities in semiconductors—materials that serve as the basis of virtually all electronic and computational products. Because neutron probing provides information on how atoms vibrate, greater understanding of the dynamic behavior of materials has also been achieved. For these and other reasons, neutron scattering will continue to be an

---

[85]Charged particles orbiting at a fixed rate through a magnetic field emit a form of electromagnetic radiation known as synchrotron radiation. Synchrotron sources are circular accelerators that can be tuned to emit radiation with a broad range of frequencies including soft and hard x-rays.

[86]See OECD Megascience Forum, *Synchrotron Radiation Sources and Neutron Beams* (Paris, France: Organization for Economic Cooperation and Development, summer 1994).

[87]Neutron radiography is used for quality control of aerospace and energy production components and to test weld seams on pipelines, ships, and offshore drilling platforms.

important technique for understanding both man-made and biological substances.[88]

Neutron beams can be produced in two different ways: from reactors in which neutrons are by-products of nuclear fission, or from spallation sources in which neutrons are generated by accelerating high-energy protons into heavy-metal targets. To some degree, reactors and spallation sources have overlapping capabilities, but each has different attributes. Reactors produce high integrated fluxes of neutrons across a broad spectrum of energies, but particularly at low energy,[89] whereas spallation sources can more readily provide pulsed high-energy neutrons. Reactors, however, can also be used to produce a variety of isotopes for medical applications[90] and for materials radiation studies.

Implications for the Future

The fact that the highest neutron flux reactors in the United States (at Oak Ridge and Brookhaven National Laboratories) are both 30 years old,[91] and that Europe and Japan have invested heavily in neutron facilities in recent years, have raised concerns that U.S. capabilities in neutron science may be lagging behind other nations. Because the most important breakthroughs in neutron research have depended on the availability of high neutron fluxes and nuclear reactors are more technologi-cally mature than spallation sources, a 1993 DOE scientific panel recommended that a new reactor, the Advanced Neutron Source (ANS), be constructed to meet the growing needs of U.S. researchers and industry.[92]

The ANS design provides for neutron fluxes at least five times higher than those of the newly upgraded Institute Laue-Langevin (ILL) neutron facility in Europe. This ANS capability would be particularly important for studying small samples (e.g., biological crystals or material fragments) or where short exposure times are necessary. However, the proposed 1996 federal budget calls for discontinuation of the ANS project, principally because of its high cost (approximately $2.9 billion).[93] A secondary factor in the Clinton Administration decision to terminate the ANS program was that the use of enriched uranium in the ANS reactor came into conflict with U.S. nuclear nonproliferation policy. Although engineers had redesigned the reactor to use lower levels of enriched uranium, even these levels were not sufficiently low to completely resolve the underlying policy problem.

In recognition of the potential contributions that an advanced neutron-scattering capability could provide to a broad range of scientific disciplines, technological applications, and industries, DOE has proposed to undertake a conceptual de-

---

[88]In the past two decades four Nobel prizes have been awarded for work relating to neutron scattering. In addition, a host of other prestigious awards in condensed matter physics and chemistry have been given to researchers that have used neutron probes as an essential part of their work.

[89]Neutrons are often slowed down to produce low energy or so called "cold" neutrons. Cold neutron research is a rapidly developing area of inquiry that could lead to major commercial applications for new classes of polymers. The importance of cold neutrons is due to interatomic and intermolecular structure and dynamics. See U.S. Department of Energy, Office of Energy Research, "Neutron Sources for America's Future," Report of the Basic Energy Sciences Advisory Committee Panel on Neutron Sources, January 1993.

[90]While some types of radioisotopes can be produced by proton accelerators, the radioisotopes used for many essential medical and technological applications are primarily produced by reactors. For example, the element californium is increasingly used in cancer therapy. Ibid.

[91]The High Flux Beam Reactor run by Brookhaven National Laboratory and the High Flux Isotope Reactor at Oak Ridge National Laboratory were built in 1965 and 1966 respectively, and are nearing the end of their useful lives. A smaller, lower power reactor was built by the National Institute of Standards in 1969, and is expected to have a somewhat longer lifetime than the two DOE reactors.

[92]U.S. Department of Energy, see footnote 89.

[93]The ANS was deleted from the 1996 budget request after a decade of planning costing about $100 million. See *Budget of the United States Government, Fiscal Year 1996* (Washington, DC: U.S. Government Printing Office, 1995), appendix, p. 435.

sign study of a 1-MW pulsed spallation source as a replacement for the ANS.[94] Although such a spallation source would offer some technical advantages over the ANS (e.g., a higher *peak* neutron flux, which allows more complex physical phenomena to be investigated), it would be inferior in other respects (e.g., a lower *time-averaged* flux, which is key for small-sample analysis and reduced cold-neutron capabilities).[95] The proposed spallation source would not produce transuranic waste or hazardous fission products.[96] However, without the ANS, DOE might find it necessary to build a dedicated reactor to meet the growing radioisotope needs of the U.S. medical community and other industries. Although some preliminary estimates have placed the cost of a 1-MW spallation source at around $500 million, the technical uncertainties[97] associated with this technology led the 1993 DOE scientific panel on neutron sources to conclude that the cost "will increase considerably with more refined estimates."[98] Some observers believe that the costs will be in the $1-billion range.[99] A 1-MW spallation facility would surpass the neutron intensity of the world's most powerful existing spallation source (the ISIS source in the United Kingdom) by roughly a factor of six.[100]

If Congress concurs with the Clinton Administration decision to terminate the ANS program and if existing facilities are not upgraded,[101] U.S. researchers could well be compelled to rely on access to foreign facilities while a spallation source is being constructed. The ANS was not conceived as an international project. Since other countries have made substantial investments in developing their own neutron-source capabilities, it is not clear whether the ANS project could have become a multinational collaborative endeavor. Although U.S. scientists and industry would have been the primary beneficiaries of ANS, there most likely would have been many users from overseas.

Assuming the ANS is not built, the United States could still maintain critical capabilities in the field of neutron scattering by exploring the possibility of joining the European ILL facility, for example. The United States could also establish its own beam line and contribute to the development of new instrumentation at ILL.[102] This would be analogous to the proposed U.S. contribution to the Large Hadron Collider project at CERN. It could be done at a fraction of the cost of the ANS but would not substitute for the capabilities that the ANS would have provided. In addi-

---

[94]Some in the neutron scattering community have called for the construction of a 5-MW spallation source, but this would be a much more challenging and expensive undertaking.

[95]It is estimated that the time averaged flux of a 1-MW spallation source would be roughly 100 times lower than that of the ANS. For cold neutron research in the areas of polymers, complex fluids, biomolecules, and magnetic materials, "the ANS would be decidedly superior compared to a 1-MW spallation source." To match the ANS flux, a 5-MW spallation source would be required, and would involve considerable technical uncertainty. U.S. Department of Energy, see footnote 89.

[96]The proposed spallation source would use a tungsten target that would produce low-level radioactive byproducts. However, if uranium is used as the target material, there would be more serious radioactive byproducts.

[97]The central technical challenge of spallation sources is cooling the target. Existing spallation sources are quite limited in the amount of heat that they can dissipate, and this problem is compounded as the power is increased.

[98]U.S. Department of Energy, see footnote 89.

[99]Colin West, Oak Ridge National Laboratory, personal communication, February 1995.

[100]See footnote 89.

[101]The Brookhaven neutron reactor, for example, could be upgraded for approximately $200 million. See "The Looming Neutron Gap," *Science,* vol. 267, Feb. 17, 1995.

[102]Developing new approaches and techniques for neutron instrumentation is a vital component of neutron scattering science. Upgrading of instrumentation at the European ILL facility has established ILL as the premier neutron center in the world. Organization for Economic Cooperation and Development, see footnote 86.

tion, the United States could also consider joining the ISIS spallation facility in the United Kingdom, which is capable of having its available beam time doubled with some modest additional investment ($60 million).[103]

Historically, use of both neutron and synchrotron facilities around the world has been based on the policy of open access to foreign scientists. Indeed, many advances in neutron scattering, particularly in instrumentation, have been brought about by multinational research teams. However, with increasing budget pressures on virtually all national science programs, this policy of open access is now being reviewed by various facilities.[104]

Since many facilities in different countries offer complementary approaches to neutron-scattering and synchrotron radiation research, there is an opportunity for improving international cooperation by having a more substantive global planning and coordination process among nations. This approach could facilitate more effective utilization of existing facilities. Paradoxically, there is a great demand for access to neutron and synchrotron facilities, but most facilities operate for limited time periods because of funding constraints. There is a need for greater international coordination in both the use of existing neutron facilities and the construction of new facilities. In particular, the European Union is now in the early stages of planning a 5-MW spallation source.[105] With the United States apparently also pursuing the devel-

opment of a spallation facility, greater interaction between U.S. and European scientists and engineers could perhaps lead to innovative approaches to spallation source design and construction. At the most recent Organization for Economic Cooperation and Development Megascience Forum on neutron sources, several participants emphasized that investments should be directed to state-of-the-art multinational facilities that have high-flux capabilities, not to smaller national facilities.[106]

Synchrotron Facilities: A Bright Future

One of the most important and powerful tools available to scientific researchers in a broad number of disciplines is x-rays. X-ray beams generated from synchrotron sources have provided the means to study a wide array of physical and biological phenomena. An understanding of the underlying molecular structure of DNA (dioxyribonucleic acid), RNA (ribonucleic acid), and viruses has come principally from x-ray research. X-ray studies of ceramics, semiconductors, and other materials have directly aided the development of a host of commercially important technologies.[107] Because of their utility to a variety of scientific fields and industries, the number of synchrotron radiation sources operating throughout the world has grown rapidly. There are about 40 partially or fully operational synchrotron facilities worldwide, with nearly the same number either in the design stage or under construction.[108] The ex-

---

[103]"The Looming Neutron Gap," see footnote 101.

[104]For example, the ILL neutron facility in Europe has established new guidelines that partially restrict facility access to researchers who come from nonmember countries.

[105]The 5-MW European Spallation Source and the ANS were viewed by many neutron scientists as complementary programs. There was an expectation among some that researchers from Europe and the United States would have reciprocal access to these facilities. If Europe builds a 5-MW source and the U.S. proceeds with a 1-MW source, then in the eyes of many, Europe would have the leading international neutron facility.

[106]Other observers, however, pointed out that smaller facilities, particularly at the university level, have been responsible for some important advances in neutron scattering instrumentation. OECD Megascience Forum, Knoxville, TN, unpublished proceedings, Nov. 3-4, 1994.

[107]Another potentially important application of synchrotron radiation is x-ray lithography. The use of x-rays might offer the most viable means of improving the performance of microelectronic devices. As dimensions of these electronic chips shrink, visible light and ultraviolet light can no longer be used. Several companies including IBM, AT&T, and Motorola, as well as a number of Japanese and European companies, are developing x-ray lithography for chip manufacture.

[108]Organization for Economic Cooperation and Development, see footnote 86.

A closeup of a synchrotron insertion device called an undulator that generates super-intense x-ray beams.

pansion of synchrotron light source capacity has been driven by a strong demand for x-ray beam time and by the desire to develop more intense sources to investigate a larger and more complex domain of problems.[109]

Three new major synchrotron facilities—the European Synchrotron Radiation Facility (ESRF), the U.S. Advanced Photon Source (APS), and the Japanese Super Photon Ring-8 (SPring-8)—will offer extremely intense x-ray beams that will allow researchers to study smaller samples, more complicated systems, and faster processes and reactions, as well as acquire data at unprecedented rates and levels of detail.[110] Researchers from industry, universities, medical schools, and national laboratories will exploit the capabilities of these machines.

At the APS at the Argonne National Laboratory, researchers will explore the following areas: structural biology, medical imaging, biophysics, chemical science, materials science, structural crystallography, time-resolved studies, basic energy science, tomography, topography, real-time studies, time-resolved scattering and spectroscopy, and geoscience. Collaborative teams from industry, national laboratories, and academia have been formed to explore new pharmaceutical products and polymer manufacturing techniques, as well as underlying processes associated with the formation of proteins.[111] The APS will be completed in 1996 at a cost of about $800 million, very close to the original estimate.[112] The ESRF and the SPring-8 have comparable construction and development costs.

Apart from the ESRF, which is a multinational effort of 12 European nations, there have not been any large international collaborative efforts in the planning and construction of new synchrotron facilities. However, a cooperative exchange agreement has been established among ESRF, APS, and SPring-8 to address common problems of instrument development. These superbright light sources require sophisticated optical components, extremely tight mechanical tolerances, and novel detector systems.[113] The technical expertise for

---

[109]As an example of the demand for x-ray beam time, the National Synchrotron Light Source at Brookhaven National Laboratory is used on an annual basis by more than 2,000 scientists representing 350 institutions, including researchers from more than 50 corporations.

[110]Each of these so-called "third-generation" synchrotron facilities will complement each other by providing a different range of synchrotron radiation frequencies and intensities. They each rely on "insertion devices" to produce x-rays of unprecedented brilliance. Insertion devices consist of alternating magnetic fields along the straight sections of the synchrotron ring. These alternating magnetic fields cause charged particles (electrons or positrons) to deviate in their trajectory giving off x-rays in the process. Insertion devices allow synchrotron radiation to be tuned over a broad spectrum of wavelengths from the infrared to hard x-rays.

[111]"Switching On a Brilliant Light," *Science*, vol. 267, Mar. 21, 1995, pp. 1904-1906.

[112]The $800 million figure is a total project cost, which includes related R&D as well as construction costs. Another synchrotron facility recently completed in the United States is the Advanced Light Source (ALS) at the Lawrence Berkeley National Laboratory. The ALS is a lower energy light source that provides the world's brightest light in the ultraviolet and soft x-ray regions of the light spectrum. The ALS complements the hard x-ray capability of the APS. It is being used for basic materials science studies, the fabrication of microstructures, and structural biology.

[113]Organization for Economic Cooperation and Development, see footnote 86.

these areas is found in many different countries and many advances in x-ray instrumentation have resulted from multilateral collaboration. The coordination agreement among the three new synchrotron facilities will no doubt enhance the networks of cooperation that have developed in recent years.

Like neutron sources, synchrotron light sources essentially serve as vehicles for small science. Because of the wide range of uses for synchrotron radiation—in particular, its role in the development of new materials, processes, and products—there has been a strong imperative for the United States and other countries to build national facilities. Having multiple facilities ensures that demands for beam time can be met and, perhaps more importantly, provides a means for competition and thus greater innovation. However, as the technology advances and the costs of constructing new facilities increase, greater attention is likely to be paid to the possibility of building international facilities.

Opportunities and Challenges of International Collaboration |4

Previous chapters of this study have analyzed U.S. science goals in an international context and examined U.S. collaboration in several scientific disciplines. Although experience has demonstrated that collaboration offers distinct advantages, it can also have drawbacks. The decision about whether to collaborate depends on an assessment of the relative benefits and disadvantages of a particular undertaking. The present chapter identifies the main benefits from, and impediments to, collaboration. It offers policymakers a framework for analyzing the appropriateness of future collaborative opportunities.

BENEFITS OF COLLABORATION

Increased U.S. participation in international collaborative research and development (R&D) ventures could offer a variety of economic, technical, political, and institutional benefits. Although these benefits may not be realizable in every case, collaboration does offer a range of potential opportunities that may justify U.S. participation in future multilateral science efforts. These opportunities include:

- reducing net U.S. costs,
- enhancing scientific capabilities,
- enhancing the stability of science goals and funding,
- supporting U.S. foreign policy, and
- addressing global science and technology issues.

These different categories are analyzed below.

■ Reducing Net U.S. Costs

In government agencies and among science policy officials, saving money is consistently cited as a principal motive for undertaking international collaboration in large science projects. Two financial trends have made international collaboration more attractive to both scientists and policymakers. First, the cost of big science has risen sharply, making it increasingly difficult for individual countries to undertake such projects alone. In the United States, megaprojects account for about 10 percent of the federal (defense and nondefense) R&D budget.[1]

Second, aggregate demands on national science and technology (S&T) budgets have also grown dramatically, outpacing government appropriations for basic science research. This has been the result of increases in the amount of R&D being conducted and in the cost of the projects (large or small) themselves. For example, since 1958, the average expenditures per U.S. scientific investigator, expressed in constant dollars, have tripled.[2] The ability of governments to meet these demands is being limited by the growing budget pressures of the 1990s. These factors have prompted policymakers to search for alternative, less expensive means of achieving S&T goals, particularly in large, high-cost projects.

One way to reduce the cost of achieving national science goals may be to undertake big science on an internationally collaborative basis. Although the international framework may raise total project costs, it is designed to lower the *net* cost to each country by distributing project tasks and expenses among a group of partners or by pooling international resources in a single project. In some cases, however, cost savings for individual coun-

tries may not be as great as expected, because participation in international ventures still requires that investments be made in national programs. Without such investments, it may not be possible for individual countries to fully benefit from the advances coming from international projects.[3]

In addition to lowering project costs for individual countries, international partnerships on large science projects may also maximize the effectiveness of each dollar spent on research. By cooperating in big science endeavors, countries can coordinate construction and optimize the utilization of large, capital-intensive, special-purpose facilities. By avoiding duplication of these major facilities, nations can also free funds for other research or for nonscience uses.

International collaboration also provides a means by which countries can share the financial and technical risks of R&D projects. This is particularly important in big science projects, where the risks are often quite high. For example, the possibility of catastrophic failure of a space launch vehicle or its payload brings high levels of risk to space-related science. And although the claims of the National Aeronautics and Space Administration (NASA) that Russian participation in the space station will save the United States money have been discounted by General Accounting Office analysis,[4] it does appear that the addition of Russian equipment and the Russians' considerable expertise in long-duration human space flight will reduce the immense technical and

---

[1]These figures are based on a selection of large projects tracked by the Congressional Research Service. See Genevieve J. Knezo, *Major Science and Technology Programs: Megaprojects and Presidential Initiatives, Trends Through FY 1996,* CRS Report for Congress (Washington, DC: Congressional Research Service, Mar. 27, 1995).

[2]Increased R&D spending can be attributed to a growing number of qualified scientists (relative to the general population) able to perform research, pressure on individual investigators to produce more research, and the increasing complexity of equipment and facilities. See U.S. Congress, Office of Technology Assessment, *Federally Funded Research: Decisions for a Decade,* OTA-SET-490 (Washington, DC: U.S. Government Printing Office, 1991), p. 199.

[3]It is important to note, however, that there have been no studies quantifying the net cost savings to individual countries from international collaboration or the value added by international collaboration of scientists. Moreover, as will be discussed below, international partnerships may increase *total* project costs.

[4]See U. S. General Accounting Office, *Space Station: Update on the Impact of the Expanded Russian Role* (Washington, DC: U.S. Government Printing Office, July 1994).

financial risks inherent in the U.S. program. According to NASA's space station business manager, the addition of Russian hardware has "reduced risk in many areas of the program."[5]

The financial savings offered by international collaboration enable countries to maintain the breadth of their national programs. For example, given NASA's substantial budget resources, the agency could, on its own, completely fund virtually any single one of the large international space research projects if they were carried out sequentially. However, doing so would severely limit the number of projects in which NASA is involved and would restrict the scope of U.S. scientific activities in space. By pursuing at least some projects collaboratively, NASA officials note that the agency has been able to spread its budget over a greater number of projects simultaneously, thereby diversifying its activities and increasing the net scientific yield of its budget. This has also enabled NASA to keep several research disciplines alive during times of budget stringency. For example, neither Cassini-Huygens (a mission of NASA and the European Space Agency (ESA) to Saturn) nor Topex-Poseidon (a U.S.-French oceanographic research satellite program) would have been possible without international participation. NASA alone could not have financed these missions simultaneously. Spacelab, the pressurized research module built for the space shuttle by ESA, has significantly increased the shuttle's research capacity. Given the severe funding pressures on the shuttle program, NASA probably would have been unable to fund Spacelab's full development cost.

Finally, some project managers voice the perception that Congress prefers that large science projects include international collaboration. For example, although NASA plans originally called for the United States to finance and build the core space station, agency executives also sought international collaboration from the beginning of the project, in part, to meet anticipated congressional requirements that some costs be shared with international partners. Planners of the Superconducting Super Collider (SSC) designed an exclusively national project. However, when cost overruns multiplied, the project was heavily criticized in Congress for failing to attract international support. Efforts to obtain foreign support failed in large part because they were undertaken too late.[6] In another case, Congress refused an initial National Science Foundation (NSF) proposal to fully fund the $176 million Gemini project to build two new eight-meter telescopes. Instead, Congress authorized only half of the amount requested and instructed NSF to internationalize the project and obtain the remaining funding from the partners. In this way, NSF successfully internationalized the venture from the beginning and the project is now proceeding on schedule. (See box 4-1.)

∎ Enhancing Scientific Capabilities

Despite the importance of reducing net costs, the desire to save money generally does not by itself motivate international collaboration. Another important reason for pursuing international cooperative research is "to do the best science." Whereas policymakers may emphasize the financial advantages of partnerships, scientists and other advocates of increased international collaboration stress as their primary motive the immense technical advantages of working cooperatively. Enhancement of scientific capabilities ranks near the

---

[5] Jeffrey M. Lenorovitz, "So Much Hardware, So Many Nations," *Aviation Week & Space Technology*, vol. 140, No. 14, Apr. 4, 1994, p. 43.

[6] For a discussion of these issues, see chapter 3. See also John M. Deutch, "A Supercollision of Interests," *Technology Review*, vol. 95, No. 8, November/December 1992, p. 66; and Bob Johnstone, "Superpowers Collide," *Far Eastern Economic Review*, vol. 155, No. 3, Jan. 23, 1992, p. 66.

BOX 4-1: Seeing the Stars: The Gemini Project

Ground-based telescopes are essential components of astronomical research. Over the past 30 years, large ground-based optical/infrared telescopes have played a key role in advancing scientific understanding of the cosmos. Further advances in the field of astronomy are expected with the construction of a new generation of even larger telescopes, including the University of California/Caltech twin 10-meter Keck telescopes, the European Southern Observatory's Very Large Telescope (VLT) project, and the Gemini Project.

The Gemini Project is a U.S.-led international partnership to build, design, and operate two 8-meter telescopes. One of the telescopes will be based at Mauna Kea, Hawaii, and the other on Cerro Pachon, in northern Chile. Initially, the project was envisioned as a purely U.S. effort. However, in 1991 Congress capped U.S. spending on the project at $88 million and directed that the U.S. contribution not exceed 50 percent of the project's total cost. As a result, Gemini was internationalized.

The United Kingdom, Canada, Chile, Argentina, and Brazil are project partners. Under the terms of the partnership, outlined in the Gemini Agreement, the United States will provide half of the funding for the $176 million project. The United Kingdom will pay 25 percent of the project costs; Canada, 15 percent; and Chile, 5 percent. Argentina and Brazil will contribute 2.5 percent each. Estimated annual operating costs for both telescopes are $12 million, of which the United States will pay half.

The National Science Foundation acts as the executive agency for the partnership, and the Association of Universities for Research in Astronomy (AURA), Inc. manages the construction of the telescopes. AURA is a consortium of 20 universities, which also manages 3 major National Optical Astronomy Observatories facilities.

The Gemini telescopes are designed to operate in the optical and infrared ranges and provide complete coverage of both the Northern and Southern Hemispheres, with spatial resolution better than the Hubble Space Telescope. Construction of the Hawaii telescope began in October 1994, with "first light" expected in 1998. The second telescope will be constructed by 2000.

---

top of NASA's policies governing international collaboration,[7] and is an integral part of U.S. cooperative research programs in fusion.

In an ideal international project, researchers take advantage of each country's strengths to ensure that the project is on the cutting-edge of science, employs the very latest in technologies, and incorporates the broadest range of technical capabilities. Science policy analysts contend that the international situation has changed and that the United States is no longer dominant in many fields of science and technology. In this context, collaboration is often necessary to keep U.S. sci-

entists abreast of cutting-edge work being conducted abroad. In some fields, U.S. scientists may remain at the cutting-edge only by conducting research internationally. As one observer has noted: "We *need* to collaborate if we are to compete, paradoxical as it may sound."[8]

In addition, the diversity of individuals and research styles encompassed by collaborative ventures may stimulate creativity and facilitate discovery. As noted by a Fusion Policy Advisory Committee report, in international collaborative work "the synergistic effects of sharing knowl-

---

[7]See discussion of NASA guidelines in chapter 3. See also National Security Council, "National Space Policy," National Space Policy Directive 1, Nov. 2, 1989.

[8]Eugene B. Skolnikoff, personal communication, Apr. 18, 1995.

BOX 4-1 Cont'd.

The project was initially troubled by a number of factors, which illustrate some of the challenges of international collaboration. The most serious challenge was sustaining partner commitments. For example, Canada reduced its initial funding commitment from 25 percent to 15 percent. Further uncertainty over the Canadian budget caused delays in signing the agreement. Increased management complexity has affected the project, too. Project managers reported that formulating an acceptable collaborative agreement and standardizing different fiscal policies and accounting practices were difficult tasks. For example, different dates for fiscal years complicate budgeting. In addition, foreign laboratories employed accounting procedures that were inconsistent with U.S. government rules.

Disagreements also arose about the mirror technology. The astronomy community was divided over whether the mirrors should be ultra-low expansion glass menisci or borosilicate honeycombs. The borosilicate honeycomb mirror was developed by the University of Arizona's Steward Observatory Mirror Laboratory, as part of a 10-year, $24 million project, about 50 percent of which is publicly funded. In 1992, the decision was made to use the meniscus mirror, which will be made by Corning, Inc. The Gemini meniscus mirror is similar to those being produced by Corning for the Japanese Subaru telescope and by Scott Glaswerke (a German firm) for the VLT. The Corning mirror was chosen for its lesser cost and, because the same technology is being proven in these other large telescopes, lowering technical risk. Some astronomers voiced strong disagreement with the decision, based on technical grounds, but these objections were laid to rest after the Preliminary Design Review.

Despite the project's financial, administrative, and technical challenges, Gemini is a good example of the benefits of collaboration and how challenges can be overcome. In this project, partners are collaborating to construct cutting-edge facilities that no single partner was willing to build on its own. Even in the case of the United States—the project's largest contributor—the $88 million cap on spending would have been insufficient to build even one of the telescopes as a national facility.[1] But as part of the international collaboration, U.S. astronomers will have access to two 8-meter telescopes that will help keep them competitive with European and Japanese investigators.

---

[1] Economies of scale make it possible to build two telescopes for $176 million. Building just one telescope would cost $106 million.

SOURCE: Leif J. Robinson and Jack Murray, "The Gemini Project: Twins in Trouble?" *Sky & Telescope*, vol. 85, No. 5, May 1993, p. 29; and National Science Foundation, personal communication, May 1995.

---

edge and trained personnel" can be quite strong.[9] By facilitating the use of the most advanced technologies, promoting consideration of the fullest range of technical ideas, and creating new research dynamics, international projects can also reduce the risks inherent in R&D projects.

In addition to the technical benefits that accrue to the project as a whole, international collaboration can benefit U.S. national R&D programs. By participating in international partnerships, U.S. scientists can widen their sphere of access to research data from projects in which they play only a contributing role. By enhancing the capabilities of U.S. science, international cooperative research also attracts the brightest American and foreign students to careers in scientific research in the United States. Although many students eventually return to their native countries to build stronger (and competitive) research programs, the continuing attraction of foreign researchers en-

---

[9] U.S. Department of Energy, Fusion Policy Advisory Committee, "Report of the Technical Panel on Magnetic Fusion of the Energy Research Advisory Board, Final Report," DOE 1S-0081, September 1990, p. 15.

The ITER San Diego Joint Work Site operations host political and scientific leaders in an unparalleled international collaborative effort.

riches high-energy physics, fusion, and space-related science research in the United States.

▮ Enhancing Stability of Science Goals and Funding

From the standpoint of scientists and partner nations, one of the most serious problems for U.S. science policy and research projects in recent years has been the uncertainty of long-term funding. All science projects—large and small, domestic and international—compete for funds in the annual congressional appropriations process. In the scientific community, this has produced uncertainty about the stability of project funding and the U.S. commitment to international collaboration. In addition, several large projects have experienced extensive mid-course revisions to meet reduced budget allocations (e.g., the space station, the Earth Observing System (EOS), and the fusion research program). A few projects already under way have been canceled (e.g., the International Solar Polar Mission and the SSC). These funding

reductions and cancellations have resulted from a variety of causes, including inadequate project planning, unrealistically low initial cost estimates by scientists and project managers, unforeseen technical difficulties, severe budget pressures, and changes in administration policies.

However, researchers also express strong dissatisfaction about what they perceive as uncertain and shifting federal funding policies, as well as the need to rejustify funding for ongoing projects each year. This has been an especially difficult problem for megaprojects, which require long-term commitment to large outlays for capital and operational costs. In conversations with the Office of Technology Assessment (OTA), some U.S. scientists working on large, long-term projects have emphasized their desire to obtain—at best—full multiyear government funding. Short of this, they have asked that other mechanisms be sought to increase the certainty of continuing U.S. government support for science projects.

Some scientists have suggested that placing megascience projects in international collaborative contexts may provide the increased stability desired. Although this motivation is not often discussed explicitly, U.S. scientists who support increased international collaboration may be doing so at least partly because of their perception that Congress would be less likely to reduce funding for or cancel an international project than a purely domestic one. As noted in recent congressional testimony, "International projects offer many significant advantages, among which are . . . candidly . . . making it difficult to back out of a project once begun."[10] This view is fueled both by perceptions of congressional priorities and by experience with past projects. Both scientists and science policy analysts have voiced the strong perception that Congress may be reluctant to reduce or discontinue funding for international projects if formal intergovernmental agreements have been

[10]Statement of Norman R. Augustine, Chairman and Chief Executive Officer, Martin Marietta Corp., *Will Restructuring NASA Improve Its Performance?* hearing before the Subcommittee on Science, Technology and Space, Committee on Commerce, United States Senate, Nov. 16, 1993, Serial No. 103-406, p. 13; and U.S.-CREST, Center for Research and Education on Strategy and Technology, *Partners in Space—International Cooperation in Space: Strategies for the New Century* (Arlington, VA: May 1993), p. 24.

signed, because of the foreign policy implications of such modifications and impacts on other collaborations.[11]

There is evidence that in some cases international cooperation has been sought at least partially to bolster project stability. In an analysis of NASA's motivations for seeking international collaboration in the space station project, it was noted that "NASA is hoping to use the 'international commitment' aspect of the Space Station to protect it from devastating domestic budget cuts."[12] Although the commitments of Europe and Japan did not protect the program from major downsizings in the late 1980s and early 1990s, the recent addition of Russia may have saved the space station from cancellation. Before Russian involvement, the U.S.-ESA-Japan project had escaped termination in the House of Representatives by only one vote in 1993. However, in 1994, after Russia had been brought into the project—partly in support of high-priority foreign policy objectives—the House approved funding for the station by a much wider margin. Administration officials and House members attributed this wider margin of support in part to the station's increased importance for U.S. foreign policy goals.[13]

It should be noted that there is no evidence that a major science project has been pursued on an international collaborative basis *solely* to bolster its funding stability. However, the perception that inclusion of an international component enhances a large science project's political stability may contribute to the decision to seek such a collaboration.[14]

■ Supporting U.S. Foreign Policy

As discussed in chapter 3, the goals of U.S. foreign policy include enhancing national security, decreasing international tensions, strengthening U.S. alliances and friendships, and increasing cross-cultural understanding. U.S. cooperation with other countries in areas of mutual interest, including scientific research, has long been an important tool in support of these foreign policy objectives. Joint scientific research pays dividends not only in scientific discovery, but also in strengthening bonds of friendship with our allies and establishing levels of trust with our rivals.

The United States has been most active in cooperating with Canada, Western European allies, and Japan in a wide spectrum of scientific research. These ties helped build and maintain allied relationships during the Cold War. Collaboration occurred in areas of both civilian and defense-related research.

During this period, the United States conducted limited cooperative efforts with the Soviet Union in fields such as space exploration and fusion. This joint research helped decrease tensions and increase cross-cultural understanding during the Cold War. In fact, analysts have contended that the political significance of the best known collaboration, the Apollo-Soyuz Test Project, far exceeded

---

[11]For example, commenting on possible cuts in the requested congressional appropriation for the Gemini telescope project for fiscal year 1993, Professor Bob Bless of the University of Wisconsin noted: "NSF has assured us that they consider the project to be very important, and the fact that it's an international effort gives it a high visibility." Jeffrey Mervis, "Gemini Telescope Project Shifts into High Gear," *Nature*, vol. 357, No. 6378, June 11, 1992, p. 430.

[12]Joan Johnson-Freese, *Changing Patterns of International Cooperation in Space* (Malabar, FL: Orbit Book Co., 1990), p. 91.

[13]According to Representative Dick Zimmer, who sponsored a measure to terminate station funding, the cooperation agreement with Russia "created considerably more support for the program on the Democratic . . . [and] Republican side." See Phil Kuntz and Jeffrey L. Katz, "Space Station Bounces Back with Strong House Vote," *Congressional Quarterly Weekly Report*, vol. 52, No. 26, July 2, 1994, p. 1803.

[14]OTA interviews with Japanese science officials indicated that such a perception does exist among scientists and policy planners in Japan.

the scientific and technical dividends that it produced. The symbolism of the two nations cooperating in a space linkup was a graphic illustration of the policy of detente, perhaps more powerful and important than the knowledge gained about space rendezvous operations.[15]

Since the end of the Cold War, joint undertakings have continued to be important to the maintenance of ties with longstanding U.S. allies. Perhaps more significantly, however, the United States has strengthened and expanded ties with its former Eastern bloc rivals. These new collaborations are important for establishing friendships with former enemies and enhancing U.S. national security. For former Soviet nations such as Russia, collaboration with U.S. scientists represents a way to sustain scientists, institutes, and research during a time of great economic stress, when previously lavish state support for the sciences has almost dried up. Collaborative work between Western and Eastern scientists also builds relationships of good will among individuals, institutes, and governments.

A longstanding example of this is the international fusion research program. Since the late 1950s, U.S., European, and Soviet fusion researchers have been engaged in productive scientific exchanges and cooperation under formal U.S.-Soviet agreements and under the auspices of the International Atomic Energy Agency. Soviet researchers developed the tokamak[16] confinement concept and shared their successful results with their peers in the United States and Europe. This information sharing quickly made the tokamak the leading magnetic confinement concept in all national programs.[17] The Russian Federation has succeeded the former Soviet Union as one of four partners in the International Thermonuclear Experimental Reactor (ITER). The ITER collaboration was launched by discussions between President Reagan and General Secretary Gorbachev at the 1985 Geneva summit.

Collaborative projects in support of science in the former Soviet Union are also important from the standpoint of U.S. national security. By engaging scientists and institutions formerly dedicated to military research in civilian projects with Western partners, the United States may support defense conversion and prevent scientists from selling their expertise to hostile countries. The United States has also used science collaboration as an incentive to former Soviet states to adhere to nonproliferation agreements. For example, the U.S. invitation to Russia to participate in the space station was conditioned on Russia's not violating the Missile Technology Control Regime by a proposed sale of cryogenic rocket engines to India.

Finally, U.S. science policy has also included collaboration with and training of scientists from developing countries, both during and after the end of the Cold War. As an illustration, large U.S. facilities, such as the Fermi National Accelerator Laboratory, have involved developing-country scientists in a variety of projects. More importantly, this scientific cooperation has reinforced U.S. foreign aid and development policies. In areas such as environmental monitoring, collaboration with scientists from the developing world has been essential to gathering data on global ecosystem behavior and establishing international policies to address global environmental problems.

∎ Addressing Global Issues

The final motive for pursuing international partnerships derives from the changing nature of the world science agenda. In the past, the United

---

[15]Johnson-Freese, see footnote 12, pp. 31-34; and U.S. Congress, Office of Technology Assessment, *International Cooperation and Competition in Civilian Space Activities*, OTA-ISC-239 (Washington, DC: U.S. Government Printing Office, July 1985), p. 377.

[16]"Tokamak" is a Russian acronym for TOroidal'naia KAMera s AKsial'nym magnitnym polem (toroidal chamber with axial magnetic field).

[17]For a description, see U.S. Congress, Office of Technology Assessment, *Starpower: The U.S. and the International Quest for Fusion Energy*, OTA-E-338 (Washington, DC: U.S. Government Printing Office, October 1987), p. 163.

States has focused most of its resources on non-collaborative national research programs, in part because the research issues confronting U.S. scientists were national in scale or did not necessitate the collaboration of other countries. However, the issues confronting U.S. scientists (in both large and small projects) are becoming increasingly global in nature. This is especially true in environmental research, where scientists are embarking on complex, long-term studies of the global ecosystem in connection with challenges presented by possible global climate change and ozone depletion.

Although some U.S. environmental R&D will continue to require only a domestic perspective, much new work will necessitate cooperation with many countries on land and sea, in the air, and in space. In many cases, ecological interdependence makes it impossible to study U.S. environmental problems in isolation from their global environmental context. The United States is taking a leading role in one of the most ambitious of these collaborations, the EOS, a multibillion dollar network of satellites to study Earth's ecosystems.

CHALLENGES OF COLLABORATION

Despite the many potential benefits deriving from collaborative research, there are also potential downsides associated with almost all of these opportunities. Such disincentives to collaboration can in some cases be quite serious. For example, although collaboration may reduce the net cost of research to each participating nation, it may increase total project costs.[18] In many cases, this cost escalation may not be a significant issue. However, in other circumstances, collaboration may result in the promotion of projects so financially disadvantageous that they would not be undertaken by individual countries acting alone.

There are additional deterrents to collaboration. Although international cooperation may enhance a project's scientific capabilities, it may also transfer critical knowledge and skills to other nations, thus enabling them to compete more effectively with the United States in both science and commerce. Moreover, although pursuing research through international collaboration could provide increased stability for large projects, this framework may also enforce an organizational and investigative rigidity that is harmful to overall research goals.

Finally, although scientific cooperation can in some cases support foreign policy, there is a risk that international scientific collaborations driven by foreign policy goals might act to the detriment of science. Politically motivated collaborations may be more likely to produce scientifically inappropriate or politically unstable projects. This has been one of the strongest criticisms of Russian participation in the space station, where analysts and policymakers have noted that the risks posed by that country's political instability may outweigh the benefits gained from its considerable technical expertise.[19] These potential downsides are listed in table 4-1.

They represent only a partial list of the disincentives to international cooperation in scientific research. Other factors that might preclude a nation from pursuing collaboration include:

- the loss of national leadership, prestige, and project control;
- the need for reliable mechanisms to guarantee long-term commitment to a project;
- the difficulty of distributing costs and benefits in an equitable manner;
- transfer of leading national technologies;
- sociocultural differences; and
- increased management complexity.

---

[18]However, just as there have been no studies documenting *savings* from international collaboration, there is no research quantifying *increased costs* from cooperative ventures. Moreover, analysts have suggested that an accurate accounting of possible additional costs would have to discount for the value added by bringing together top scientists from different countries for work on the project.

[19]See, for example, Jeanne Ponessa, "Wariness Over Russia's Role," *Congressional Quarterly*, May 7, 1994, p. 1114.

TABLE 4-1: Opportunities and Potential Downsides to International Collaboration	
Opportunity	**Downside**
Reduce net U.S. costs.	Increase total project costs.
Enhance U.S. scientific capabilities.	Enhance competitive capabilities of U.S. partners.
Enhance stability of science goals and funding.	Increase rigidity of goals and funding.
Maintain U.S. science leadership.	Dilute U.S. scientific leadership.
Support U.S. foreign policy.	Distort or undermine science because of political goals.

SOURCE: Office of Technology Assessment, 1995.

■ Loss of National Leadership, Prestige, and Project Control

In the words of one observer: "Very large facilities are symbols of power. Consequently, individual countries will only agree to cooperate in constructing them if they have no other alternative."[20] Although this somewhat overstates the point and discounts other reasons for collaborative undertakings, large science projects are closely related to feelings of national leadership and prestige. While the desire to maintain U.S. scientific leadership can motivate collaboration in some cases, it is usually a much stronger disincentive to cooperate with other nations in large science ventures. The goal of establishing and maintaining leadership in scientific R&D is deeply embedded in the culture of U.S. science; it is reinforced by the system of financial and intellectual incentives that govern the activities of U.S. scientists and research institutions. Among the most important of these incentives are the criteria for awarding research grants and academic tenure, competitive salaries for top research scientists, and review criteria for publications.[21]

This culture can act as an obstacle to international collaboration. Since the highest rewards (e.g., the Nobel Prize) are generally based on individual achievement, many U.S. scientists prefer to conduct research independently. They are often very reluctant to participate in joint projects—

domestically as well as internationally—in which rewards and recognition are shared. Even when budgets are severely constricted and research goals can be achieved at lower cost through international collaboration, U.S. scientists have sometimes pressed for strictly national research programs. For example, U.S. scientists, supported by NSF funds, are conducting gravitational wave experiments through the Laser Interferometer Gravitational Wave Observatory, completely independent of parallel research efforts in Europe. In addition, U.S. astronomers initially advocated that the two Gemini telescopes be strictly national projects. As noted above, foreign partners were sought only when Congress denied funding for strictly national telescopes and mandated international collaboration. Many attribute termination of the SSC—perhaps the most prominent failure of a big science project—partly to physicists pursuing a strictly national project too long, despite the financial advantages of building such an expensive project collaboratively. In this case, to researchers, the competition for scientific discovery outweighed the potential for saving public funds.

When U.S. scientists and institutions do participate in collaborations, the "culture of national leadership" may strongly influence the character of these cooperative ventures. Then too, the desire to maintain national leadership is often accompanied by the desire to maintain project control.

---

[20]Francoise Praderie, Project Head, OECD Megascience Forum, *Megascience and Its Background* (Paris, France: Organization for Economic Cooperation and Development, 1993), p. 35.

[21]Although foreign scientists are governed by similar incentive systems that encourage individual achievement, they are subject to often stronger countervailing incentives (e.g., limitations on national funding abilities) to collaborate with other scientists both at home and abroad.

For example, NASA has been the U.S. agency most actively involved in international collaboration and has employed an explicit set of rules to govern its collaborative efforts. (See chapter 3, box 3-3.) At the heart of NASA's approach to collaboration is a preference for maintaining control over critical paths.[22] This policy was designed to ensure that the United States minimizes technical risk and maintains both leadership and project control in its collaborative space efforts.[23] However, this approach has also meant that most U.S. space partnerships have been compartmentalized, value-added projects, rather than integrated collaborative work.

This approach has worked relatively well at NASA, where the building of instruments for scientific activities in space is conducive to compartmentalization and where the United States continues to enjoy a very strong lead in scientific and technical capabilities, as well as higher levels of funding. However, it may not be easily applicable to other scientific areas, where the research enterprise is more integrated and where other nations have comparable scientific and technical capabilities.

As their domestic science programs grow more sophisticated and competitive, potential partners in Western Europe and Japan are demanding more substantive involvement in collaborative research and a share of at least some leadership roles. In fact, Europe's two principal collaborative science organizations, the European Laboratory for Particle Physics (CERN) and ESA, were established explicitly to bridge the technical gap that emerged between Europe and the United States in the post-World War II era and to place Europe in a position

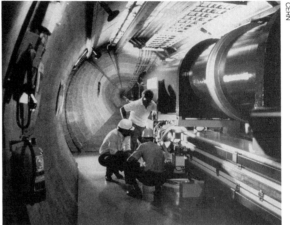

Mock-up of the CERN tunnel that will be the home of the Large Hadron Collider.

to cooperate with the United States from a position of strength, as equal partners. In this, ESA and CERN have been largely successful. They have stopped the "brain drain" of European scientists to the United States, and they have developed high-energy physics facilities, telescopes, and space systems at least comparable and, in some cases, superior to those of the United States.[24]

Maintaining scientific leadership and project control may also conflict with a primary motive for undertaking international collaboration—saving money. As other countries contribute a greater share of project funding, they will demand greater control. Even when the United States funds the bulk of a collaboration, partners are unlikely to cede complete discretion in project management. Writing about the lessons learned from the space station experience thus far, space policy analysts at NASA and the International Space University

---

[22]NASA policies on critical-path technologies are discussed in chapter 3. Prior to Russian participation in the Space Station, the Canadian robot arm for the space shuttle was the only exception to these policies. However, NASA maintained ultimate control over critical pathways by stipulating in the contract for the robot arm that the Canadians provide full access to all production plans and materials should they not fulfill the agreement.

[23]NASA has been able to establish collaborations under these guidelines in part because the United States has usually provided the bulk of project funds.

[24]John Krige, "ESA and CERN as International Collaborative Science Organizations," contractor report prepared for the Office of Technology Assessment, January 1995, p. 1.

noted that although the space station partners agreed from the beginning that the United States would be the senior partner, "there was considerable discussion on the level of protection for the minority partners in the preservation of management roles."[25]

In contrast, the ITER project conceptual and engineering design phases have been true quadripartite collaborations from the beginning. Each partner has contributed one-quarter of the costs, and decisions have been reached through consensus. The project is overseen by the ITER Council, consisting of two representatives from each party. Engineering design activities are being coordinated by a multinational central team that has been tasking the respective national fusion programs to provide supporting R&D and technology development. Except for a relatively modest amount of funds transferred to support the Joint Central Team administration, the ITER parties have met their commitments through in-kind contributions of personnel, services, and equipment. That structure may have to evolve if and when the project moves into a construction phase to accommodate the management demands of overseeing and directing a large ($8 billion to $10 billion) construction project.

Nevertheless, U.S. goals can create a basic conflict with collaboration. This conflict is related less to money than to scientific leadership. To structure successful partnerships, the United States must provide adequate incentives for other parties to collaborate. Yet U.S. desires to maintain scientific leadership may undermine these efforts and provide a substantial disincentive to collaboration. As one European science official commented to OTA, "Why should I, as Europe, collaborate with the United States to maintain [U.S.] leadership?"[26]

The Need for Reliable Mechanisms To Guarantee Long-Term Project Commitment

One of the most often-cited impediments to future international collaborations has been the difficulty of guaranteeing long-term commitments on the part of all project partners. Countries are reluctant to agree to expensive, long-duration research projects unless they are confident that their partners' commitments are reliable. Once projects are under way, uncertain or changing commitments can complicate project planning, contracting, and budgeting. Questions about the commitment of a partner government can have a domino effect on the other partners, making it more difficult for them to raise money and sustain political commitment to the project at home. Lack of confidence in the reliability of partners also makes it difficult to establish the mutual trust necessary to do the best science in the most efficient manner.

Perceptions that it is an unreliable or unpredictable partner have been a particular problem for the United States. Yet these perceptions are based in part on recollections of only a few cases in which the United States has withdrawn from cooperative science projects. The cases usually cited by Western European and Japanese partners are the U.S. decision to withdraw from the Solvent Refined Coal Demonstration Plant-II (SRC-II) and the Solar Polar project. SRC-II was a joint project of the United States, Germany, and Japan to build a demonstration plant to produce liquid fuels from coal. (See chapter 1, box 1-2.) The project, established in 1980, was terminated by joint decision in 1981. The Solar Polar Project is described in box 1-3. Although these two cases occurred more than a decade ago, they are remembered and are cited frequently by our European and Japanese partners to

---

[25] Lynn F.H. Cline and George Van Reeth, "Space Station—An International Venture," prepared for the Workshop on International Space Cooperation: Learning from the Past, Planning for the Future, November 1992, p. 5.

[26] OTA Workshop on International Collaboration in Large Science Projects, Sept. 13, 1994.

bolster claims that U.S. commitments are unstable.

An even more prominent issue among U.S. partners is the U.S. budget process, in which funding for all projects must be rejustified yearly. In virtually all of OTA's discussions with U.S. partners, foreign governments, and organizations, the annual uncertainty over U.S. appropriations was cited as among the most formidable challenges to prospective and ongoing collaborations.[27] It is important to note that differences in budget processes contribute to foreign perceptions that the U.S. process promotes instability. Our major partners have parliamentary systems in which the combination of legislative and executive authority gives majority political parties greater power to control the agenda and implement policy. For partners accustomed to this system, the U.S. budget process seems to lead to greater uncertainty.

The U.S. budget process frequently creates tensions for collaborations already under way. In the case of the space station, continuing struggles over funding have increased tensions between the United States and its partners. Even in less contentious cases where appropriations are virtually assured, U.S. partners report concern about what they perceive as an annual process that calls U.S. funding formally into question. Although international projects are rarely canceled in the yearly budget process, the cancellation of domestic science projects such as the SSC has contributed to uncertainty about the strength of funding for international projects as well.[28]

The annual budget process does allow flexibility in planning that European countries and Japan lack. Having made multiyear commitments to science projects, these countries often find it difficult to revise or terminate inefficient or nonperforming projects.[29] However, some partners see a contradiction between U.S. claims of world scientific leadership and its annual budget process.

In contrast to instabilities in the U.S. funding process, funding for science research in Europe—by country or in multilateral organizations—has generally been more stable. This increased stability cannot be attributed to different statutory procedures, such as multiyear appropriations for science projects. Like the United States, European countries generally appropriate science funds yearly, as part of the annual budget process. Instead, two other factors account for this increased stability. First, although these countries and organizations generally do not provide multiyear appropriations, their planning processes, both for research programs and individual large science projects, are more extensive, which results in more realistic funding estimates and research time lines. Once governments commit to a project—and this is generally a longer process

---

[27] This perception is prominent in public discussion of international science projects as well. For example, commenting on the Gemini telescope project, Julie Lutz, Director of the National Science Foundation's astronomy division, said "[I]t is harder for the United States than for other countries to sustain a long-term scientific collaboration because the entire U.S. budget is reviewed annually by Congress." Mervis, see footnote 11, p. 430.

[28] In an analysis of 30 selected projects, several of which were canceled, the Congressional Research Service notes that "One . . . tentative conclusion is that significant technical, cost, political, foreign policy, and other events following an initial authorization and/or appropriation may overshadow initial congressional support." Sharp escalations in project cost or lower agency appropriations were an especially significant cause of project terminations. See William C. Boesman, *Big Science and Technology Projects: Analysis of 30 Selected U.S. Government Projects* (Washington, DC: Congressional Research Service, Aug. 24, 1994), p. 7.

[29] It should be noted that although individual countries lack flexibility, multinational European scientific organizations such as CERN, ESA, and ESO have in recent years shown flexibility in canceling, reducing funding for, and restructuring projects.

than in the United States—funding and participation are virtually guaranteed.[30] Second, almost all basic science research in Europe contains a significant international component. This applies not just to research conducted in multilateral organizations, but also to national research projects. Given their extensive interdependence in science research, stability of funding and adherence to international commitments are absolutely vital to the viability of European national research programs. The strength of international commitment in Europe has a nonscientific and historical component as well—the countries' relatively small size, close proximity, and closely interwoven economies. Moreover, the European Union treaty encourages joint research efforts among member states. The consequences of breaking an international commitment would likely be much more serious for a European country than they would be for the United States.

Similar factors apply in Japan. Projects receive approval only after undergoing a rigorous technical and financial evaluation that typically occurs over a three- to five-year period. Although Japan is generally slow to enter into commitments, once having agreed to a project, it adheres strongly to its commitments in part because of the desire to maintain and foster good international relations. However, participation in large international projects is usually not pursued by the Japanese unless there is a sound scientific or strategic motivation.[31]

Nevertheless, growing budget constraints within Europe may weaken multiyear funding arrangements or commitments to collaborative projects. Signs of strain are already showing with-

in CERN, where Germany has lobbied successfully to reduce its yearly contribution and where the future of the Large Hadron Collider (LHC) was complicated by heated disputes over funding contributions. ESA itself has recently undergone dramatic budget reductions in its optional programs, necessitating project cancellations. Disagreements about funding priorities have delayed approval and resulted in a downsizing of the organization's plan to build a pressurized laboratory and other compenents for the space station.

However, despite the concern among partner nations that the United States can sometimes be an unreliable or unpredictable partner, some question whether the United States has actually paid a price for being perceived as unreliable. Although this perception has unquestionably complicated U.S. negotiations in prospective collaborations, OTA cannot identify a case in which efforts to collaborate or initiate a project have failed because of questions about U.S. reliability. In fact, concerns about U.S. reliability may be ameliorated by the disproportionately large share the United States has paid into some collaborations. Nevertheless, future partnerships may have to be more formally structured to address the concerns of potential U.S. partners.

Finally, reliability is not related solely to the ability to deliver promised funds. Reliability also has a technical aspect—the ability to deliver properly designed and tested project components in a timely manner. In a purely domestic project, oversight and project control may be much simpler than in an international venture, where multiple agencies and firms in various countries have technical responsibilities. If there are only a few items

---

[30] European countries employ four- to five-year long-term planning processes for R&D decisions. Programs that have been approved at the cabinet level in these countries are reviewed on a two-year basis and generally can be canceled only if feasibility studies have not been conclusive or if the country is under economic constraints. Moreover, "[T]he most striking difference between the United States and other democratic countries is the action of Congress which can, more easily than anywhere else, shut down or create new programs without the agreement of the Administration/White House. In other countries, such behavior for major programs could lead to a political crisis." Center for Science, Trade and Technology Policy, George Mason University, "Large Science Project Priorities in Selected Countries," contractor report prepared for the Office of Technology Assessment, January 1995, p. 13.

[31] For a detailed discussion of this process, see Kenneth Pechter, "Assessment of Japanese Attitudes Toward International Collaboration in Big Science," contractor report prepared for the Office of Technoloy Assessment, December 1994.

on critical paths or if critical technologies are distributed among a smaller group of countries and firms, technical risks and concerns about the reliability of partners are reduced. However, the greater the number of partners that have responsibility over items on critical project paths, the more difficult it will be to ensure technical control. NASA's policies and preferences governing critical paths and project control are designed in part to meet these concerns.

■ Difficulty of Equitably Distributing Costs and Benefits

Apportionment of funding contributions and contracts can also impede cooperation. Successful collaboration requires convincing all international partners that project financing is structured fairly. Partners must also be satisfied with the policies that determine how and where money is spent. Distributing costs and benefits has been a continuing and difficult problem. The equitable allocation of costs and benefits has generally been a more serious problem for collaborative science organizations, with pooled funding and contracting operations, than for ad hoc collaborations in which there is often no exchange of funds or contracts.

The United States has collaborated more often using the latter arrangement and has placed heavy reliance on "clean interface" collaborations with no exchange of funds. This has reduced potential problems over the distribution of project costs and benefits. The Europeans, with their reliance on joint research organizations, have dealt with the problem more often and in greater depth. However, if the United States collaborates more actively in the future, it too will have to grapple with the issue of how to distribute project obligations and benefits. The United States may face this in awarding contracts and making the siting decision on the ITER project. The issue has also arisen at

CERN over potential U.S. participation in the LHC project. CERN has informed the Department of Energy that U.S. physicists may be unable to conduct research on the Large Hadron Collider if the U.S. government does not contribute to the capital costs of building the LHC.[32] U.S. policymakers may therefore benefit from an assessment of the challenges that Europeans have encountered in this area.

In practice, it has been easier to formulate systems for determining each country's funding contribution than to apportion project contracts. ESA and CERN employ formulas based on the gross domestic product to determine each country's funding contribution. This system is designed to ensure proportionality: each country contributes funds relative to its resources. In ESA's case, the proportionality formula applies to the organization's "mandatory" science programs. ESA allows countries to contribute additional funds to "optional" projects in which they are especially interested.

Yet even in this area, there has been substantial difficulty in assessing and compensating for the costs and benefits that may accrue to a country hosting a science facility. Some organizations spread their facilities among participating countries. In areas of ad hoc collaboration, there may be informal agreements among governments about which country is next "in line" to host a major facility. The benefits of hosting a facility may also be factored into a country's funding contribution to a facility or organization. In the case of the European fusion community's Joint European Torus (JET), Great Britain agreed to pay an additional 10 percent as its share of project costs in exchange for hosting the facility. However, there was recently sharp disagreement at CERN between Germany and Great Britain, on the one hand, and France and Switzerland, on the other, over how much the latter two countries should

---

[32]C. Llewellyn Smith, Director General of CERN, letter to U.S. Department of Energy Secretary Hazel O'Leary, Feb. 15, 1994.

contribute to the LHC in exchange for being its hosts. Final approval for building the LHC was held up while CERN members negotiated over this issue.[33]

Ensuring some balance in the procurement of goods and services has been even more difficult. There is a fundamental tension between each country's desire to receive financial returns commensurate with its contribution and the need for the project itself to contract work most efficiently and effectively. ESA, for example, has attempted to satisfy member demands for equity in contract apportionment by instituting a system of "fair return" (often referred to as *juste retour* or, in ESA's case, "equitable geographic return"), whereby each country receives a percentage of project contracts proportionate to its funding contribution, both for mandatory and optional projects. Observers report that this system worked relatively well in the past because ESA managers were allowed to meet the fair-return requirement by calculating contract distribution over several years and over a series of projects. ESA managers report that this gave them leeway to meet the distribution requirement and to place contracts where they were most technically and financially appropriate.

However, others argue that fair return discourages competitiveness and efficiency, and may prevent organizations from contracting with the best or most appropriate firms.[34] Recent experience at ESA may support this point. Although ESA's system of fair return appeared to work well in the past, political and budget pressures in member countries in recent years have led to demands for equitable returns on *each* project, reducing the

organization's flexibility and possibly increasing costs.[35]

To avoid this problem, which can affect even the best functioning fair-return arrangements, CERN until recently had no requirement to distribute contracts among partners. CERN was mandated instead to place contracts where most appropriate—technically, logistically, and financially. However, the following factors have resulted in pressure on CERN to enact some variant of fair return as well: budgetary constraints among member countries of CERN; the fact that host-states France and Switzerland have consistently won almost 60 percent of CERN contracts; and the fact that about 8 percent of CERN's annual budget is spent outside its member states (more than 5 percent is spent in the United States). CERN now employs a relatively loose return coefficient of 80 percent and contracting rules that keep prices of fair-return contracts close to the lowest bid. These provisions allow much greater flexibility than ESA has for placing contracts where they are most technically and financially advantageous.[36]

Fair return is an issue of contention not only because each country seeks to recoup its immediate contribution to each project. Differences also arise over the distribution of contracts because of the possible commercial potential of the technologies involved in developing megascience projects. For example, contracts to develop superconducting magnets for a collider or for Earth-observing instruments on an orbiting vehicle may finance new technologies with commercial implications

---

[33]In December 1994, the CERN Council approved the construction of a $2.3 billion Large Hadron Collider to be built in two stages. France and Switzerland, who will host the facility, agreed to pay proportionally more than they have for previous CERN projects. If additional funding is received from the United States and Japan, the LHC will likely be built in one stage and completed around 2004. If CERN is unable to secure funding from these and other nonmember states, construction will be stretched out into a second phase, which will end in 2008. See Dennis F. Cioffi, "CERN Reaches Consensus on Two-Stage LHC," *Physics Today,* vol. 48, No. 2, February 1995, pp. 48-50.

[34]See, for example, "Will Europe be Lost in Space?" *Nature,* vol. 373, Feb. 16, 1995, p. 545.

[35]ESA increased its overall country-by-country fair return goal to 95 percent in 1993 and is trying to reach 96 percent by 1996, with a goal of 90 percent within each of its programs. Krige, see footnote 23, p. 4.

[36]Ibid.

far beyond the initial science-oriented project goals. For this reason, not only are countries anxious to receive contracts for path-breaking technologies, they are also reluctant to finance, through their project contributions, contracts that develop these technologies (and create jobs) elsewhere—in effect, financing foreign commercial competitors.

Because of the differing commercial potential of various technologies, distribution of contracts has been a more important issue in some fields than in others. European collaboration has worked most smoothly when the science or technology concerned is not of direct commercial importance. For example, CERN's success, its lack of a fair-return policy, and the absence of large national facilities in all member states except Germany reflect European governments' perception that high-energy physics is a field of research with little potential for practical application, at least in the short to medium term. In space research, the situation is different, as evidenced by the existence of several independent European national space programs in addition to ESA, by ESA's industrial policy of fair return, and by the demand, particularly from the smaller or technologically less advanced member states, to move even closer to 100-percent return on their contributions.

Intellectual property issues also complicate collaborative arrangements. In structuring a research venture, managers must decide how to acquire, use, and safeguard technologies that are necessary to the project, but proprietary to a certain firm or country. Research projects must also design intellectual property mechanisms for processes and products produced by the venture itself. These issues may be even more complex than deciding where to assign contracts because they require, additionally, mechanisms for dispute resolution.

Ironically, the most difficult benefit to assign may be the least commercially important: where to site a project. There are unquestionably many

financial benefits to be derived from hosting a major science facility, most of which come from construction, operation, and maintenance contracts, as well as payrolls, that can give a significant boost to a local economy. Also, a major science facility could attract new companies to an area. However, rather than the benefits derived from hosting the facility and its infrastructure, contracts to produce path-breaking technologies with commercial implications or spinoffs may actually be much more beneficial to a country's economy as a whole, helping to create entirely new sectors of industry and employment. Thus, for example, the United States might place a much lower priority on hosting ITER than on maximizing opportunities to develop and produce the magnets, other reactor components, integration systems, or advanced materials that could have considerable commercial potential beyond fusion. In effect, the United States could use the siting decision as a bargaining chip to obtain concessions for critical advanced technologies and services.[37]

Nevertheless, siting remains an important issue in collaboration because it is so closely related to prestige—the national prestige of the country hosting the project, as well as the status of a nation's scientific community. Thus, decisions about siting are a challenge to collaboration due to questions of *both* national prestige and distribution of project benefits.

∎ Transfer of Leading National Technologies

The potential for transfer of technologies that have national security or commercial implications represents another impediment to collaboration. With respect to scientific and commercial considerations, the challenges presented by technology transfer are closely related to those posed by the distribution of benefits and the maintenance of national leadership. Countries and firms are reluc-

---

[37]Even site-related contracts, such as construction and management services, need not accrue solely to the host country.

tant to participate in projects that may result in the transfer to potential competitors of technologies in which they hold a scientific or commercial advantage.

Countries with cutting-edge technologies essential to a project have used a variety of means to protect their edge while participating in collaborative research. For example, a country can try to safeguard its lead by compartmentalizing work in collaborations or by stipulating project rules that clearly spell out the ways in which the technology may be used. NASA has employed this approach through the rules described in box 3-3. When it is impossible to safeguard a technology, a country may still participate in joint research because it derives other scientific or commercial benefits that compensate for the costs of sharing its leading technologies.[38] For example, the United States has developed considerable and unique expertise in the design of superconducting magnets as an outgrowth of the SSC program. By participating in the LHC effort, this important expertise can be utilized and sustained over the next decade. Not sharing this expertise could hurt overall U.S. capabilities in hadron accelerator technologies, because U.S. physicists would not have access to a machine (LHC) that is at the edge of the energy frontier.

However, despite all precautions, technologies may still be "leaked." Moreover, when countries sacrifice a lead in one technology for the sake of access to other technologies or benefits, calculation of the relative tradeoffs is difficult and imprecise. Countries, institutions, or firms may also choose to solve the potential technology transfer problem by withholding their leading technology and using less advanced technologies on a collaborative project.

The national security aspects of technology transfer—the transfer of technologies with proven or potential military applications—may be even more formidable. It is difficult to proceed with scientific collaborations that involve the transfer of militarily relevant technology. The United States has encountered serious obstacles in joint government-level military-related research with its allies.[39] This type of technology transfer is out of the question if the partner is a potential U.S. enemy or rival. Yet even when the United States is willing to share these technologies with friends, it may prove too difficult to design a collaborative and regulatory framework that would prevent further transfer or proliferation of the technology or technical capabilities.

■ Sociocultural Differences

Although often given short shrift in policy-related reviews of collaboration, sociocultural differences among scientists in an international research venture can pose obstacles to a successful collaboration. These impediments range from the obvious to the more subtle.

The first set of sociocultural obstacles involves daily life-style changes. Of these, the most obvious is the difference in language. For scientists working together in a single research venture, clear communication is vital, not only in daily scientific discourse, but also in establishing the mutual trust and collegiality that can foster creative synergies. Other differences in life-style, including working habits, housing, and cuisines, can also have negative effects on a scientist's ability to feel relaxed, "at home," and able to devote maximum mental energy to the project.

---

[38] In the private sector, IBM, Toshiba, and Siemens have decided to pool resources to develop the next-generation semiconductor DRAM (dynamic random access memory) technologies. Each of the companies has developed leading-edge capabilities in semiconductor design and fabrication. However, the financial and technical challenges associated with the 64-megabit and 256-megabit memory technologies compelled these companies to share the risks and costs of development. Each is revealing important information to the other in order to make this effort successful. In so doing, these companies are hoping to achieve synergies and new technical approaches that will reduce manufacturing costs.

[39] See U.S. Congress, Office of Technology Assessment, *Arming Our Allies: Cooperation and Competition in Defense Technology,* OTA-ISC-449 (Washington, DC: U.S. Government Printing Offfice, May 1990).

The stress of living in a foreign culture can increase in direct proportion to the "distance" of that culture from a scientist's own. Thus, it may be easier for a Western scientist to adjust to life in another Western country than in an Asian country, and vice versa. Furthermore, scientists from the countries of Western Europe, which are smaller than the United States, as well as more closely interwoven geographically and culturally, share a long history of collaboration in economics, politics, and culture, as well as science. These scientists often adapt more readily to life abroad than scientists from larger, more geographically isolated countries. For example, some U.S. citizens have a more difficult time adapting to life abroad because preparation for international living played a much smaller role in their personal and professional upbringing than it did for their European counterparts.

Perhaps the most serious of these sociocultural challenges—highlighted by international participants at OTA's workshop on international collaboration—is the retention of cultural identity within families, especially among children. Scientists from the United States, Europe, and Japan noted that the biggest problem they face while working abroad is finding culturally appropriate educational services for their children. Whatever the difficulties and rewards of foreign life for them as adults, they place strong emphasis on being able to educate their children in their home culture or provide employment opportunities for spouses.

Officials at Fermilab, an institution with a strong history of international cooperation, say that to ensure a successful environment for collaboration, a host institution or country must invest resources to address the needs of foreigners. These include not only education, but also housing, food, and other areas. Addressing these sociocultural issues can be an unanticipated expense in an international partnership, in both large and small science projects. Fermilab, for example, employs someone full time to work exclusively on these matters.

■ Increased Management Complexity

Managing an international venture is a more challenging and complex enterprise than managing a strictly national project. Increased management complexity can manifest itself in several ways. These include increased transaction costs, increased complexity of multinational decision-making at both the administrative and the scientific levels, and in some cases, reduced financial scrutiny and accountability. All of these factors make international projects more costly than purely national ones, in terms of both budgets and management time. The factors that increase management complexity are reviewed below.

Transaction costs take many forms. These include the cost of constructing and maintaining multiple, parallel, and geographically disparate administrative structures on the national and international levels. International projects also involve higher expenses for certain overhead line items, such as translation services and travel. Differences in equipment and standards may create costly and confusing obstacles to joint research. Moving and maintaining scientists abroad can be extremely expensive, much more so than the cost of maintaining the same scientists at home on exclusively national projects.

Transaction costs in international collaborations can be considerable, far beyond normal expenses for exclusively national projects. Critics of international collaboration maintain that due to these costs, international collaborative projects are always more expensive (in the aggregate) than national ones. However, it should be noted that since these higher costs are spread among all participating countries, the net project cost to each country is still likely to be substantially lower than the cost of undertaking the project alone.

In addition to the transaction costs of collaboration, increased management complexity can be reflected in complex, binding international agreements that reduce project flexibility (and serendipity) and increase the time required to reach decisions collectively. For projects in which policy and funding decisions require consensus or the approval of several different countries, it can be difficult to make decisions and change direction as needed in the course of the project. With science projects that have important commercial implications for their member states, policy decisions may require high-level meetings. For example, major policy decisions at ESA are made by meetings of the ministers for space-related affairs from all member states. At CERN, an organization with more limited commercial applications, decisions seldom require such high-level meetings. Other aspects of increased management complexity include boundaries to the movement of people and materials across borders, problems in obtaining work permits for spouses of scientists, and so forth.

More serious in its consequences for scientific discovery is the greater difficulty in reaching consensus decisions. Although this type of consensus may compel greater care in research before the publication of new discoveries, it may also produce a conservatism that is counterproductive to the basic mission of scientific discovery. Thus, innovation and individualism may be discouraged. For example, some analysts have criticized ITER's planners for using a fairly conservative design in an effort to ensure that the ignition of fusion fuel can actually be achieved.[40]

In some cases, international projects are complicated by differences in management and accounting systems, which make it difficult to evaluate the contributions and activities of each member country or institution. U.S. public science institutions, which operate under extremely tight and well-elaborated rules, have at times had particular trouble obtaining the necessary financial information from partner institutions abroad. This makes it difficult for them to account for expenditures of collaborative funds and time.

CONCLUSION

The decision to pursue scientific research on an international cooperative basis is complex. It involves balancing the relative benefits of collaboration against the disadvantages of international research. OTA has found that the most concrete benefits of partnerships include opportunities to reduce net U.S. costs and to enhance a project's scientific capabilities. The desire to reduce costs and/or "to do better science" has featured prominently as a motive in all the collaborations that OTA investigated. In addition, some collaborations have also been motivated by the desire to enhance funding stability, to support U.S. foreign policy goals, and to address global scientific questions.

Although these motives to collaborate can be attractive, the potential disadvantages of scientific cooperation must also be considered. In the past, the strongest disincentives to U.S. participation in collaborative endeavors have been the potential loss of national leadership and project control, difficulty in distributing a project's costs and benefits, and the risk of technology transfer. From the standpoint of U.S. partners, the inability of the United States to guarantee long-term political and funding support for international projects has been the most serious challenge to collaborations with the United States. However, there is evidence that these concerns have been overstated. There is also reason to believe that U.S. partners may soon experience the same types of instability. Finally, some sociocultural challenges may exist that complicate collaboration. These problems, however, are almost always outweighed by the benefits that can be derived by pooling intellectual talent from around the world and by the increased understanding that results from the close interaction of diverse groups of people.

---

[40]Because ITER is an ambitious, very expensive international collaboration (one of the first), a conservative and probably more expensive design is being used to reduce the chances that the machine will not perform as intended.

Appendix A: Science Goals of Other Nations | A

International scientific activities influence U.S. science policies and vice versa. This influence is likely to become more pronounced as research costs rise and the technological expertise of other countries increases. Since World War II, Europe and Japan have developed world-class scientific research programs and facilities. For example, the European Union has assumed a leadership position in high-energy physics research with its facilities and programs at the European Laboratory for Particle Physics (CERN). The Japanese have made important strides in their work on linear electron-positron accelerators and silicon tracking detectors used in particle physics research. Such advances in these and other research areas make it necessary for the United States to examine other nations' science policy goals and to reassess ours in terms of both the potential for international collaboration and our own goals. Accordingly, this appendix discusses other nations' science goals and funding priorities.[1]

Table A-1 presents a comparison of research and development (R&D) spending in the United States and several other nations. In 1991, the United States spent nearly $150 billion on R&D. Industry was the leading source of funding, contributing 56 percent of the total. Defense-related R&D commanded the largest share (more than 50 percent) of the federal contribution.

As a share of gross domestic product (GDP), U.S. R&D expenditures rank second. Japan's rank first. If only nondefense R&D is considered, the U.S. position would be lower. (See figure A-1 for a comparison of the Organization for Economic Cooperation and Development (OECD) countries' R&D expenditures as a share of GDP.)

GERMANY

In basic science, Germany's main goal is to secure its place as a major player in the world science arena. Closely linked to this goal is the commitment to maintaining and enhancing the quality of science.[2] The Federal Ministry for Research and Technology (BMFT) reports that international recognition of Germany's scientific achievements has grown in the last decade. Germany has

---

[1] For an indepth discussion of international research organizational structures and mechanisms, see U.S. Congress, Office of Technology Assessment, *Federally Funded Research: Decisions for a Decade,* OTA-SET-490 (Washington, DC: U.S. Government Printing Office, May 1991).

[2] Federal Ministry for Research and Technology, *Report of the Federal Government on Research 1993* (Bonn, Germany: July 1993).

TABLE A–1: Comparative R&D Spending (1991 data)

	Germany	France	Russia[a]	India	China	Brazil[b]	Canada	United Kingdom	Japan	United States
GERD (million dollars—PPP$)	35,562	25,033	20,200	6,000	22,500	3,180	7,804	19,137	67,349	149,842
GERD/capita (PPP$)	446	439	136	7	20	21	289	332	543	593
GORD (million dollars—PPP$)	14,058	14,295	26,000	4,680	13,500	2,540	3,195	7,943	10,540	65,897
GORD/GERD (percent)	40	57	95	78	60	80	41	42	16	44
Civilian GORD (million dollars—PPP$)	12,512	9,149	13,400	3,510	NA	2,184	3,003	4,369	9,908	26,359
Civilian GORD (percent of total GORD)	89	64	52	75	NA	86	94	55	94	40
Industrial development (percent of civilian GORD)	26	33[c]	22	13	47	NA	35	29	34	22
Health and environment (percent of civilian GORD)	13	10	4	9	4	4	16	22	6	43.5
Space (percent of civilian GORD)	6	14	NA	13	NA	11	9	5	7	24.5
Other research areas (percent of civilian GORD)	17	24	NA	8	27	NA	16	9	9	10
University research (percent of civilian GORD)	37	19	NA	NA	NA	23	22	34	45	NA

[a] During this transition year, substantial government outlays were diverted to non-R&D uses.

[b] In 1992, the defense budget dropped to 7 percent of GORD, whereas the health budget increased to 5 percent.

[c] In 1992, 24 percent.

KEY: GERD = gross domestic expenditures on R&D; GORD = government outlays on R&D; PPP = purchasing power parity; NA = not available.

NOTE: PPPs are used to convert national currency data to U.S. dollars by comparing the growth in prices in each country with that in the United States. The conversion used in this table was made by the OECD Economic Statistics and National Accounts Division.

SOURCES: Orgnization for Economic Cooperation and Development, *Main Science and Technology Indicators* (Paris, France: 1994) No. 1; and Center for Science, Trade and Technology Policy, George Mason University, "Large Science Project Priorities of Selected Countries," report prepared for the Office of Technology Assessment, December 1994.

FIGURE 1-A: Gross Domestic Expenditures on Research and Development in Selected Countries as a Percentage of GDP

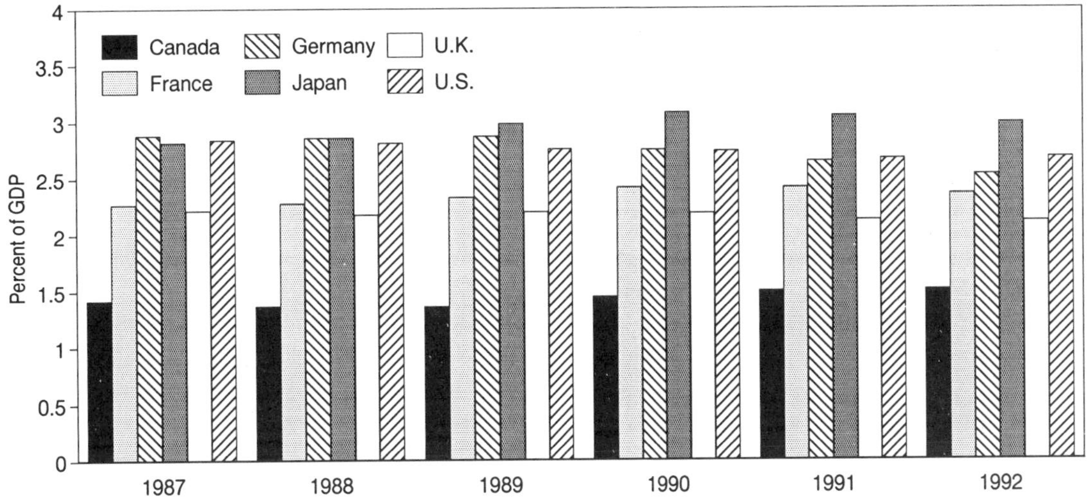

SOURCE: Organization for Economic Cooperation and Development, *Main Science and Technology Indicators,* No. 1 (Paris, France: 1994), p. 15.

developed and maintained a high profile in several disciplines, including nuclear physics, high-energy physics, and synchrotron radiation research. The Hadron-Electron Ring Accelerator (HERA) electron-proton collider has attracted physicists from around the world. Germany is also looking to expand its role in other areas such as bioscience and materials science.

Although basic science continues to serve as the foundation for technological innovation and economic competitiveness, applications-oriented research is growing in importance. Priority is given to scientific endeavors that translate into marketable processes and products (e.g., computer sciences, materials, bioscience, and environmental research). Agricultural research is also a top government priority. In the future, this trend may translate into fewer national large-scale basic science projects.

Because of budget constraints, BMFT has indicated that over the next few years, the government will focus on utilizing existing large-scale facilities and equipment rather than financing new ones. For example, Germany has no plans to upgrade its synchrotron facility (DESY) in the near future. In this regard, building cooperative partnerships and networks may intensify. Germany already has science and technology (S&T) agreements with more than 50 countries. Bilateral S&T agreements with the United States cover space research and technologies, biotechnology, nuclear reactor safety research, and energy technologies. The German government views these cooperative arrangements as important components of its overall research program. The government also promotes international scientific collaboration as a way to exchange information, pool resources, and tackle thorny global problems. Moreover, international collaboration may be necessary to sustain existing big science projects.

Germany is a member of several international organizations, including CERN, the European Space Agency (ESA), the European Southern Observatory, and the European Research Coordinating Agency (EUREKA). Germany contributes 22.5 percent of CERN's budget, the highest percentage of all member states. As a major contributor, Germany has played a pivotal role in recent decisions about the Large Hadron Collider (LHC) project at CERN.

In 1991, Germany spent a total of $35.6 billion on R&D. Most of the budget was earmarked for medium- to long-term research projects with high technology and economic potential.[3] Like the United States, German industries fund more than half of its nation's R&D. However, Germany expends considerably less on defense R&D. (See table A-1.)

FRANCE

France's primary science goal is to maintain a presence and, in some cases, to be competitive in several fields. Scientific excellence is closely tied to this goal. World leadership is neither a motivation nor a goal of French science. The concept of leadership is viewed only in the context of the European Union. To achieve its goals, France looks increasingly to international collaboration in big science projects. The pooling of financial, technical, and intellectual resources is the main motivator to participate in international projects.

In France, the science community plays a major role in setting the nation's scientific agenda. Projects generally move from the bottom up, and science budgets are estimated in five-year cycles. Unlike the United States, French government agencies do not have to go through the annual budget process once project commitments are made.

France has strong science programs in high-energy physics, space, astronomy, fusion, biological science, and nuclear physics. In the field of high-energy physics, national projects are funded by the Institute for Nuclear Physics and Particle Physics. Although France does not have a large, national high-energy physics facility, it is a major participant and contributor to CERN. France is also the host nation of the Institute Laue-Langevin (ILL) neutron facility, the preeminent neutron-scattering facility in the world. In addition, France hosts the 12-nation European Synchrotron Radi-

ation Facility (ESRF) in Grenoble, the first of a new generation of high-intensity x-ray sources.

Among European countries, France is the leader in space science. Also, France was a driving force behind the creation of ESA. The National Center for Space Research is responsible for national space projects, which focus primarily on providing assistance at Ariane launches, spacecraft acquisition, long-range planning, and managing contractors. Most scientific research is carried out at ESA or through bilateral agreements, primarily with the United States and Russia. France commits about 60 to 70 percent of its space budget to ESA.[4]

France has actively pursued collaborative projects with many countries, including the United States, Japan, India, and several in Eastern Europe and Latin America. The United States and France have a long tradition of scientific cooperation and numerous cooperative projects. Franco-Japanese scientific collaboration is more recent, but it is growing in importance. As part of the European Union, France is a partner in the International Thermonuclear Experimental Reactor (ITER) project.

In 1991, gross domestic expenditures on R&D totaled $25 billion. Government outlays accounted for 57 percent of the total. Large science projects account for about 9 percent of the total science budget.

RUSSIA

The former Soviet Union (FSU) has a well-developed and respected scientific research community. During the Cold War, the Soviet government targeted several priority areas for extensive scientific research, partially in support of potential military applications, but also as part of the competition with capitalist countries to prove which system was the more innovative and productive.

---

[3] Glenn J. McLoughlin, *International Science and Technology: Issues for U.S. Policymakers,* CRS Report for Congress, 94-733 SPR (Washington, DC: Congressional Research Service, Sept. 16, 1994), p. 20.

[4] Gerard Petitalout, National Center for Space Research, personal communication, Nov. 9, 1993.

Basic research in priority areas including space, high-energy physics, high-temperature superconductivity, and oceanography was well financed, and scientists working on these subjects enjoyed social status, high remuneration, and preferential access to goods and services.

Since the breakup of the Soviet Union, fundamental changes have occurred in the political, economic, and social orders. These changes have had a profound impact on S&T policy in the former Soviet Union. The huge military budgets of the Cold War, which underwrote much of the research, have been slashed, and the competition with the West to prove which system is the best (through science or by other means) has ceased. With civilian budgets strained to the limit, many research institutes lack the financial resources even to pay salaries. According to one expert, funding for Russia's S&T programs has declined significantly in recent years: 26 percent from 1991 to 1992; 17 percent from 1992 to 1993; and 8.7 percent from 1993 to 1994.[5] In addition, the skyrocketing cost of living and the more lucrative financial opportunities in the commercial economy have driven thousands of scientists out of research completely. Even where scientists remain at their posts, there is often no money to finance the research itself. For example, oceanographic research ships are stranded for lack of funds, and no new research reactors have been funded.[6] Even subscriptions to foreign journals are beyond the means of some institutes.

Nevertheless, efforts to reconstruct and continue research are under way. Russia inherited the bulk of the FSU's scientific expertise, although other former republics have research facilities and well-respected scientists. In 1994, Russia funded 38 S&T programs. The programs selected were chosen from a group of 150. Top-priority items on Russia's scientific agenda include space, high-energy physics, global climate change, and synchrotron radiation sources. Russia's space program is given special priority—a separate line item budget, and funding almost equal to the entire S&T budget. High-energy physics also commands a huge share of the total Russian S&T budget, accounting for about 27 percent.[7]

The Russian government is trying to integrate some of its scientists into the world scientific community, and is attempting to use international collaboration and support to preserve the country's scientific and technical expertise. For example, in high-energy physics, Russia has signed a bilateral scientific cooperative agreement with CERN. Russia is interested in becoming a full member of CERN and is supportive of plans to build the LHC. In space, the Russians have become a critical partner in the International Space Station project. Russia will provide expertise and equipment developed from its long-duration activities in orbit, for which it will be paid $650 million by the United States. Russia will use the payment to partially finance its involvement in the project. Additionally, Russia is one of the four partners in ITER.

The U.S. government has undertaken several activities to support Russian scientists. Given the proliferation risk represented by unemployed former Soviet arms scientists, the U.S. government has financed a program, the Moscow International Science and Technology Center, to reemploy them in peaceful uses of their expertise.

The outlook for Russian science is troubled by continued economic and political uncertainties, and difficulties are likely for the next several years. However, stabilization of the Russian economy and successful transition toward markets could provide a sounder economic basis for the government to finance an effective, though much smaller, basic research program than in the Soviet era. Under these circumstances, Russian scientists would increase their engagement with the world

---

[5]Irina Dezhina, "Russia's Science and Technology Priorities," n.d.

[6]Sergei P. Kapitza, "Russian Science: Snubbed and Sickly," *Bulletin of Atomic Scientists,* May/June 1994, p. 48.

[7]Dezhina, see footnote 5.

scientific community, and international collaboration would become essential to the Russian research enterprise.

INDIA

The goal of India's science policy is a practical one: to apply scientific knowledge and its related benefits to advancing the well-being of its population. Tied to this goal is the development of a self-reliant S&T base.[8]

India has a strong tradition of basic science research, and its scientists are highly respected. Science gained even more prominence after independence in 1947, with the goal of developing economic and political power. Nehru's government developed large programs in physics, astronomy, chemistry, and nuclear energy, and several national laboratories were built. With the help of the United States, India developed a highly sophisticated nuclear energy program.

Also, India has successfully developed its own satellites and launch vehicles. Its first experimental satellite was launched on a Soviet rocket in 1975. India's space program is oriented toward Earth observation, weather prediction, and telecommunications; space exploration is negligible.

India has no high-energy physics facility, but its scientists participate in experiments at other nations' facilities. India had agreed, in principle, to contribute to the proposed, and now defunct, Superconducting Super Collider and has expressed interest in contributing to the LHC project at CERN.

Indian scientists are also actively involved in other international science projects, including astronomy, nuclear physics, and materials science. It has S&T agreements with many countries, and its collaboration with the United States is particularly strong.

In 1991, R&D expenditures totaled $6 billion, which is modest by industrialized country standards but above average for developing countries. The Indian government funds the lion's share of R&D and conducts most of the research. Defense-related R&D is the top priority for India, followed by space and health research. In recent years, government support for R&D has been declining. The outlook is for further cuts in government funding and more reliance on commercially funded projects.[9]

CHINA

Basic science has long been an important part of Chinese culture. Scientific achievements in astronomy, mathematics, medicine, and chemistry date as far back as ancient times. In fact, Chinese leadership in science was not challenged by Western countries until the 17th century.

In recent years, however, economic reforms have dictated China's emphasis on applied, rather than basic, science research. The primary goal of scientific research today is to contribute to the economy and provide a foundation for international competitiveness. Research that can contribute to doubling the gross national product (GNP) by the year 2000 and programs aimed at developing new high-technology industries are given the greatest government support.

In 1989, the Chinese Academy of Sciences issued a report on the status of basic research in China. The report characterized China's basic research structure as weak and its programs as well behind other nations in several fields, including biology, chemistry, and mathematics. Basic science has taken a back seat in China's changing economy.[10]

A bright spot is in the field of high-energy physics. Completion of the Beijing Electron-Pos-

---

[8]McLoughlin, see footnote 3, p. 39.

[9]"Time To Catch Up," *Far Eastern Economic Review,* vol. 155, No. 49, Dec. 10, 1992, p. 45.

[10]Chinese Academy of Sciences, *Investigation of the National Basic Research Disciplines of the Natural Sciences* (Beijing, China: Beijing Science Press, 1989), as reported in *World Science Report 1993* (London, England: UNESCO Publishing, 1993), p. 105.

itron Collider in 1988 provided a boost to China's high-energy physics program. However, other disciplines, such as condensed-matter physics, and atomic and molecular physics, remain weak.[11]

Another bright spot is China's space program. China is one of a few countries that has a national space program. It has been marketing its launch capabilities in international markets, and its satellites have been used for Earth observation and telecommunications.

Annual expenditures on S&T have averaged about 1 percent of the GNP, with basic science funding accounting for about 4.8 percent of the total. Both of these figures are well below the world average.[12] Given China's goals, it is not surprising that industrial development commands the largest share (47 percent) of R&D spending. Other priority items for funding are health and agriculture (about 10 percent of civilian R&D outlays).[13]

In the past, S&T projects were funded by the central government, according to state economic plans. Since 1986, funding has diversified somewhat, with several state ministries and private sector organizations supporting science research. However, limited funding remains a thorny problem for science. In addition to funding constraints, China's science community faces another serious problem—its aging scientists. Moreover, there is a dearth of younger scientists due, in part, to past political policies (e.g., the Cultural Revolution), and the decision of Chinese scientists trained in the West to remain rather than return home.

Most of China's scientific endeavors are national projects. The desire to tailor scientific projects to national economic needs, the reluctance to provide access to research work and information, plus the need to build up its own scientific infra-structure all contribute to China's high rate of unilateral projects. Nevertheless, China does have a large number of S&T cooperative agreements with other nations. For example, China and Brazil are jointly building two remote sensing satellites to collect weather data. Also, China has a broad range of bilateral S&T agreements with the United States and Europe. U.S. and French scientific cooperation with China is particularly strong. The foundation for U.S.-China scientific cooperation was established by the 1979 U.S.-China Agreement on Cooperation in Science and Technology. Agreements cover space technology (the National Aeronautics and Space Administration (NASA)), high-energy physics (the Department of Energy (DOE)), medicine, earthquake studies, nuclear safety, aeronautics, transportation, and telecommunications. Activities are generally funded under existing agency budgets.

BRAZIL

Budget constraints, the lack of human resources, and limited regional and international cooperation have hampered scientific development in Latin America. Therefore, science policy goals in Latin America focus primarily on building up its scientific infrastructure through education, cooperation, and integration or coordination with other sectors of the economy, particularly those having strong scientific components. Attracting young people to science professions and actively pursuing collaborative projects are important strategies for achieving scientific goals.[14]

Of all Latin American countries, Brazil has the largest R&D budget and the highest rate of scientific publications. In 1991, Brazil's science R&D expenditures were about $3.2 billion, roughly 0.7

---

[11]Ibid.

[12]United Nations Educational, Scientific and Cultural Organization, "China," *World Science Report* (London, England: UNESCO Publishing, 1993), p. 104.

[13]Center for Science, Trade and Technology Policy, George Mason University, "Large Science Project Priorities of Selected Countries," report prepared for the Office of Technology Assessment, Jan. 23, 1995, p. 18.

[14]Ibid., pp. 39-40.

percent of its GDP. The largest R&D expenditures are for agriculture, accounting for about 20 percent of government outlays. Health research and space research are also R&D priorities.[15]

In 1992, Brazil's civilian space budget was $98 million, a significant drop from the $247 million funded in 1991. Exploration accounts for about 36 percent of the total space budget.[16] As noted earlier, Brazil and China are jointly developing satellites to gather weather data.

In the field of high-energy physics, Brazil's budget is rather modest. It has no large facilities but does participate in programs in other countries. Brazil does, however, have a synchrotron radiation facility.

CANADA

Industrial and economic goals dominate Canada's science policy. The 1991 Science Council report noted the importance of the linkage between scientific research and technical innovation and competitiveness. Several research areas have been identified as vital to sustained economic growth in Canada. These include biotechnology, space, advanced industrial materials, and environmental and marine sciences.[17]

In 1991, total R&D expenditures totaled $7.8 billion. The private sector funded nearly 60 percent of Canada's R&D activities. Industrial development commanded the largest share of funds. Other priority areas included defense, space, and energy.[18]

Faced with growing budgetary pressures and the need to pool resources, Canada's basic science programs have both national and international elements. In high-energy physics, national efforts have centered on the construction and development of a relatively large national facility called

TRIUMP. This national facility is funded by several government agencies and managed by four universities. Foreign experts serve as members of the facility's planning and advisory committees. Canada's investment in high-energy physics has been about $300 million per year, with annual operation costs budgeted at about $35 million.

Canada's space program is oriented toward Earth observation, including weather data, and communications. On the international level, Canada has alliances with NASA (e.g., for the space station) and with ESA. In the latter case, Canada submits proposals to the ESA board that, if accepted, are included in ESA's programs.

Canada has a strong tradition of scientific cooperation with the United States, Europe, and more recently, Japan. Canadian scientists are participating in international projects, such as the Global Climate Change Program, the Ocean Drilling Program, the Human Genome Project, the Gemini project, and ITER.

UNITED KINGDOM

Science policy in the United Kingdom focuses on two primary goals: 1) maintaining and enhancing the quality of science, and 2) providing economic and social benefits to the nation. In recent years, the government has strengthened the link between science and the creation of wealth. In its first review of science policy in more than 20 years,[19] the government outlined a strategy for ensuring the success of the industry-science marriage. The strategy hinges on developing stronger relationships between science and industry, participating in international research efforts, and improving the training and education of scientists and engineers. In particular, the research councils responsible for funding science projects have been re-

[15]Ibid., pp. 14, 38.

[16]Ibid., table 10, figure 6f.

[17]Science Council of Canada, "Reaching for Tomorrow: Science and Technology Policy in Canada, 1991," 1992.

[18]Center for Science, Trade and Technology Policy, see footnote 13, table 4.

[19]Chancellor of the Duchy of Lancaster, *Realising Our Potential, A Strategy for Science, Engineering and Technology,* presented to Parliament by Command of Her Majesty (London, England: Her Majesty's Science Office, May 1993).

organized and given the explicit mission of enhancing industrial competitiveness. In addition, the Technology Foresight Programme (TFP) was created to identify strategically important technologies and high-priority research areas. Information collected by TFP contributes to long-range R&D planning and funding decisions.

In 1991, total expenditures on R&D amounted to $19.2 billion, or 2.1 percent of GDP.[20] This percentage has remained fairly stable over the last decade. Defense research is given high funding priority, followed by industrial development, health, and the environment. Not surprisingly, the Ministry of Defense is the leading government supporter of R&D, contributing about 40 percent of total government outlays for R&D. Industry funds about half of all R&D activities. The electronics, chemical, and aerospace industries receive the largest share of industrial funding.[21]

Basic science is viewed as an international enterprise that depends on the pooling of intellectual and financial resources. The United Kingdom has been active in international activities at all levels in all areas of science, including high-energy physics, astronomy, fusion, and space. Collaboration ranges from informal agreements among scientists and institutions to bilateral agreements between governments, to international partnerships. The United Kingdom is a member of CERN, ESA, ILL, ESRF, and EUREKA. In addition to its membership in European consortia, the United Kingdom has a strong tradition of cooperation with the United States.

The United Kingdom has significant national research programs in fusion, astronomy, and nuclear physics. The reputation and expertise of its Culham Laboratory for fusion research contributed to the decision to site the European Union-funded Joint European Torus (JET) facility in England. It is also a member of the ITER project team.

Although the United Kingdom does not have a major high-energy physics facility, its scientists are actively involved at CERN. The United Kingdom contributes about 14 percent of the CERN budget.

JAPAN

Technology is the driving force behind science policy in Japan. Science is viewed as a foundation for technological and economic development and international competitiveness. Japan's focus on applications-oriented research can be attributed, in part, to industry's large share of R&D funding. In 1991, industry contributed 84 percent of the total R&D funds.

Another priority of science programs and industry is to "catch up" to the West, specifically the United States, in areas in which Japan feels it lags. National prestige and capacity building also figure into decisions about undertaking expensive national projects, such as the B-factory, and collaborating on international big science projects.

Research priorities are set at the highest government levels and are reached after extensive interagency consultation. Consensus decisionmaking drives this consultative process. The Council for Science and Technology (CST), which is chaired by the Prime Minister, is the cabinet-level coordinating body for S&T. It consists of distinguished representatives from academia, industry, and government. The Science and Technology Agency is the secretariat for CST, but other powerful agencies, such as the Ministry of Science, Education, and Culture, the Ministry of International Trade and Industry, and the Ministry of Finance, are also members of CST. CST is responsible for outlining the national research agenda, approving government agency plans, and ensuring that funding is appropriate to meet needs. New materials research (particularly superconducting

---

[20]Center for Science, Trade and Technology Policy, see footnote 13, table 4.

[21]McLoughlin, see footnote 3, p. CRS-54.

materials), biotechnology, space, fusion, and high-energy physics are top priorities.

In recent years, government support for basic research has increased, although industry is still likely to continue to fund and do the bulk of the work. This increase in support is viewed as a way to build Japan's science infrastructure and develop its standing in the world scientific community. The Japanese have come to believe that being leaders in technology innovation, manufacturing, and marketing is not sufficient to gain the respect of other major industrialized nations.

The government promotes international collaboration in big science projects as another way for Japan to develop as a world science leader. Also, the Japanese view international collaboration as an opportunity to pool resources and to address global issues. Japan has extensive cooperative agreements in space, fusion, high-energy physics, astronomy, ocean and environmental sciences, and health. The United States and Japan have a strong tradition of scientific cooperation. The U.S.-Japan Science and Technology Agreement fosters scientific information exchange and access to facilities, and provides for the protection of U.S. intellectual property rights.

The International Space Station project is the largest cooperative space venture in which the Japanese are engaged. Japan's contribution to the space station—an experimental module—is its most expensive space project to date. The module will cost about $3 billion to build, and Japan will share in operating costs as well.[22] National space efforts, directed by the National Space Development Agency, concentrate on developing satellites and rocket launchers. Satellites are used for Earth observation and telecommunications. In fiscal year 1994, funding for space was $2.18 billion.

Japan is also a partner in ITER. The potential for an unlimited, economical energy source and the development of advanced materials and magnet technologies are among the driving forces behind Japan's participation in this project. However, enhancing Japan's stature in science was an important selling point for both the space station and the ITER projects. In 1991, Japan spent nearly $300 million on fusion research.[23]

Japan has a very respected national high-energy physics program. Its National Laboratory for High Energy Physics (KEK) has attracted scientists from around the world. Japan also sends scientists to CERN facilities and has decided to contribute $60 million toward the construction of CERN's LHC project. KEK has cooperative agreements with the Stanford Linear Accelerator Center, the Brookhaven National Laboratory, and the Fermi National Accelerator Laboratory. Japan's top-priority national project is building the B-factory machine. Development of the B-factory machine is one area of high-energy physics in which Japan and the United States are pursuing parallel paths. Both countries can afford to build their own machines, which will not only provide their scientists with more opportunities to conduct experiments, but will contribute to national prestige. Japan's 1993 budget for particle physics was about $350 million.

In 1991, Japan spent about $67 billion on R&D. Industrial development accounted for the largest share of funds.[24] As a share of GDP, Japan's R&D expenditures are the highest. Unlike the United States, Japan spends less than 2 percent on defense-related R&D.

---

[22]John M. Logsdon, "US-Japan Space Relations at a Crossroads," *Science,* vol. 295, Jan. 17, 1992, p. 299.

[23]Center for Science, Trade and Technology Policy, see footnote 13, figure 8c.

[24]Ibid., table 4.

Acronyms | B

ADEOS	Advanced Earth Observing Satellite
AEC Act	Atomic Energy Commission Act of 1954
ANS	Advanced Neutron Source
APS	Advanced Photon Source
ASTER	Advanced Spaceborne Thermal Emission and Reflection Radiometer
AURA	Association of Universities for Research in Astronomy
AXAF	Advanced X–ray Astrophysics Facility
BMFT	German Federal Ministry for Research and Technology
CAT	computerized axial tomography
CDA	conceptual design activities
CGRO	Compton Gamma Ray Observatory
CERN	European Laboratory for Particle Physics
CST	Council for Science and Technology
DAAC	Distributed Active Archive Center
DESY	Deutches Elektronen–Synchrotron facility
DNA	deoxyribonucleic acid
DOE	U.S. Department of Energy
D–T	deuterium–tritium
EDA	engineering design activities
EOS	Earth Observing System
EOSDIS	Earth Observing System Data and Information System
EPACT	Energy Policy Act of 1992
ESA	European Space Agency
ESO	European Southern Observatory
ESRF	European Synchrotron Radiation Facility
FSU	Former Soviet Union
GCRP	Global Change Research Program
GDP	gross domestic product
GLSP	Group on Large Scientific Projects
GNP	gross national product
HEPAP	High Energy Physics Advisory Panel
HERA	Hadron–Electron Ring Accelerator
HIRIS	High–Resolution Imaging Spectrometer
IAEA	International Atomic Energy Agency
ICF	inertial confinement fusion
IEOS	International Earth Observing System
ILL	Institute Laue–Langevin
ISPM	International Solar Polar Mission
ISSA	International Space Station Alpha
ITER	International Thermonuclear Experimental Reactor
JCT	Joint Central Team
JEM	Japanese Experimental Module
JET	Joint European Torus
KEK	National Laboratory for High Energy Physics (Japan)
LHC	Large Hadron Collider
LIGO	Laser Interferometer Gravitational Wave Observatory

MFEEA	Magnetic Fusion Energy Engineering Act of 1980	OECD	Organization for Economic Cooperation and Development
MIMR	Multifrequency Imaging Microwave Radiometer	OMB	Office of Management and Budget
MOU	Memorandum of Understanding	POEM	Polar–Orbit Earth Observation Mission
MSS	Mobile Servicing System	POES	Polar–Orbiting Operational Environmental Satellite
MTCR	Missile Technology Control Regime		
MTFF	Man–Tended Free Flyer	SAR	synthetic aperture radar data
MW	megawatt	SLAC	Stanford Linear Accelerator Center
NASA	National Aeronautics and Space Administration	SPring–8	Super Photon Ring–8
		SRC–II	Solvent Refined Coal-II Demonstration Plant
NASDA	Japanese Space Agency		
NIF	National Ignition Facility	SSC	Superconducting Super Collider
NLC	Next Linear Collider	STA	Science and Technology Agency
NOAA	National Oceanic and Atmospheric Administration	TFTR	Tokamak Fusion Test Reactor
		TPX	Tokamak Physics Experiment
NOAO	National Optical Astronomy Observatories	TRMM	Tropical Rainfall Measuring Mission
		VLT	Very Large Telescope

Index

☆ U.S. GOVERNMENT PRINTING OFFICE: 1995 - 387-789 - 814/37414

Superintendent of Documents **Publications** Order Form